TSUNAMI
AND
THE SINGLE GIRL

TSUNAMI
AND
THE SINGLE GIRL

ONE WOMAN'S JOURNEY TO BECOME
AN AID WORKER AND FIND LOVE

KRISSY NICHOLSON

ALLEN&UNWIN
SYDNEY·MELBOURNE·AUCKLAND·LONDON

First published in 2013

Copyright © Krissy Nicholson 2013

Allen & Unwin
83 Alexander Street
Crows Nest NSW 2065
Australia
Phone:	(61 2) 8425 0100
Email:	info@allenandunwin.com
Web:	www.allenandunwin.com

Cataloguing-in-Publication details are available from the National Library of Australia
www.trove.nla.gov.au

ISBN 978 1 74331 694 8

Set in 12/18 pt Berkeley LT by Midland Typesetters, Australia
Printed in Australia by Griffin Press

10 9 8 7 6 5 4 3

CONTENTS

NOTE TO THE READER

Thanks for reading my book. I decided to write *Tsunami and the Single Girl* in the hope that I could use my own stories—as a single, everyday girl—to highlight important issues about social justice, gender, poverty and disaster. Serious issues are addressed, but I have also interwoven fun (and not so fun) stories of my search for 'Mr Right' and the craziness of the expatriate lifestyle.

All the events and stories in this book are true. I have, however, taken some creative licence in merging some of my characters and on the rare occasion have added true events into inaccurate time frames to ensure important points are made. I have changed the names of most of my friends, lovers, colleagues and some towns in which I worked.

While I have tried to portray information and events as accurately as possible, most of the stories are personal recollections and therefore are biased to my point of view. All the facts and figures I have used are referenced at the back of this book for further exploration. The thoughts and opinions in this book are mine only and do not represent Oxfam or any of the people I have met along the way.

I feel blessed to have the opportunities I have had in my life. The people I have met, the communities I have worked with and the places I have been. I have learnt so much on my road to become an aid worker and in my search for love.

I hope you enjoy the journey.

Krissy xxx

CHAPTER 1

IN A MATTER OF MINUTES

BOXING DAY TSUNAMI, SRI LANKA 2005

I always imagined by 30 I'd have met the man of my dreams and be starting a family. Instead, here I was, 29 years old, still single and smack bang in the middle of the world's biggest disaster. The universe obviously had different plans for me. The chilled champagne at my farewell party the week before seemed a lifetime ago.

White flags, symbolising death, fluttered in the breeze as I passed makeshift graves in the sand. It was 35 degrees Celsius, yet the breeze sent a shiver down my spine. I couldn't imagine what this place must have looked like before. The stench of rotting bodies had disappeared, yet death and destruction was still raw and all encompassing.

Five weeks after the 2004 Boxing Day tsunami, Oxfam sent me to one of the hardest hit areas in Sri Lanka. Examining the ruins in Batticaloa, my brain tried to process what my mind couldn't. All I could see was absolute destruction.

I swallowed hard, willing myself not to cry. The shore was covered in debris. The debris of people's lives.

It was difficult to fathom the reality of the situation. I imagined poorly constructed mud and straw huts that were easily washed away. But in this area it had been solid brick houses that were dragged out to sea. Houses, cars, boats, shops and, most devastatingly, people, had all disappeared. Entire communities and generations of families. Gone in a matter of minutes.

Walking among the rubble, I got a feeling for the people who had lived there. Mud-soaked clothes wrapped around trees, demolished temples, fishermen's boats in pieces. Broken tiles from bathroom walls, decorated with hand-painted flowers. I stopped to pick up a toy monkey half-buried in the sand. It looked identical to one I owned as a child.

I flicked through a waterlogged photo album I found amongst the debris, and stared at washed-out images that had survived the water: a young man smiling at the camera, a smudged picture barely showing a father kissing his son. The pictures gave faces to the disaster. Did they escape? Were they the lucky ones who were able to run to high ground or climb a tree? Or were they one of the mothers, fathers, sons, daughters, neighbours who were violently taken by nature? A part of nature they had grown up with and knew so intimately. The sea provided them life, food, jobs. They played in it as children and it formed the backdrop to their everyday lives. But that December, the ocean became their enemy.

I walked in silence with my local colleague, the only sound was the waves lapping at the shore. What words could possibly be appropriate?

Throughout the day we met people who wanted to tell their story. One mother told us how she clung to a tree, holding tightly to her three children. The water rushed around her ferociously. As her strength weakened she had to make a choice. She was forced to let go of one child so she could hold on to the tree and other children. The alternative was for them all to die. She had saved two of her children, but would live with the guilt of the one she let go for the rest of her life.

Another man was aimlessly wandering the streets, still searching in hope for his wife and daughter. He was a carpenter and was looking for work to start building a life again, for their return. I am sure in his heart he knew they were gone.

'The dead ones are the lucky ones,' cried one woman, as she told her story of losing her entire family and all her belongings.

Walking back to the car, my interpreter stopped.

'Krissy, stop and listen . . .' he said. 'What do you hear?'

I couldn't hear anything, so I shrugged my shoulders.

'You hear the waves. The tide going in and out, right?'

I nodded.

'Just before the tsunami, there was absolute silence.' He paused. 'The tide stopped completely—absolute silence.'

I couldn't speak. *What am I meant to say to that!*

'And then minutes later the sound was like a roar from a football match—but instead of cheers of joy, it was cries of absolute terror.' *Oh God!*

I'm sure that sound will stay with him forever.

Sitting on the guesthouse balcony that evening, I tried to process all I'd seen. As a thunderstorm began to rage, I watched a frog jump around a puddle. Dogs howled at the flashes of lightning highlighting the palm trees in the background. For me, the rain brought relief from a hot and humid day. I tried to relax and plan for the day ahead. But I couldn't stop thinking of the people in the camps. Tens of thousands of people living in small tents. It would be horrendous. Damp, crowded and maybe even scary. Scary, because although rain and thunderstorms are natural and nothing to fear—so once was the ocean.

Later that night I lay under my mosquito net watching the fan twirl slowly overhead.

My dreams of becoming an aid worker were playing out in full swing and I knew that this was just the beginning. Sure, that meant my dream of finding Mr Right was on the back-burner. But there wasn't any other place I'd rather be. Plus, you never know where Mr Right might be hiding!

I smiled thinking of the fateful night that changed the direction of my life, that led me to this very moment.

It all started on a dance floor in Vietnam . . .

CHAPTER 2

FATE ON THE DANCE FLOOR

VIETNAM 2001

'You Spin Me Round (Like a Record)', Dead or Alive's song, blared over the crackly speakers. Lights flashing, waves crashing, tequila shots and cheap cocktails running freely. Footloose and fancy free at a beach party in Nha Trang, Vietnam 2001. A cute backpacker spun me around with the abandon of a Ho Chi Minh City bus driver. He twirled me until I dropped. I literally dropped. SPLAT! Right in the middle of the dance floor.

'Here, grab my hand.'

'I'm not sure I . . .'

'Come on, I'm strong, give me your hand.'

'No, I mean I don't think I . . .'

'Oh my God!' he stepped back.

The shock on his face confirmed there was something really wrong, and this time it wasn't just too many tequilas. Frozen on the ground, I looked down to see my knee protruding at right angles to the rest of my leg. *ARGHHHHHHHH!!!*

At the hospital the doctors spoke to me in broken English. I signed a variety of documents that I didn't understand, and what could have been days or hours later I awoke, feeling groggy, to a young nurse taking my blood pressure. I scanned my body, thanking God that my right leg was still in place and I hadn't signed up for an amputation. Yep—vital organs still in place as far as I could tell. I watched the flickering lights and paint peeling off the ceiling while I was being wheeled on a stretcher to my room. To my relief Cam was sleeping in the bed next to mine.

Cam is my stepbrother. He was three when Dad met his mother, Christine (my stepmother), and they joined my brother Paul and me in what became our relatively functional dysfunctional family.

'Cam, wake up.'

Cam had been travelling with me through Thailand and Cambodia. The Vietnamese hospital was a new addition to our three-month itinerary of South-East Asia. Cameron groaned. The smell of hospital disinfectant couldn't drown out the stale beer and cigarette fumes on his 'same same but different' t-shirt.

Cam being there was reassuring. The dirty walls were not. But at least it was a private room and he was allowed to stay.

'Cam, please get me out of here!' I yelled down the hallway, as the nurses wheeled me away again.

Heading to an unknown destination down a long hallway, I was handed over to two men in white coats (presumably doctors). They began putting my leg in a full plaster cast. I'm not a doctor, but I was pretty sure that plaster was only used for broken bones, not dislocated knees. I pushed these thoughts aside and tried to ignore the blood splattered on the walls and the high-pitch screeching of electric saws in the adjacent room. The gooey white plaster was cold and wet on my skin.

'Excuse me, I think the plaster is too high up my leg.' The doctors looked at me cheerfully, obviously not understanding a word.

'No problem.' They both smiled and continued to wrap me in goo.

'I won't be able to go to the toilet.' They looked at me blankly.

'Um . . . too high . . . psssssss . . . urine down leg,' I said, motioning my hand from my groin outwards as I made pissing sounds.

The doctors just laughed. 'No, no, no, it okaaaay.'

But 'it NOT okaaaay'. As predicted, two hours later I was holding my breath and my bladder, having the plaster sawn off. All sense of dignity went out the window as I relieved myself in an emergency potty right there and then.

Over the next few days the nurses brought me drugs in little white cups. I swallowed obediently after realising that they couldn't understand my questions of 'what is the drug?' and 'what are the side effects?'

'No problem, you have,' they always said without a smile and promptly left the room.

That is when we actually saw the nurses. Cameron had to do what goes beyond the boundaries of any sibling relationship and empty my bedpan on a couple of occasions.

'Cam, look the other way and sing a song please.'

Then again, backpacking in Asia meant that we already knew way too well each other's toilet habits, including all the joys of traveller's bowel movements.

The next day a doctor sat with me—an assistant by his side, presumably because they felt he spoke better English—and explained:

'You . . . Ho Chi Minh City!' he said cheerfully. *Me Ho Chi Minh City!?!*

'Ok,' I said, wondering how on earth I was going to make the eight-hour trip down south. It was certainly not going to be by motorbike or the crowded buses that we travelled here in last week. 'Do I organise that or do YOU organise that?'

'Yes,' they said in unison.

'Hold on, let me get this clear . . . so, do I organise that?'

'Yes.' They nodded enthusiastically.

'Or do YOU organise that?'

'Yes.' More nodding.

'Do I take a bus or a plane?'

'Yes.'

All I can say is thank God for Cameron and for travel insurance. After days of trying, Cam ended up getting in contact with the insurance company and an American doctor picked us up and escorted us in an ambulance back to the craziness of Ho Chi Minh City.

The joys of private hospitals in Vietnam (yes, I'm a glass half full girl). After backpacking in $3 a night accommodation for the past six weeks, we felt like we were living in luxury. Crisp white linen, hot running water and even our own toilet!

I was told I would have to end my trip a couple of months short, and I was disappointed, but I knew immediately it was meant to be. The universe had something in store for me, I just wasn't sure what. Maybe I would meet that doctor I was supposed to marry?

When I was sixteen, a clairvoyant told me I would marry a doctor. She said I'd meet him in a hot, far away land—maybe somewhere in Africa. Perhaps she got it slightly wrong and it was meant to be an accident in a faraway land that led me back home to meet him? And maybe it was Vietnam and not Africa? Who knows, but since then it's been a teenage fantasy that I have held on to. I wondered if this accident was fate.

Cam continued his travels solo, and alone on the plane I had time to reflect. Doing the obligatory Aussie thing after university, I had based myself in the United Kingdom to earn money and travel the world. I led a kind of double life—wearing a suit working in a sales-driven corporate recruitment company in London, then backpacking like an intrepid hippie, in purple fishermen's pants and with a nose piercing.

Six months work funded six months travel on a shoe-string budget. All my possessions on my back. Sleeping on everything from rooftops to twenty-bed dorm rooms or under the desert stars free of charge. I shared public transport with locals and their chickens and prided myself at getting off the beaten track.

I'd clocked up over 40 countries in Europe, South America, the Middle East and the first leg of South-East Asia (excuse the pun). It was nearly three years since I'd been home. I was returning with a bung leg, yet a healthy dose of self-awareness packed up with a full heart, expanded mind and nourished soul that only independent travel can provide.

'Wow, three years, hey. So what are you going to do now?' asked the 50-something-year-old woman sitting next to me on the plane.

With my leg stretched out in a full brace on the business class seat the insurance company had paid for, I had limited chance to wander the cabin, so I told my life story to the passenger next to me.

'Good question.' I watched the flight attendant down the aisle reapply her bright red lipstick. 'Well, I'm over the corporate world. I think I'd like to work for Oxfam or something like that. Somewhere that I can make a difference.'

I had always felt strongly about social justice. My adventures through the developing world and witnessing the conditions so many people live in had strengthened my desire to actually do something about it. Travelling taught me so much, but while I was richer with knowledge and insights into the world and myself, I left the countries just as poor.

My experience in Peru a few years earlier had whet my appetite for aid work. I was in a quaint bar in the middle of Cusco, 'Pisco Sour' in hand and sharing stories with other travellers. I had toyed with the idea of aid work over the years, but that was before I had really been exposed to poverty in third world countries.

Walking through villages across South America, the poverty was evident. Too many children on the streets begging. I gave pockets full of lollies, stickers and small change but it felt meaningless. A little something that would appease my guilt at my own affluence.

Sipping my drink in the dimly lit bar that night, I watched some young children and their mother huddling in the cold street outside. As if in a trance, I stared through the window at the children settling down to sleep in a gritty doorway. While they were oblivious to my stares, I refocused to find my reflection in the window, wavering with the flicker of the scattered candles around the room.

My focus came in and out like waves. The children, my reflection, my friends, the candle, the children, my reflection, my friends. The clinking of glasses, laughter, music. The lighting of a cigarette, the smell of candle wax, sweet juices from the cocktails. The mother tucked her children under some rags. The kaleidoscope of moving images made me dizzy. I took a deep breath and my focus became fixed on my reflection.

I met my own eyes in the window and burst into tears.

It didn't feel right. My cocktail cost more than the family earnt in a week, possibly a month. As I blurted out my feelings of discontent with the injustices of the world, the party agreed. They all shook their heads and lowered their eyes momentarily.

'Nothing a tequila won't fix,' someone yelled as another round appeared.

I continued to drink and smile politely at the jokes but remained acutely aware of the family on the street. Something had moved inside me. I resolved to myself that one day I would give something back. I felt such a sense of gratitude to the people and cultures of the countries in which I had travelled. But as a tourist, there wasn't much I could give.

I knew that the odd bit of money or food was pointless. And although I didn't know when I'd be in the position to be able to make a real difference, that night, over a cocktail in Peru, the desire to work towards real change was cemented in my core.

So three years later and on a plane heading for home, I knew it was my time to stop talking about injustice in the world and start acting. As for how, I didn't know.

Tears ran down my cheeks during touchdown, as the captain announced our arrival.

'. . . and to those returning to Melbourne, a very warm welcome home.'

⌒

The one good thing about being in a wheelchair is that you get past all the queues at immigration, and I was wheeled straight into my mother's arms: an unexpected homecoming for such an independent traveller. I was soon back at Mum's house, on crutches and reliant. My medical dramas didn't stop there, as I discovered I had developed deep vein thrombosis (DVT) from the flight.

Extra complications meant more specialists and more doctors but to my disappointment they were old enough to be my father, female, or just . . . NOT. My fantasy of fate leading me to the love of my life started to dissolve. The next month saw Mum unceremoniously chasing me around the loungeroom, trying to inject me with DVT drugs, while I wondered what on earth I was going to do with my life.

My mother, a nurse, is a hippie earth goddess who has taught me to be open-minded and accepting of everyone regardless of their background. She is the type of woman who became the 'adopted' mother of many of my friends, well, of anyone she met really. Arms always open. I can confide in Mum about anything.

Growing up with Dr Jim Cairns as my great-grandfather, I belong to a family whose members are passionate advocates for social change. Jim was the Deputy Prime Minister of Australia with the Whitlam Government in the 70s. Among many other great feats, he led the Vietnam War Moratorium, one of the biggest social move-ments in Australia's history. As a child I'd curl up next to Jim and listen to stories of the 100,000 people he led in a peaceful protest through the streets of Melbourne. Mum and I were both inspired by his intelligent mind and his unwavering commitment that had him writing books and selling them at Camberwell market well into his eighties. Jim was a hero to many, including me.

Alongside stories of activism and social justice, I was also fed fairytales—Cinderella, Snow White, Sleeping Beauty—all stories ending with Prince Charming sweeping the Princess off her feet and living happily ever after. That's what's meant to happen. My Mum said so. Well, I tell you what, I had searched far and wide and kissed a lot of frogs—but none of them had turned into a prince.

It was good to be home but the reason perplexed me. Why had I been brought home so suddenly? What did the universe have in store for me if not a spunky doctor?

A couple of weeks later Mum plonked the *Age* classifieds in front of me. She'd highlighted a job in bright yellow:

Humanitarian Relief Register Officer
Oxfam Australia

'A dynamic professional required to recruit humanitarian specialists to deploy to disasters around the world.' Tingles went up and
down my spine as I read the ad.

'Mum, this is it!' I squealed, as I spoke at her a hundred miles an
hour. 'Oh my God, it's what I said I wanted and here it is . . . Oxfam!
. . . I've got the recruitment background . . . YAY . . . Mum . . , I'm
so excited . . . but hold on, I don't have the humanitarian experience . . . do you think that matters? . . . no . . . surely not . . . it says
"desirable" . . . my travels mean something right . . . MUM!!! What if
. . . oh my God . . . I'm going to apply . . . I can't believe it.'

If I could dance I would have, but all I could muster was an
uncoordinated jig on my crutches.

This was it. This was the reason I had to come home. It wasn't
Mr Right after all. I was sure of it. I was still on crutches and having
daily injections, but nothing was going to stop me from applying for
this job.

∽

Struggling to look relaxed as the receptionist eye-balled me, I sat
upright on the coffee-stained seat. This was certainly not like the
flash offices I was accustomed to in London. I pretended to read
the annual report, noticing the frayed carpet and the rudimentary
Oxfam sign that looked as though it had been stuck on the wall with
sticky tape. Public donations were obviously not going to interior
decorators.

Staff skipped by, grinning at me in their stripy coloured socks
and hippie skirts. The starch in my obviously inappropriate grey suit
became stifling. I casually folded my jacket into my black leather

handbag and took a deep breath. My palms slipped on the crutch handles and my smile was far too wide as I hobbled into the windowless board room. I felt like I was in a quirky kind of firing line when I saw the panel of three sitting behind a large white table. Awkwardly, I lay my crutches on the floor and took a seat.

BANG! 'What skills can you bring to this job?'

BANG! 'Tell us about a recruitment process you led.'

BANG! 'What are the key issues to consider when sending someone to a disaster?'

Throughout the interview my voice waivered and the room seemed to echo when I swallowed. *Oh my God, is that a bead of sweat dripping down my face?*

To make it worse, when the dreaded question came up, I went against all my friends' advice.

BANG! 'So what happened to your leg?'

Don't say it. Don't say it. Don't say it . . .

'I dislocated my knee on the dance floor in Vietnam.'

BANG! BANG! BANG! *Shit.*

The panel smirked, holding back what could have been laughter or disapproval. I wasn't sure.

'Must have been some moves you were pulling!'

They put their revolvers down.

Breathe out.

I staggered out on my crutches thinking I'd blown it for sure.

CHAPTER 3

DATES AND OTHER DISASTERS

MELBOURNE 2003

'Get the fuck out of the car and put your hands on your heads.' An AK-47 was pointed straight at my chest. There were six of them, two sporting massive guns and the others rusty machetes. Wearing a mismatch of military gear and grubby t-shirts, our aggressors also wore black bandannas to hide their faces. We had just passed a military checkpoint on our way to a location where we had been told 20,000 refugees were crossing the border. These guys must be the off-shoot militia we had been warned about.

'We're from Oxfam, trying to help your . . .'

'Shut the fuck up and get on the ground.'

The ringleader with wild black eyes spat words into my face and pushed me to the ground while the other militia forced my colleagues into the dirt next to me. My hands were yanked behind me and I felt scratchy rope tie my wrists together. I didn't try to speak again. All I could do was concentrate on the mud two centimetres in front of my face. Suddenly I was in darkness, when a black smelly cloth bag was pulled over my head. I could hear my colleague next to me whimpering.

'Please, Sir.' The head of mission, a tall Scandinavian man, started to talk. 'We are aid workers trying to bring water to your . . .'

'Silence!' the ringleader shouted.

Dazed and confused and in darkness, with a sharp stone sticking into my hip, I could hear the militia making jokes and laughing in a language I couldn't recognise. Next thing I heard something dripping and felt warm fluid dribble down my neck. The militia laughed loudly—they seemed to be urinating on us.

Just breathe, Krissy. Just breathe. In and out. In and out.

My brain raced a million miles an hour trying to remember what we had learnt, what to do in this situation. Next thing, I heard my colleague Kathy scream and what sounded like her being dragged away. The tinkling of buckles being undone, animalistic grunting and a high pitch scream coming from my right. Or was it my left? A gun shot. *Oh no . . . Kathy . . .*

Just breathe, Krissy, just breathe . . . it's just a simulation. It's just a simulation.

But I wanted to get out of it. Even though I knew it wasn't real I had to talk myself into being calm. This was all part of our training, but it could be real one day. So I breathed through it until we were finally out of the six-hour simulation and being debriefed in the humanitarian training room.

The ten-day 'RedR' course was hard going yet exhilarating. If you couldn't cope on this course, you couldn't cope in the field and the trainers kept a watch out for those who'd be weeded out. While some may have left the course thinking 'this isn't for me', I left with a strong resolve that humanitarian work was exactly what I wanted.

I'd been working at Oxfam for a few months and this course was part of my induction. I would be deploying aid personnel to emergencies in often dangerous places, and I needed to understand how humanitarian programs operated. It was part of my job to provide security briefings and prepare workers for the field.

Oxfam was another world. I learnt a new language filled with TLAs (three letter acronyms), a new culture, new skills. Despite feeling like a kid learning to ride a bike without training wheels, I loved every minute of it. I loved how friendly and open people were. I loved being surrounded by incredibly talented, experienced and motivated professionals committed to overcoming poverty. I loved that I could wear whatever I wanted and that the local pub was known as 'Meeting room 3'.

'What the hell are RBA, GNA and RTE anyway?' I slurred to my colleagues after sharing our fourth jug of beer.

'Rights-based Approach, Gender Needs Analysis and Real Time Evaluation,' they chanted in unison.

'WTF?' I still had no idea what they were talking about.

We all laughed.

I stood in awe of other staff who had worked in the many inspiring Oxfam programs around the world. They came back from the field with lively stories. Health programs in East Timor, gender programs in the Solomons, water and sanitation in Mozambique, emergency needs assessments in Iraq. I felt like a teen meeting her favourite movie star. I wanted to be like them.

I loved the way that Oxfam worked with communities at a grass roots level, but that it also integrated advocacy into its work, seeking to influence government and policy makers as well. That it was secular, with no religious affiliation, and offered assistance to all. And it operated using a rights-based approach with the premise that people globally don't 'need' food, water, health, safety and equality—but they have a fundamental 'right' to these things. This was a different way of thinking from old school charity of 'giving to the poor people'. It meant working together with communities and recognising and utilising their strengths to provide a hand up rather than a hand out. This approach made sense to me. I thrived on learning the ropes and couldn't believe I was now operating in this new international world. And I loved how, after a while, I started to understand its language.

Among the staff were some older tainted aid workers who were disillusioned with the system, and after so many years of working hard couldn't see enough real change. Regardless, they tirelessly worked on for the cause they believed in, with little monetary compensation. I was always aware that I could be making tens of thousands more in the corporate world, but none of us were there for the money. I knew I was in the right place. I thanked whatever god was responsible for that night on the dance floor in Vietnam.

I learnt so much working on the humanitarian relief register. Recruiting and training professional aid workers and preparing them for rapid deployment in case of an emergency. In the first couple of years our work revolved around East Timor, Afghanistan and the Iraq war. Post 9/11 we were acutely aware of the new type of warfare and terrorism that aid workers were contending with, particularly in conflict postings. No longer could aid workers move safely in areas of conflict under the banner of humanitarianism. The lines had been blurred with growing militias, war lords and United Nations conventions that were being trampled on from both sides. Western armies were also blurring the line between combatants and non-combatants by doing 'aid work' out of uniform. Many soldiers and militia would have never heard of the Geneva Conventions outlining the laws of war, or would blatantly choose to ignore them. Deaths and kidnappings of aid workers were on the rise.

I was busy preparing people to send into war zones, but I was passionate about the West not being involved in these wars in the first place. On 14 February 2003, in solidarity with millions of protesters world wide, a few of us drew some handmade peace signs and took Dr Jim Cairns to join 200,000 Melbournians in protesting against Australia's involvement in Iraq. We walked down the same streets Jim had when he led the Vietnam moratorium march. Hadn't we learnt anything in 30 years? It made it that much more special to have Jim with us.

When Jim sent a message of solidarity to the crowds, the streets exploded in exhilaration. As we walked slowly with our fellow Melbournians, countless people came to shake Jim's hand.

'You started all of this, Jim.'

'Wow, is that Jim Cairns?'

'We love you, Jim.'

It made me realise just how important he had been in Australia's history. Sadly, Jim died later that year.

Beyond participating in Australia's biggest public protest, working for Oxfam gave me a sense that I was doing something for the people affected by wars and other disasters. I no longer looked at the news feeling guilty and helpless. Some would call it naïve, but I wanted to be a part of making the world a better place, even in my own small way.

My new manager, Lucy, was English, with spiky blonde hair and bright blue eyes. Lucy showed me the ropes and patiently answered my million and one questions. Friendly enough but quite serious to start with, Lucy took a while to open up. But it wasn't long before we were like old friends. She'd joke that the only reason I got the job was due to my crutches—to improve disability numbers. Unfortunately for our colleagues across the hall, we found a shared love of musicals. Songs from *The Sound of Music* and *Phantom of the Opera* rang out in our little broom cupboard of an office.

In between teaching me the ropes of the Register and interviewing emergency workers, Lucy and I would sing to our hearts' content. On Monday mornings, she would pop her head up and sit up straight like a meerkat, poised and ready for my latest gossip. In a serious long-term relationship, she lived vicariously through my romantic interludes. Or should I call them comedy skits?

Often there was nothing going on. Zero. Boring. Kaput. I was like a thirsty explorer, lost in the desert with no water in sight, only mirages. When I did start dating someone, suddenly there would be an onslaught of men and I could hardly keep up. Most of them weren't serious, but at least I was dating and had some stories to tell.

Like Tom. A sweet, tall and lanky boy I met at Meeting room 3. We went to a Japanese restaurant in Brunswick Street and talked about music, culture, likes and dislikes. Things were looking good—and then he told me he liked wearing dresses. I had no problem with men wearing dresses as a rule, but I didn't really like the thought of my boyfriend going through my wardrobe. Next . . .

Like Gordon. I met him at a doctors' and nurses' house party. I figured if I couldn't find a real doctor then someone who could play the part would suffice. And I tell you what, he certainly gave me the medicine I needed. Pity about the rest, though. He proceeded to tell me his life story, including his professions as everything from a sniper with the army, to a hot-shot city lawyer, to an environmental conservationist, to a personal trainer. His stories reminded me of *Forrest Gump*. He gave me his card when he dropped me home. It read:

Gordon's Guys

'Want to do what your husband's doing?'
Services include:
Exotic dancers
Intimate liaisons
Scantily clad home cleaning services

I nearly engaged him in a conversation about morals, and that he was actively encouraging women to cheat on their husbands, but who was I to talk—I got a free service and I was happy. *Scantily clad home cleaning services!!!* The flashing lights around his four-poster bed, his different 'characters', his extravagant orgasms and the G-string he strutted around in started to make sense. Next . . .

Like 'Airport Man'. I met him at Melbourne Airport bar. He was a great conversationalist and an even better kisser. My excitement dissolved fairly quickly on our first date when he told me he still lived with his mother and showed me the tattoo of Jesus on his chest. I politely declined his offer to take me to the Born Again Christian weekly sing-along. Next . . .

And of course there were several Mr Married Men, who failed to tell me they were married and tried to seduce me anyway. Where is the sign on my forehead saying 'If you're married, please come on to me?' Why can't I just find Mr Right without baggage—like a wife!!! I have always held strong views about fidelity. Whatever temptation was put in my way, I was determined not to succumb.

Unfortunately, most of my efforts to find Mr Right resulted in a few dates here and there, or drunken one night stands, but none had that spark—the chemistry I was yearning for.

Between my dates and a busy social life, you'd think I had no time to work, however my job at Oxfam was the most rewarding role I'd ever had. I worked hard and loved every minute of it. But the more you know, the more you realise you don't know and I started to feel that I lacked the kudos and experience required. I'd be briefing and debriefing aid workers about situations I had only read about. Without field experience I couldn't really relate to them, even though I tried.

After a year or so I started to feel removed. I wanted to get out there, to actually experience what my colleagues spoke about. The thought of public health work appealed to me the most. I always loved interviewing the public health advisers. It was something I could see myself doing: working with communities to improve their health and ensuring the basics of hygiene and sanitation were met. I pictured myself with little babies on my knee, surrounded by women, working together to make healthy families. While there was no way I was going back to study, which meant public health was out of the question, I did want my own stories to tell. So I started planting the seeds for my deployment.

~

'Have you met Mr Right yet?'

While Dad was supportive of my work, he was much more interested in the idea of having grandchildren. And this was the opening question to most of our conversations.

'No, Dad, not yet.'

My father, a self-made business man, was a hard worker with a strong sense of fairness. He taught me to aim high and that I could achieve anything I put my mind to. 'Work hard, play hard' was the philosophy he instilled in me and he would often be out partying later than me. I was Daddy's little girl. I looked up to him and we had a close relationship. Brought up a strict Catholic, Dad was more conservative than Mum. He always questioned me as to why I followed the Dalai Lama rather than the Pope. Actually, Dad was generally pretty open-minded but retained the 'guilt complex' of most Catholics of his generation.

It was my best friend Stephanie who started to question my own Catholic religious beliefs at age thirteen.

'Do you think babies are born as sinners?'

'No.'

'Do you believe that a woman has a right to choose?'

'Yes.'

'Do you think non-believers will go to hell?'

'No.'

'Do you think contraception should be legal?'

'Yes.'

'So do you believe in sex before marriage?'

'Yes.'

'So how can you say you are Catholic?'

'Mmmmm . . . good question!'

Stephanie—my best friend, my mentor, my soul sister. Stephanie always checked that my actions were true to my values. We had met in year 7 at a conservative private girls' school. She was super intelligent, musical, creative, philosophical and had strong opinions on everything. We experienced many firsts together—school dances, first period, first bra, first kiss, first U2 concert, first date, first job. We shared movie star crushes, family dramas, growing pains and childhood secrets. There wasn't a story we didn't know about each other. She was like a sister to me and we united through a galaxy of laughs and a Milky Way of tears.

Steph had found her Mr Right years ago. Her fairytale actualised. So I knew it was possible. True love wasn't just in children's books or movies.

I had a wide range of friends and was a part of many social circles. People used to joke that they had to book me months in advance to get a space in my social calendar. A social butterfly, I was always instigating parties, barbecues and picnics. I wasn't religious, but I was a bit of a new age hippie and into crystal healings, sound meditations and alternative festivals. Sometimes I struggled with the paradox of my life. I was just as comfortable sitting in the dirt around a camp fire drinking cheap red wine as I was sipping French champagne out of crystal glasses in a five-star restaurant. I could converse with a dread-locked lefty on how to heal our chakras and out of body experiences as much as I could talk about how to develop a high-performing team to a corporate man in a suit. Growing up, I used to feel confused—was I a socialist or a capitalist—but as I grew more confident in who I was I figured I didn't have to fall into any category. As long as I had balance, was open-minded and acted with integrity in a way that would not hurt anyone, then I felt I could float between both worlds.

With a focus on my deployment, I put dating onto the back seat and accelerated towards my dream of becoming an aid worker. Although it was Africa I always felt a calling for, the offer that came from Pritha, the Oxfam Human Resources Manager in the South Asia office, was too good to be true. So instead of preparing others to go to the field, I started preparing myself. Lucy supported me on a three-month secondment to Bangladesh. I knew she would miss me and my Monday morning dating stories, but she was a supportive manager and a good friend.

With a healthy mix of apprehension and excitement, my bags were packed, official documents, piles of program information and the *Bangladesh Lonely Planet Guide* in my hand. My whole family and Stephanie were in tears with me as I said goodbye. Walking through those giant metal doors leading to the 'other side' at Melbourne Airport, I knew this was the start of something big.

CHAPTER 4

THE CULTURAL DIVIDE

BANGLADESH 2004

Brrring, brrring, toot, toot. Negotiating my way from the hotel to the office was an adventure in Dhaka, Bangladesh. One of the poorest countries in Asia, the poverty was evident. The dust kicked at my heels and tickled my nostrils, as I squinted into the blaring sun. I readjusted the *dupatta* scarf to cover the chest of my new *shalwar kameez*, the comfortable outfit of pyjama-type pants worn underneath a knee-length, shoulder-covering top common in South Asia. I trod carefully to avoid colliding with the tinkling bicycle rickshaws, three-wheeler tuk tuks and the myriad of old cars clambering the streets. The symphony of obnoxious honking horns staccato'd with the high pitch ringing of bicycle bells. *I should have brought ear plugs.*

I dodged potholes, ducked under the dangerously low electricity lines, and tried not to breathe through my nose. Open sewer pipes spewed into the small creeks around the city and the streets were littered with rotting piles of rubbish. I watched as grubby faced, barefoot children wearing nothing but rags sifted through the debris, and tried not to stare as legless beggars scuffled their way between commuters, dragging their torsos on the gravel.

I passed concrete buildings, many still under construction using centuries old techniques. Bamboo tied together to make up scaffolding and pulley systems to haul up the next pile of concrete. Men in flip flops and traditional sarongs, sweating as they laboured. An Australian contractor's occupational health and safety nightmare.

I wondered how the women wore those beautiful coloured saris—bright greens, blues, yellows, pinks. Jet black hair falling out of their head scarves. Unlike other Muslim countries I had visited in the Middle East, Bangladesh seemed to be more lax regarding headdress. Saris revealed the brown midriff skin of the women who wore them effortlessly. Spicy aromas wafted from the makeshift stalls on the side of the road. Chapatis, curry, sweet milky tea. A man walked past selling washing baskets and brooms made out of straw, the lot piled on his head, towering higher than his own height. The sticky air made it difficult to breathe, and the pollution and open sewers didn't help.

It was only 48 hours ago that I was sipping a chilled sauvignon blanc on Brunswick Street with my friends. Now I was in another world. I had travelled to over 40 other countries, yet the fact that I would be working in this one was new and exciting. I didn't have my usual air of traveller's freedom and nonchalance. I had to abide by Oxfam's strict ten-page security guidelines, making me overly cautious and slightly nervous.

'If you're ever involved in a car accident where someone has been injured, just drive off and get help afterwards. Local people will take matters into their own hands and you could be beaten and killed,' read one of the guidelines. *Gulp* . . .

No such thing as blending in here, I thought, as people stopped to stare. No inconspicuous side looks or trying to hide it; apparently in Bangladesh it's not rude to stare. Well, it may not be rude, but it sure was uncomfortable. Sometimes I'd smile, but I rarely got a smile in return. I stepped slowly on the uneven road, like a toddler learning how to walk. In other developing countries in which I had travelled, I had attracted endless people coming up to sell me things, beg for money or try to propose marriage to me. But here, on my first day on the way to work, it was just a curious yet unnerving stare. Bangladesh was not used to tourists, and besides aid workers and diplomats, there weren't many white people around.

After fifteen minutes of walking that felt like an eternity, I reached the security of the office compounds. My manager Pritha met me with a gentle smile. It was great to finally put a face to the name from all those emails I'd received to organise my deployment. Pritha was a quietly spoken, middle-aged Indian woman with wire frame glasses that she pushed back on her nose before she spoke. Shy, yet highly efficient, she briefed me on my work. The Oxfam Regional Management Centre in Dhaka was a central office that managed six countries in the region: Sri Lanka, Pakistan, Afghanistan, Nepal, India and Bangladesh. My role as Human Resources Executive meant advising managers in these countries on general HR issues. That meant everything from policies regarding recruitment and selection, how to hire more women, how to manage staff performance, to inputting on the development of regional strategies to improve program quality. Basically, to have the right people in the right jobs to work with communities in poverty and disaster.

My job was diverse and challenging. From supporting emergency responses such as the conflict in Afghanistan, to our work with the thousands of displaced people from the floods in Bangladesh. Agricultural programs in Nepal, to peace building initiatives in Sri Lanka. I struggled enough trying to remember how to pronounce the sixteen-syllable names of my colleagues let alone getting my head around the enormity of the programs.

At the time, the Regional Management Centre was going through a big change process, and the whole office was moving to New Delhi with only the Bangladesh country program staying based in Dhaka.

This meant a lot of people losing their jobs and my team was trying to lessen the blow. I felt for the staff, as unemployment was high in Dhaka and new job prospects were low. We did our best to run training programs, help develop CVs and network with other organisations to explore opportunities. I really valued the incredible pool of local staff who were working directly with the communities. And I was learning more about the regional programs. It was a lot of office work and not the romantic notion of being in a remote field surrounded by children that I had held of being an aid worker. Mainly, I was in an office behind a computer. Before starting in the sector, I hadn't considered the business side of aid work. I was doing a lot of administrative tasks behind the scenes as well as training staff and developing strategy for the HR department.

I was welcomed warmly by the Bangladesh team. I made friends with everyone from the guards, drivers and cleaners to the senior managers. It was apparent after just a few days in Bangladesh that this was not normal practice. Hierarchy was prominent here and people of higher class did not socialise with lower classes. Despite Oxfam's 'equality principles' I found that cleaners and drivers were treated with less respect by local staff. I also quickly discovered the expatriate and local divide that reminded me of old colonial movies. This divide didn't sit comfortably with me at all.

There was the American Club, the British Club and the Australian Club that all the white people would go to on the weekends to use the tennis courts and swimming pools and have big parties and drinks at the bar. This in itself didn't bother me. I knew it was important for people living away from home to have some fun times, and bars were illegal here. What did bother me was that it seemed that locals were not welcome. I remember a sign in one of the clubs directed at the nannies who spend their lives looking after the western children, indicating they were not allowed to enter through the same door. I couldn't believe it. But, new to the scene, I wanted to fit in and was pleased to be invited to the expat parties, despite feeling uncomfortable about it.

Riding in the back seat of a taxi on my way to a party, I would routinely be bombarded by an onslaught of beggars with gross disbilities. Women pushing their disfigured babies in my face. Disabled men sitting on low wooden planks with wheels. Women with mutilated, scarred faces from acid burns most likely inflicted by their husbands. Hands outstretched from every direction. Desperation and in-your-face poverty that didn't sit well. Usually, I'd politely refuse and look the other way, other times I'd surrender and give some loose change. Sometimes I'd buy the street kids a drink or some lollies. Mostly, however, I didn't want to encourage beggars and felt there were long-term sustainable solutions. I'd been told that some people made their injuries worse to attract more money. I definitely didn't like the practice of sending small children into the traffic to beg. But it illustrated the extreme levels of poverty and desperation.

Sometimes I'd wind up the windows as I saw one approaching. Looking the other way, sinking further into my seat, overcome with guilt. But if you gave to one, it would bring over another ten, all just as needy as the next. I made myself feel better by saying to myself that I was employed by an organisation that worked with the poorest of the poor. But that was in rural communities. None of our work was directed at the little boy asking for ten cents, or the blind mother with a malnourished baby sucking at her breast in front of me.

Once, on my way to a party, I saw a couple of two year olds playing on the curb at dusk, centimetres from rushing cars. Entire families slept on traffic islands in the middle of busy roads. Rolling over in their sleep could be fatal. I'd witnessed urban poverty, but I'd never seen anything like this.

And then I'd arrive at my destination—a grand house with lavish gardens, serviced by cleaners, gardeners and drivers. And I'd smile and order a gin and tonic. Drinking the images to the back of my consciousness. Pretending to be interested in discussions on how hard it is to hire reliable house help around here. Don't get me wrong, everyone was lovely. It was just a weird world and I felt I'd landed in some sort of parallel universe.

Back in the office, I tried to balance my living paradox with strong ideologies clearly badged on my forehead. I tried as much as possible to 'do as the locals do'. I wore local clothing (although the saris were too hard to put on, let alone walk around in). I invited all staff to Friday night parties at my house, and I even learnt how to eat with my hands. Mmmmm . . . rice and runny curry. This was not the kind of curry with lots of chunky bits that could be easily picked up. It was the local variation of dhal that was pretty much like muddy water with a few floating lentils.

Much to my colleagues' amusement, they watched as I gathered a ball of rice into the palm of my hand, rolled it in the curry and, as instructed, levied it into my mouth with my thumb. It was all about the flicking action from thumb out of palm to mouth or, in my case, chin, clothing and back on my plate. Remembering of course to only eat with my right hand, as the left was for 'hygiene habits'. Despite laughing at my efforts, I could tell they appreciated it and I finally got the hang of it.

It's amazing how much little things like this, and learning to say 'hello, how are you' make in being accepted into a new culture.

⤸

'Are you married?'

   'No.'

   'Why not?'

   'Well, I just haven't found the right man.'

   'How old are you?'

   'Twenty-eight, I've got plenty of time.'

   'Twenty-eight! You're too old now.'

   'Well, it's hard to find a good man!'

One of my colleagues, Fazal, was interrogating me as we waited for the bride at our colleague's wedding. While I am sure Fazal's questions were well intentioned, I was bombarded with questions about my marital status more often than I could count. Meeting someone on the street, enquiring taxi drivers, nosy older colleagues and basically anyone I spoke to. At first I thought it was men trying to pick me up (which often it was) but it seemed to be a part of a general greeting. 'Hi, how are you? What's your name? Are you married?'

As to why everyone was interested in my marital status I don't know, but I did learn that according to Bangladeshi culture, at 28 I was already 'bad meat', 'dried up', 'over the hill', and would illicit looks of horror when I answered 'no'. I guess as the life expectancy here is about 64 then it makes sense. But to me, I was at the prime of my life. An independent woman focusing on her career and discovering the world. Yes, I wanted to find Mr Right but I figured I had more time. Thirty would be the perfect age to meet someone, settle down and have children. I still had some time.

The bride walked into the crowded room. Layers of deep red sari laced with intricate gold weaving, draped elegantly over her petite frame. Decorated by gold necklaces, fine bracelets tinkling on her arm and detailed henna on her delicate hands. An elaborate chain hung from her nose piercing to her ear. It crossed her heavily made-up face, reminding me of an Egyptian goddess. A tapestry of fresh flowers was held by men in suits over her head as she walked demurely to centre stage, where her husband was waiting. Her eyes always to the ground. Despite her beauty she looked like a scared little lamb.

'Why isn't she smiling?' I whispered to Fazal.

'It's rude to smile. The bride is meant to be upset that she is leaving her parents' house and will be the property of this new family now. She has to show remorse.'

'But doesn't she know the new family, isn't she happy?'

'She has only met her fiancé twice and chatted on the phone. Their parents arranged it all and his parents probably only met the girl once. But they are a reputable family and they got a good dowry.'

I'd read a lot about dowry in South Asia and was fascinated and slightly appalled by the practice of a woman's family paying a 'gift' to the groom's family to marry their daughter. It was like a transaction and although it is now illegal in Bangladesh it is a common practice, often with severe consequences. If they were lucky, the couple would get along and be happy, but often the woman ended up at the beck and call of her new family and had limited choices.

Acid burning and violence against women is often as a result of insufficient or unpaid dowry and hundreds of 'dowry murders' are recorded annually. From birth, the girl child can be seen as a financial burden that has to be dealt with later on in life. At least this bride was over eighteen and from an educated family. Child brides are

32

common, with over half of Bangladeshi girls being married before the age of eighteen, a large percentage of those before they reach their fifteenth birthday. It adds to an already entrenched cycle of poverty. A girl forced into early marriage is less likely to stay in school, and is more likely to suffer abuse and to experience premature pregnancy, increasing her risk of dying during childbirth. Thinking back to when I was fifteen, I can't even imagine what that would be like.

'It's ok, I'll help find you a husband.' Fazal had obviously been thinking about it and taken pity on me. 'What are your requirements?'

Mmmm . . . that got me thinking. What are my requirements? I tried to remember the list Stephanie and I had written when we were fourteen. Her list was made up of four things; mine—twenty! But now, at 28 and wanting to find Mr Right, I thought this a good time to make a new list. Positive visualisation. Put it out to the universe.

Mr Right will be (not in order):
Tall (at least 6ft)
Broad shoulders
Handsome (*to me*)
Confident
Successful in what he does
Intelligent
Good sense of humour
Wants children
Likes animals
Similar values to mine
Musical
Gives great massages
Open-minded
Good in bed

Kind

Romantic

Good cook

Believes in feminist values, for example, helps around the house, women's rights

Generous

Good manners (puts knife and fork together at the end of a meal)

Gets along with my friends and family

Honest

Loyal

While I still held some hope of the clairvoyant's prophesy that I would marry a doctor coming true, it never made it to my list as that would just be ridiculous! The fantasy remained in a secret recess of my mind like a bear in hibernation, just waiting for the first signs of spring.

Unlike some of my friends who were unsure if they wanted to marry or have children, I was so sure that it was scary. I have known since I was about fourteen. I repressed my basic instinct to try on wedding dresses in preparation for my prince charming. I felt like Muriel from *Muriel's Wedding*, who kept a scrap book of wedding dresses, pretending that she was getting married. While I didn't keep a scrap book, I wouldn't allow myself to look through wedding magazines. Sometimes I'd imagine my dad walking me down the aisle and it would bring tears of joy to my eyes.

But for now, those wedding magazines seemed like they would never get a look in. Even my 'back-up plan' was no longer an option. I thought back to the proposition I had received from my friend Scotty a few years before.

'If you get to 35 without meeting anyone, I'll marry you,' joked Scotty.

'Ok, it's a deal,' I laughed. Although I was confident that by 35 I would have met Mr Right.

Scotty was a dear friend who I lived with in the travellers' share house in London. He was the token Englishman among fourteen other Aussies, Kiwis and South Africans. Scotty was a long-haired, dope-smoking, guitar-playing hippie. When we first met I thought he was cute, but he had a girlfriend therefore he was out of bounds. Over the years, after his relationship ended, we would fall in and out of bed together—friends with benefits. There were a few times when my emotions spilled over into the 'oh shit, I think I might be in love with him' category, but we were just really good friends. He was a bit like my grounding stone. Chilled out and comfortable, he gave the best hugs of anyone I knew. Although after London we only saw each other every couple of years, we would exchange long, deep and meaningful emails about what was happening in our lives.

'I want to opt out,' he said to me as I spent a couple of nights with him while visiting England for a human resources conference.

'What do you mean?'

'I can't be your back-up plan any more . . . I don't want any more kids—' (he already had a child from a previous relationship), '—and I don't want to get married . . .'

'I can't believe you're backing out,' I laughed. I never really thought it was serious anyway and found it amusing that he even remembered.

Although I had never really taken it seriously, I found it slightly depressing that even my back-up plan had reneged on the deal! What hope did I have if my 'back-up plan' didn't want me?

Whatever! It wasn't the right time for me anyway. I was in the midst of beginning a serious career, and I couldn't afford to be in love. It would only bring me home and hamper my other dream of being an aid worker. And I had only just arrived in Bangladesh. The journey was just beginning.

⌐

It seemed that Bangladesh was somewhere that people either stayed for years, or only for a few months. Nothing in between. After three months, I hadn't even scratched the surface of the complex issues facing the people and their country. I barely understood the expatriate world. The cliques, alliances and 'who knows who' were a culture in themselves. Many expats were lovely and I'm still friends with them today, but the whole colonial thing didn't sit comfortably with me.

When my boss Pritha offered me a six-month stint in Pakistan, I accepted with a personal oath that I'd try to fit in. I'd make an effort to hang out with the locals and integrate with the culture. Very soon, I was to discover some virtue in the expat world that would challenge my judgemental notions of right and wrong.

CHAPTER 5

IN THE NAME OF HONOUR

PAKISTAN 2004

'I'm sorry, Miss, you can't bring alcohol into Pakistan.' The immigration officer at Islamabad Airport stared at me.

'But I'm not Muslim.' I'd heard that expatriates were allowed to drink alcohol in Pakistan and was reluctant to let go of my bottle of gin.

'Yes, Miss, but it's the law.'

I argued with him for a while but in the end had to relinquish the bottle. As the gin was prised from my tightly gripped fingers I told him I hoped he would enjoy it. Where else would this alcohol go? I am sure they don't throw it in the bin! *It's ok, Krissy, you wanted to integrate, well, this is it. Six months without alcohol won't kill you . . .* I swallowed hard.

The immigration officer ran after me as I left the terminal.

'Sorry, Miss. I'm so sorry you can't bring alcohol in.' He passed me a business card. 'But if you want marijuana I would be happy to be at your service.' *You have to be joking!*

37

'Er . . . no thanks.'

'Peace, Unity, Faith' stood out in big Hollywood-style letters on the manicured lawns as I drove away from Islamabad Airport. This was the place that I would call home for the next six months. Marvelling at the new buildings and colourful gardens, I wondered why so many people in Pakistan lived below the poverty line. This place looked like Canberra. And in fact, similar to Canberra, Islamabad was a purpose-built city to house the Pakistan Government and was filled with State buildings, High Court Houses and diplomatic enclaves. 'Islamabad is ten minutes from the rest of Pakistan,' was a common saying that made sense when I realised how privileged Islamabad was compared to the rest of the country.

Although Pakistan and Bangladesh used to be one country, a bloody war had led to Bangladesh's independence in 1971. Islamabad was a far cry from Dhaka's potholed dirty streets and Pakistan had a different feel all together. I couldn't breathe as easily, because conservatism and a stricter sense of Islamic rule permeated the streets. Similar to Bangladesh, walking to work brought a lot of stares . . . or was it glares . . . I couldn't quite tell. The stares came predominantly from workmen wearing their light blue *jalabiyas*, more tailored but less colourful than in Bangladesh.

Except for shopping precincts, it was rare to see women walking in the streets. When I did see them, they were well covered with their stylish head scarves framing their pretty faces. I made sure I dressed conservatively, always covering my shoulders and ankles, but I may as well have been wearing neon lights flashing 'LOOK AT ME'. Anyone would have thought I was walking down the street in a bikini! Although I tried to fit in, my mismatched *shalwar kameez*, my lighter hair or the fact that I occasionally modernised the look with jeans, clearly had me labelled as an outsider.

In Islamabad itself, I never covered my hair and many of the more modern women chose not to as well. It was in the rural areas that I would wear a head scarf. Accustomed to being stared at in Bangladesh, although not completely comfortable, I became used to it and I looked forward to exploring the country and learning more about Islam. I have always found it a fascinating religion that brings with it a lot of strengths, although it challenges my feminist notions of freedom and women's rights.

Unlike the Bangladesh Oxfam office, here I was the only expatriate on staff. This suited my desire to fully integrate with the people and their culture. The staff were highly educated and friendly and they made me feel welcome. The Pakistan program had a couple of different offices and worked to build the capacity of local partner organisations and respond to emergencies such as droughts and floods.

Programs worked in different ways depending on the context. Oxfam would either be directly operational, which meant activities were organised and implemented by Oxfam staff, or we would work with local partner organisations. Our partners were generally smaller community based organisations managed and run by local people in their own communities. Oxfam would support local partners through funding their activities, capacity building (working with them to improve their skills, knowledge, systems), and through monitoring and evaluation to ensure they were on track and the funds were being spent appropriately. Other stakeholders we worked with included government departments to help strengthen systems and advocate policy and practice change. So while we worked in grass roots organisations operating with communities, we also worked with the government to bring about change and promote ownership. It was a comprehensive approach to ensure that changes made at community level would be supported by higher level policies, laws and systems. The programs covered everything from long-term agricultural programs, to small-scale emergency responses for drought relief with a focus on safe drinking water, sanitation and hygiene.

While the program staff worked at changing behaviour and systems at community and government level, it was my role to change organisational culture and ways of working. Thinking about systems and processes at office level sounds boring, but it's when they are weak that things can go wrong and program quality and accountability can suffer. For example, nepotism was common in the region and pressure from local leaders wanting us to 'hire their second cousin's son's brother' was something that staff had to contend with. My first job was to hire and train a human resource officer who would then be responsible for HR practice after I left. We ran training on good recruitment policy and practice, providing staff with the tools and language to resist these types of pressures, and make sure that the best person for the job would be hired. Training was a core part of my role: performance management, recruitment and selection, coaching and feedback. Essentially—good management skills.

Sometimes I would take a step back and look at myself. Here I was, a young Australian woman in Pakistan, training highly experienced professional aid workers. Using participatory methodologies, throwing in games as icebreakers and seeing staff engage in conversation, problem-solving and practical exercises. It brought me so much joy to see staff putting into practice what they learnt in my training. Whether it be ensuring gender was a consideration when recruiting staff to allow women the best chance to apply for and be considered for roles, or seeing managers provide their staff with critical feedback to improve their performance. It all made a difference to how the organisation ran, the motivation of the staff, the quality of work and therefore stronger accountability to the communities in which we worked and the donors who provided us the funds to do the work in the first place.

I still felt distance between myself and the communities in which Oxfam worked, but I knew that a stronger staff who were clear on their roles and responsibilities, felt empowered and were managed well would translate to the best possible practice on the ground. And it felt good to be a part of that.

And wherever possible when working in the field offices to run a training program or assess office systems, I would make sure that I visited programs within the communities so that I could see the real difference that Oxfam was making. One of the most fascinating programs to me was a part of our gender equality work: the 'campaign to stop honour killing'. I'd read about honour killing at university, but talking to women in a country where the practice is prevalent and accepted brought my awareness to a whole new level.

Honour killing is when members of a woman's family, usually the father or brother, murder their daughter or sister due to actions that they say 'dishonour' the family. It's estimated in Pakistan that about 1000 women are killed every year in the name of honour. A woman can be targeted due to a number of reasons that are unimaginable to me—from allegations of adultery to refusal to enter into an arranged marriage, to women wanting to leave an abusive relationship, being a victim of rape, or even wearing clothing that doesn't fit the cultural norm. The truth of the matter is irrelevant. A mere allegation is enough to bring 'dishonour' to the family and therefore the slaying is justified. It's harmful, misogynistic practices like this that make my blood boil, and highlight the extreme outcomes of gender inequality and how ignorant cultural doctrines try to rationalise it.

On a field visit to Sindh province, in the south-east of Pakistan, we stopped to monitor the progress of one of our partners—a small, community based organisation. Their key focus was on stopping honour killing.

'It's complex,' explained the young female project manager pouring me a cup of green tea. 'You can't just go into a village and say, "Hi, we're here to talk about honour killing." If we did that, we'd be outcasts.'

'So how do you encourage the women to open up?' I asked.

'We usually start talking about health. More acceptable casual topics and eventually, after time, when the women feel more comfortable with us, we gently raise the issue or sometimes it will just come up.'

'How big is the problem around here?' I enquired, still in disbelief that the practice actually took place.

'Well, in Sindh province alone, there have already been over 250 cases in the first half of the year. But we are sure there are more. These are just the ones that are reported. The killings are often covered up and the police don't take any action.' *Oh my God—stay professional, Krissy!*

'That must be hard to work with, particularly if the police aren't even on board.'

'Yes, it is. Like last month, we were told about a young woman in a nearby village. She was dragged naked along the ground by a rope tied to the back of a horse until she was dead. No one stopped to help her.'

I shook my head and looked into my green tea.

She continued. 'It wasn't reported to police so the incident doesn't even show up on official records.'

I watched a little boy leading a donkey laden with wood past the window. Lost for words. This is just one of many stories I heard about the practice. It's hard enough to fathom people killing at all, let alone killing their own flesh and blood. But honour killing just highlighted the limited worth of women in some parts. On this occasion, the woman in question was accused of an affair, yet she may have simply been speaking to a man outside her family, which caused the rumours that lead to such brutality.

The local women running this organisation were so brave. Their strength and determination was impressive, leaving me humbled.

On the car ride back to the Sindh office, my colleague told me about the rest of the campaign. This organisation's work with women in villages was an important grass roots component of the program, but talking to women alone would not change the practice. It was also the men, the Mullahs, the legal system and the government that needed to be engaged with the issue to effect change.

Mullahs—the Islamic equivalent to Christian priests—hold a lot of power in villages but are often illiterate and uneducated themselves. Oxfam ran workshops with the Mullahs to change attitudes and behaviours concerning the practice. Some Mullahs would say 'but it's in the Koran', however, this was a misinterpretation. The program involved getting more educated, well known Mullahs in the workshops to dispel these harmful myths. At the same time, our advocacy team worked with human rights groups and the government to encourage impending changes to unjust policies that often let these crimes slip under the radar.

I tried to be open-minded and see all the good that Islam brings. There were many unjust laws being made 'in the name of Islam', but it's the same with any religion: the ideology and practice are often contradictory, and this is one of the reasons that I rejected my own Catholic religion so many years ago.

I thought about my upbringing and rights as a woman at home in Australia. It's really easy to be critical of other cultures, and honour killing was extreme, but I reminded myself that it's only recently that women have had more rights in the West. And we still have a long way to go. Even now, women are judged by what they wear. Comments like 'she was asking for it', 'well, of course she is going to get harassed if she wears that skirt' are still common. Sexual abuse and domestic violence are rife in Australia. In the West, up to 70 per cent of female murder victims are killed by their partners. It's like women are blamed for the irresponsibility of men, 'they can't control themselves', 'it's in their nature', 'it's the alcohol that did it'. *Bullshit!*

I tell you what though, I am so thankful for the work of feminists up until now. I just think of the changes made since even my mother's generation. I'm a strong advocate for equity in whatever society in which you live. It was encouraging to see Pakistani women at the forefront of social change here, and while change may be slow every step is vital, no matter how small.

I often consulted the learned accountant, Fahid, about Islamic doctrine. A kind intellectual, Fahid's door was always open for my questions about his religion.

'What is this about then? How can this be fair?' I slumped into the chair next to Fahid's desk, pushing the latest quote from the newspaper under his nose.

'Yes, I can see out of context this does not look good. But if you think about it with the rest of the paragraph, it actually means . . .'

This became a daily practice, as I struggled to learn more about Islam. Fahid was a patient and willing teacher. I didn't agree with everything he said and still found many of the quotes from the Koran harsh and discriminatory (particularly concerning women), but in general the teachings of the Koran made sense. Fahid would listen carefully to my point of view, and in some cases even agreed with me. It strengthened my understanding to learn so many negative practices in Muslim countries are actually more of a 'cultural' practice, rather than religious. However, over the years these cultural practices, such as honour killing or forced marriage, have been viewed as religious and therefore encouraged by local leaders and Mullahs in the name of Islam.

~

Back in Islamabad, a few months into my stay, I was finding being the only expatriate challenging to my usual social repertoire. Pakistani hospitality was always generous and people were accepting and welcoming. I had some lovely experiences with local staff. Weekends away and trying new cuisine such as sparrow. *Eeeeek!!* Breaking fast with families during the fasting season of Ramadan, and some refreshing walks through the surrounding Margalla hills. It was generally work colleagues I was socialising with and always as a guest and having to be on my best behaviour, aware of breaking cultural taboos and making a good impression. I couldn't completely relax. Plus most had families to go home to and I found myself alone most evenings—something unheard of for the one who was usually the instigator of parties at home in Australia.

One weekend, a female neighbour, Faiza, invited me for a girls' weekend with a few of her friends. In most Pakistani circles, girls' weekends away were forbidden without male chaperones. Faiza was a pretty woman with a slight build and long hair she wore held back in a ponytail. Her *dupatta* (a long scarf worn either to cover hair or draped over shoulders) was slightly crumpled and, to look at, you would never imagine such a strong, confident personality and professional demeanour.

Her two friends Nagma and Nafisa were sisters. Nagma, the more elegant of the two, had high cheek bones and manicured eyebrows.

Her long wavy hair fell against her immaculate lemon *shalwar*. Nafisa, the younger of the two, had unruly hair and was a great deal pudgier, and it was obvious that she lived in her sister's shadow and couldn't quite emulate Nagma's style. These three beautiful, strong women in their mid to late twenties had no problem telling off any passers-by who would stare and whisper about the likes of 'us' without a chaperone.

'Don't yell at them, Faiza,' I exclaimed, as she screamed at passers-by to mind their own business and stop staring, for the third time that day.

'Krissy, you don't understand our culture, ok? We have to put up with this every day. Why shouldn't we be able to come out by ourselves without stares. I'll say what I want to them.' I kept my mouth shut from then on, feeling I had crossed over some invisible cultural line. In fact, they too had crossed over a line of social expectations for women just by being out alone so far from their home.

Saying that, however, we did have a male driver for the car we hired and he took it upon himself to look out for us as we drove towards the scenic north-east Mansehra district and the picturesque local tourist spot of Naran Valley. But these women were progressive, independent and intelligent and it was clear to me, if not the society in which they lived, that they could be just as strong and powerful as their male counterparts.

We hiked up to the stunning glacial lake of Saiful Muluk, watching the more respectable Pakistanis drive the easy path. The lake was filled with mystery that had our hearts longing for love. As the ancient story goes, a Persian prince falls in love with a fairy princess he meets in his dreams and journeys for years to reach the lake. Alas, he finds her already bound to an evil man who he fights to the death to win the fairy's affections. In fear of retribution, yet madly in love, they hide in a cave under the lake for protection. Legend has it that they are still beneath the water and during the full moon nights they emerge, mounted on a flying white horse. *Ahhhhh . . . how romantic . . .*

As with most girls' weekends, we sat in our PJs eating chips and chocolates, and recalling the funny stories of our day. We talked about the same topic that interests straight women the world over— men. Although the conversation was quite different to that of any girls' weekend I had previously been on.

'Krissy, it's just not fair. My parents are trying to arrange a marriage for me. I have met so many men and played the dutiful daughter. I have to pour tea and then sit in the other room so they can talk about me. It's like I'm invisible.' Faiza grabbed another handful of chips. 'Already the fact that I am independent and have my own point of view is a cross against my "suitability as a wife". I'd be expected to give up my job completely if I got married. I want to travel, develop my career, see the world, but that's not what "a good Pakistani woman" does.'

'Can't you find a progressive educated man who wants a professional woman?' I asked.

'They are few and far between, Krissy,' Faiza continued, 'and if they are that progressive they have usually moved to the States or UK by now,' the girls laughed. 'I think Nagma must be the only one to get lucky. She already has a lovely man . . . Nagma, doesn't your fiancé have a brother or something?' Faiza jeered at Nagma, who had snuggled up with a pillow on the couch.

Nagma was in the throes of organising her own wedding.

'No, and keep away from my fiancé,' Nagma laughed, as she threw the pillow at Faiza.

'Is it a love marriage?' I asked.

I used to think this was such a strange question, but in contemporary South Asian society it was a common one. Most marriages were arranged by the parents, where the couple had varying amounts of choice depending on how conservative or educated the family was. With more women starting to gain independence, getting an education, joining the workforce and gaining more rights, there were increasing numbers of love marriages. If you were lucky, your parents would like the partner. In this case they did and Nagma told us about the wedding plans.

'Yes, it's looooove,' teased Nafisa, as she reached for another handful of chips. 'I wish I had such luck. I'm begging my parents to find me a husband.'

'Really?' I was intrigued. 'But don't you want to choose for yourself? Don't you want to fall in love?'

'My parents know me. They know what I like and I'm sure they'll choose a man from a good family. There have just not been many good offers around.'

'What's the big deal about love marriages anyway? Where you're from, one in three marriages end in divorce. Here you can get lucky and fall in love after the mariage, and have the blessing of your parents'.

'What if you're not lucky, though?' I asked.

'Yes, well, that's the problem. There aren't many options for women once they are married. You can't just get divorced here. You'd be an outcast.'

We talked about the pros and cons of arranged and love marriages and agreed that the main issue was the ability for women to choose, which in Pakistan depended on your family. Although it didn't affect these women, 'forced marriage' where women were stolen, raped and forced to marry their aggressors to save their family from dishonour was still prevalent and, in Pakistan and much of Asia, child marriage was a major issue.

I must say, though, considering my luck in finding Mr Right on my own, I thought about sending my 'list' home to my parents!

Back at home in Islamabad I looked through the photos of our adventure. Weekends like this were fantastic. I was always appreciative when people took it upon themselves to take me away, meet family in their villages, have dinner at their houses and in general show off the infamous Pakistani way of welcoming strangers. I learnt a lot about local traditions. So different to my own culture, drinking was a no no and a fun night for some of my friends consisted of a trip to the local KFC and then home and in bed by 10 p.m. And that was a Saturday night. The rest of the week my TV, which I rarely watch at home, got a good work out and I filled pages in my diary.

Well, I wanted to integrate into the local culture and do as the locals do, didn't I? But the locals I knew all had big families to go home to—that was the difference. I had nobody waiting at home for me and I was lonely. Three months went by and while the work was interesting and the occasional outing with a kind colleague was nice, I started feeling restless. It was three months into my deployment when I was introduced to a young Canadian woman called Emma, who ran a yoga class. So it was from the humble pose of the 'downward dog' that I entered into a completely different world of Islamabad—the expatriate world.

CHAPTER 6

THE POWER OF WATER

PAKISTAN 2004

Champagne flowing, costume parties, poolside barbecues and at least weekly functions at one of the embassy clubs housed in the diplomatic enclave. I was entering a world I had criticised in Bangladesh. Most of the frivolity took place in the heavily guarded and fenced off diplomatic enclave that housed the international embassies and clubs.

I found my groove with a great bunch of friends from all around the world. They ranged from diplomats, to businessmen, to other non-government organisation workers. Many of them were musical and I was in my element at sing-alongs and performances with some great musos at Emma's fortnightly jam sessions. I felt like I had entered a secret world, and while it was exclusive and not really in tune with Pakistani culture, I felt ok with it.

It made me realise the importance of maintaining links with other expatriates. Living in another country, with a new culture and different language, having to cover up all the time and watch every movement can be tiring and lonely. So now I had the best of both worlds. I maintained my local friends, continued to learn the language and visit local families, but I was also able to let off steam, completely relax and have fun among people with a similar culture. And I definitely made up for those three months of not drinking or socialising much!

My new set of friends and I even had our very own 'bootlegger', who delivered alcohol underground. I felt like I was living in 1920s prohibition America and it was exciting.

'Who is THAT?' I asked, motioning towards the striking dark horse whose mere presence filled the room.

'Oh, that's Zakir. Come, I'll introduce you. He's a fantastic singer.'

Emma led me over to the group sitting on Afghani woven cushions in the corner. A guitar and a few *darbuka*—traditional Arabic hand drums—lay among the group. They were sharing a *shisha* pipe. The apple tobacco smelt sweet as it bubbled through the elaborately designed glass water pipe. Drawn smoothly up the long, golden, threaded mouthpiece into the pipe, the exhaled smoke contributed to a sultry mood. It took me back to my travels around the Middle East.

'Zakir, this is Krissy. Krissy works for Oxfam and has been here for a few months.' Emma introduced me around the circle, but I wasn't interested in the others.

'Hey, Krissy, how ya going?' Zakir's hands were rough. His eyes black. His voice as deep as an operatic baritone. 'Join us.'

Emma and I found some cushions and the circle widened to make space for us. The *shisha* was handed to me and I inhaled deeply, feeling the familiar light-headedness and tingling skin. I sank further into my cushion. The first drummer began.

Takata takata takata taa . . .

Others joined in and Zakir picked up the guitar and strummed gallantly, complementing the rapid beat of the drum. I wanted to dance but didn't feel comfortable (or drunk) enough in the new crowd.

Takata takata ta takata takata ta . . .

The rhythm was short, sharp and addictive. The beat fastened and the energy in the room heightened. A few people relented and started to dance, their movements casting shadows on the wall from the flickering candles.

And then it happened.

Zakir began to sing.

It was a sound like I had never heard before. I was transfixed and transformed. Breathless, I stared in awe. He was strong, confident, comfortable. His eyes were closed and locks of thick, dark, curly hair swung around his masculine face. It was Qawwali music—Sufi inspired, poetic, passionate and philosophical. Watching Zakir, the hairs on my arms stood up and shivers went down my spine. In a musical reprieve, Zakir's eyes met mine. I smiled and nodded in appreciation of his music as I inhaled once more on the *shisha* pipe. I felt dizzy but I wasn't sure it was the pipe. Zakir stirred a part of my being that had not been stirred in a long time.

⌒

The following week I was back in the Sindh office to conduct a human resources audit: check that all the systems and records were up to scratch and run a few management training sessions. The office was responsible for our drought response program and I took the opportunity to visit some communities. Rolling up in our dusty white 4WD, we arrived at a small village that seemed to pop up out of nowhere. From afar, I hardly noticed it was there. The mud houses with straw thatched roofs were made of materials from the surrounding environment, and the colours melted into the desert landscape. As if from out of nowhere, there was a hoard of people surrounding our car. Men in dusty *shalwars*, women in faded yet colourful saris and barefoot children giggling and fighting to hold the hand of the white woman. I was here to assess the conditions under which our staff were working and deliver some training, and took the opportunity for a field visit to see the impact we were having on people's lives.

The village leader proudly showed me the new Oxfam well and buckets, as I stretched out my fingers to accommodate three children holding each hand. I ducked my head to look into a small, round mud brick house made up of a single room for an entire family of eight. It smelt of mud and smoke from the small fire in the centre. A couple of beat-up water containers in the corner, blackened pots and that was about it. The only clothes they had, they were wearing. I was given a small wooden stool to sit on as about 100 villagers sat around me. Women to one side. Men to the other. Children at my feet. Flies everywhere in between.

I shifted on my seat, smiling at everyone. Silence. *What now? I didn't realise that I had to say anything . . . I am just here to observe.* But expectations were too high and I felt a hundred sets of eyes waiting for what the white woman was going to say.

'Er . . . *assalam alaikum*,' I mumbled the traditional Islamic greeting of 'peace be with you'.

'*Wa alaikum salam*,' they replied, delighted that I spoke some of their language.

'How are you?' Everyone nodded their heads and touched their hearts.

'I'm from Australia.'

Blank looks as many in this remote community hardly knew they were in the continent of Asia.

'It's a country a long way away,' I explained.

Adjusting my head scarf as I noticed a curl escaping, I switched to English, asking them about the new well and health program.

Ahmed, the Oxfam public health officer, translated for me.

'It has made our lives so much easier,' said a young man, smoking a roll-your-own cigarette.

'We used to have to walk for hours to collect water,' added a young woman with a naked baby tied to her back. 'Now the well is here, we are so happy and it gives us more time for our other duties.'

An old woman yelled something at the children, who were taking turns to touch my white skin followed by muffled giggles. Much to the amusement and pleasure of the group, I picked up a little girl wearing a worn, oversized t-shirt and put her on my knee. She stared at me with adoring eyes and played with the hairs on my arms.

'We want to say thank you to you. The Oxfam people came and taught us about how to look after our water and our children are not sick any more.'

This is what it's all about. This is why I came here. I swallowed hard and smiled softly.

'Before, many of our children died from diarrhoea,' the tooth-less woman explained, eyes glistening. 'Now our children are much healthier.'

My eyes glistened too as I held back tears.

'Do you have clean water in your country?' they asked.

I talked about the drought in Australia and how in many parts of the country there is desert and little water, just like this. I wanted to find some common ground. But I also told them that most people could get water to drink and clean themselves. I did not tell them that the water in our toilet bowls is cleaner than what they used to drink. Or how each time we flush our toilet, it is equivalent to the amount of water a whole family here uses in a day. Or how I can just turn on my tap and out comes water that I can drink without getting sick.

'You have a beautiful village,' I told the group as we walked around getting ready to leave.

A woman came running over and presented me with a coloured scarf, in bright greens, blue, pinks and yellows. It was newer and brighter than anyone in the village was wearing. I knew it would be rude to refuse the gift. I was touched but also felt guilty that they had so little, yet still offered me a gift. I wished I had something for them in return.

As the community leader and children followed me excitedly to the car, my heart was warm. This was the image I had of myself when I imagined being an aid worker. Surrounded by gorgeous children and hearing people talk about the difference that a program I was working on had made in their lives. We pulled away and the children ran as fast as they could, yelling their goodbyes until we lost sight of them. Despite the poverty and lack of the basics, people were still positive and thankful just to have water.

The next week I visited our Quetta office in Balochistan. The area was known to be rougher than Sindh, with regular bombs going off in town and eruptions of violence. Balochistanis are a proud semi-nomadic people, living in harsh desert conditions. It was dry and dusty, and people here were more aggressive and guarded in their manner. Driving five hours through the arid desert, the mountains of Afghanistan in the background, the blinding sun reflecting off the sand, we arrived in another community. The feeling here was different. Straight away, I understood that this experience was not going to be the touchy feely sort that I encountered in Sindh. I was with a junior male hygiene promoter from Oxfam who was enthusiastically showing off our programs, but I wasn't warned that we might not be well received. As our car approached the village, the children and women seemed to run away and hide.

Sitting cross-legged on the dirt floor of a small mud brick hut, I wasn't sure where to look. It was quite cool inside despite the unrelenting 45 degree Celsius heat outside. My left leg started to go numb against the hard ground. Opposite me sat the village chief and two other male leaders.

'*Assalam alaikum*,' I smiled.

'*Wa alaikum salam*,' they replied without interest.

Silence.

'My name is Krissy and I'm from Oxfam . . .' They barely looked at me. 'I'm here to look at the water system we worked with you to install.' More silence. 'To see how it's going. What impact it's had on your community?'

I noticed a small hole in one of the men's discoloured white *jalabiya*. The men looked uninterested and unwilling to engage. Was it because I was a woman? Was it because Oxfam's program had finished? My efforts were greeted with cold, blank expressions.

'Yes, now there is water, but we need much more.' The leader told me abruptly. 'There are no schools for our children, there is no food, there is no health clinic, there is no transport, there is little firewood. How can you help us more?'

What am I meant to say to that? I swallowed hard. There was nothing I could offer, nothing I could do. I didn't have the authority to promise a new program here. The funding had dried up. The initial money was to install wells and pipes to ensure clean water, but there was nothing left. What do I say, what could I say? All I knew was the worst thing to do was to make false promises as many agencies had done over the years.

'I'm sorry, I am just here to have a look at the water system and see if it is helping.'

'But what else are you going to do? You can see the situation here!'

I could see. There was nothing here. I had no idea where they would even get vegetables from as the dry sand would be hopeless for any type of crop and besides the odd goat, I couldn't see any animals. There were no proper roads leading to this village; it is a wonder that they survived out here at all.

I looked at my colleague desperately but he didn't seem to know what to say either. It was up to me. 'All I can do is pass on your message to my manager. I'm sorry, I'm just here for a visit.'

The men nodded and remained silent.

'Is it ok if we see the water installation?' I asked meekly. The men called on another villager to show us around.

The villager was friendly and enthusiastic and I began to breathe again. I'm not an engineer but it seemed like quite a feat to have pipes deliver water to such a remote area where the ground water had all but dried up. The pipes had been installed and were connected through several villages that were scattered kilometres apart. Considering we were in the middle of the desert, this was miraculous!

Returning to the mud hut, I saw the village leaders again. 'Can I talk to the women and children?' Knowing that it is the women and children who collect the water, wash, cook, clean and so on, then this installation would have had the most impact on them.

'No.' Why would he bother with niceties if there was no more that we were offering to this village?

I thanked them for their time and drove away feeling like an absolute fraud. *What the hell am I doing here? How can I even start to help these people?* I felt like a voyeur, an aid tourist who was just here to see how the poor people live but had nothing to offer. Nothing. Yes, they now have water, but what else could we give when there is no funding available. No health, no education, no transport . . . no nothing . . .

You naïve idiot, Krissy. What good can YOU do? I felt hopeless, sad and disappointed. I stared off into the desert, flat and stark as far as the eye could see.

I thought about my friends in Melbourne. They would probably be just finishing work and going for drinks at Meeting room 3. I felt alone and useless. We sipped hot green tea back at the office, but all I wanted to do was run to my room and cry.

Such diverse experiences within the same week were a great lesson to me about the ups and downs of aid work. Sometimes you can leave a situation feeling great about small changes, at other times you feel depressed that it is just not enough.

CHAPTER 7

BOMBS, BANDS AND BURKAS

PAKISTAN 2004

Scrunching my curls in front of the mirror, I wondered if Zakir would be at Emma's party that night. I thought he would be more of an au naturel kind of guy, so I put my bright red lipstick to one side, choosing instead a subtle lip gloss and a touch of mascara. I was not really into make-up, but I liked to make an effort when going somewhere special. I had kept replaying our meeting in my head over the last week. Not that anything happened. We hardly said two words to each other, but my attraction to him was palpable.

I felt good in my little black dress. A far cry from the *shalwar* and head scarf I wore in the field, it had just enough cleavage and hung just above the knee. Sexy yet sophisticated. My mum always taught me to buy matching underwear and it was at times like this that I appreciated the advice. I always felt a little more special with matching lingerie. I checked the lace wasn't visible through the dress.

I turned the lights off in my house and shut the door behind me. I quite liked my place. When I first moved here it was a bit lonely, but now I had an active social life it was great. I was even used to the minaret speaker right in front of my bedroom window. The 5 a.m. wake up call that was once annoying was now quite comforting.

There was a chill in the air. I wrapped a deep red pashmina around my shoulders and walked down the street to catch a taxi.

'*Mujhe Sector D jana hai.*' I proudly used my new language skills to ask to be taken to Emma's house.

I had been studying Urdu and taxi drivers were great to practise on. But my language had limits and slipped between English and Urdu as the drivers practised their limited English on me. The conversation, however, was always the same.

'Where are you from?'

'Australia.'

'Oh, Australia, Ricky Ponting.' I had no idea about cricket but quickly learnt the Pakistani Aussie favourites.

'Yes, yes,' I smiled.

'You married?'

'No, I'm not married.'

'Why?'

'Because I haven't found the right man yet.'

'Why not?'

'I don't know.'

'How old are you?'

'Twenty-nine.'

'You are too old now. You better find a husband.'

'Gee, the weather was nice today, wasn't it?'

The party was in full swing by the time I arrived. I immediately joined Emma and the rest of our gang chatting in the kitchen.

'Champagne anyone?' The cork popped with a bang. 'Woo hoo . . . the best sound in the world!' I shouted.

I'd purchased a dozen from my bootlegger before the last party.

'How are you?'

'I just got back from Quetta . . . it's so full on.'

'Isn't that where all the bombings were last week?' asked Tim.

Tim was a close friend. He had lived in Islamabad for a couple of years, working at the Australian Embassy. One of his jobs was to know and advise on the latest security incidents.

'Yeah, but it was fine when I was there. Just a very different culture. Tough!'

I scanned the room for Zakir and spotted him talking to a pretty Pakistani girl who I hadn't met before. *That better not be his girlfriend!*

'Emma, let me help you with that.'

I took the food platter off her and started handing it around the room. I knew most people at the party. Many just by face, from the British Embassy costume party the week before and others with whom I had spent many a hungover Sunday brunch by the pool at the Canadian club.

'Hi, Zakir, how are you?' I held the food platter steady as he took a *pakora* (a fried, battered vegetable snack). 'I'm Krissy.'

'Yeah, Krissy, I remember.' *He remembers!* 'Krissy, this is my cousin, Ghazala.'

Thank God!! Although, it's not uncommon to marry cousins here . . . should I be worried!!!???

'Great to meet you . . .' I motioned towards the food as I started to move on with the platter. 'Chat to you later.'

Really, I didn't know what to say and needed more champagne to calm the clowns doing cartwheels in my stomach.

'Of course.' Zakir smiled, sipping his whiskey.

A Pakistani artist and singer, Zakir was on the fringe of society. A part of a young, progressive, alternative Pakistani culture, Emma had become friends with him and his crew. It was open mike night tonight and someone started playing some funky riffs on the base guitar. The room soon exploded into a jam session. Guitars, drums and even a saxophone came out. We danced, drank and chattered through the night. Later in the evening as the crowd started to thin out, the window sill became the backdrop of a stage and individual acts began. And then it was my turn. I had been practising 'Fever' with Sven the Norwegian guitarist all week, and I had enough alcohol in my blood to give it a go.

'Never know how much I love you. Never know how much I care,' I swooned, 'when you put your arms around me, I get a fever that's so hard to bear. You give me fever. With your kisses . . . fever when you . . .' I started slowly but built my confidence by the end, clicking my fingers and rocking to the sultry beat.

'Wow, Krissy, we didn't know you could sing, that was fantastic,' a few people came up after the song. Embarrassed but on a high, I looked around for Zakir. He was smoking a joint, in deep conversation with some guys by the door. *Damn, did he even notice?*

Later, Zakir performed. I could feel his passion oozing from every note. It was captivating and penetrated the core of my being. Again, I was lost in his magic.

This was one of many nights to follow and soon they all merged into one. Singing, dancing, music. Zakir and I developed a strong friendship. We were often the last ones up at a party. Singing together, smoking a *shisha* pipe, sharing the odd joint and sipping our bootleg booze til all hours of the morning. I had discovered he was actually training professionally as a Qawwali singer and was recording some albums. His passion went beyond his music. He was passionate about the state of the world, of local politics. He had strong views on religious doctrine. We discussed issues such as gender and culture, why the sky was blue and what is the meaning of happiness. The more I got to know about him, the more I liked him. But we always went home in separate taxis.

'Where are you from?' *Here we go . . . !*

'Oh, Australia, Ricky Ponting.'

'Yep,' my eyes rolled involuntarily.

'You married?'

'Yes.'

'Where is your husband?'

'He's waiting for me at home.'

End of conversation.

~

'Don't you feel guilty?' asked my stepmother, Christine, as we sipped red wine from china tea cups. We'd just settled into the Chinese restaurant at the Marriott Hotel in Islamabad. A bottle of wine was never allowed in plain view on the table and everyone seemed to be enjoying 'tea'. Dad and Chris had come to visit from Australia and we had just returned from a five-day road trip in the beautiful mountains of Swat Valley. 'I feel bad drinking and eating good food after what we've seen. I can't imagine how you must feel all the time.'

'I used to but not any more.' I poured myself another cup of red.

A lot of people have asked me this question over the years and it's something I used to struggle with. Working with such poverty and then coming back to a comfortable bed and good food. Or going to a party after walking through a village where children are dying from malaria. It doesn't seem fair and it's not. But guilt is an emotion

I have had to learn to deal with. If I felt guilty constantly I wouldn't be able to do my job. In fact, if I didn't have the space to socialise with people I had something in common with I would probably go crazy—particularly on longer-term deployments.

I feel empathy, and I feel sad, and I feel angry and I feel hopeful . . . but I try not to feel guilty. I also understand that I need to be a happy, healthy person to be able to work effectively in the field. I am here, I feel active. Walking into a village where others only see poverty, I see hope, resilience and strength. I am continually surprised by the human spirit and how much we can endure.

No, it's not right, it's not fair—people in a world where there are enough resources to share should not be starving to death, or dying from easily preventable diseases. Where there is no clean water, education or health care. We should have our eyes wide open to this. But it's important to recognise the strengths that every person has to offer. To provide space and a platform in which they can rebuild their own lives, and their own countries. And not take the paternalistic view of 'those helpless little poor people' who we have to save. I do believe we are global citizens and people need to support each other, but we need to do it in a way that is respectful and empowering.

'I feel guilty sometimes,' I continued, 'but I think it's important to have a balance. Just let my hair out sometimes.'

'Literally!' Christine laughed. 'I don't know how you keep this scarf thing on your head. Seriously, it kept slipping off me.'

'I know, it's a fine art. They do it with such ease and manage to look elegant.'

'Yep, where I feel like a rag doll! And I wish everyone would stop staring. It scares me.'

'Well, I tell you what, Krissy, you are a better person than me,' said Dad. 'I could never live here. Give me Brighton Beach any day. We are so proud of you.'

'Thanks, Dad.' He reached over the table and gave me an affectionate pat on the hand.

Negotiating the streets of Peshawar a few days before had been an eye opener. Dad and Chris had both travelled in the 70s but had never experienced such in your face poverty and cultural differences. Particularly in the old city, where we stayed as a pit stop to Swat. It was like stepping back in time. Horse-drawn carts, donkeys, narrow, winding and dusty streets.

Christine in particular found it quite confronting and, after entering a mosque where no women were to be seen and receiving constant stares, she opted to stay in the hotel with her book. It was interesting to witness such culture shock as for me, the more different the culture the more intrigued and fascinated I am. But I understood the fear as Peshawar in particular was known for extremism. Car bombings and gunshots were not uncommon. There was still a war raging in Afghanistan and anti-western sentiment was high in much of the region.

Dad and I traversed the narrow alley ways, lined with shops of spices and gold.

'How can there be so much gold among so much poverty?' asked Dad. 'Who buys this stuff?'

'Good question.' The gold bracelets, pendants and chains shimmered in the windows as a barefoot, blind beggar held out his hand in the street. A stark declaration of the gap between rich and poor and the emerging middle class in Pakistan. Out of the corner of my eye, I noticed two women looking at me. Well, I couldn't really see whether or not they were looking at me as they were in full burka, but I felt it.

'*Assalam alaikum*,' I offered tentatively. It's hard to talk to someone you can't see.

'*Wa alaikum salam*,' they giggled, obviously happy to speak to the only other woman in sight—and a westerner at that. Dad stayed back as I explained they wouldn't talk to me with a man around.

'How are you?' I asked in Urdu.

'Good.' I heard them giggle some more and talk excitedly to each other.

I practised the little language that I had and then said my goodbyes, but I left them feeling a mix of warmth and anger.

As culturally sensitive as I try to be, no matter how much I see a woman in full burka, I still find it challenging. How can a culture dictate so much of a woman's life? Down to whether she can speak, who she can speak to, whether she is seen or not seen. I don't agree with the subtle (and not so subtle) ways discrimination plays out in my own culture and I certainly don't agree with it here.

I questioned my own cultural bias. Was I being racist? Was I merely forcing my own western values on to another culture? I try to understand cultural differences regarding gender, but I struggle with what I consider such lack of freedom of movement and expression. For me it is about human rights and choice. In a country where 74 per cent of women are illiterate, I wonder whether many women even understand the concepts of 'rights', let alone the ability to demand them.

'When are you coming home, darling?' Dad asked, as he polished off the last bit of fried rice.

'In a couple of months, but I wish I had more time here.'

'Come home, Krissy. It's time. You've done your bit now. It's time to come back and make me a grandfather.'

'Dad!'

'What?' he laughed as he paid the bill.

'Thanks for coming, guys, I really appreciate it.' Tears filled my eyes. Dad and Christine were leaving the following day.

'Well, next time can you make sure you are deployed to Paris?' asked Chris. 'I'm not sure I could handle this head scarf again.'

While I was thriving in my workplace and had a great social life, my Dad and Chris's departure made me reflect more on life. I wanted to provide Dad with grandchildren as much as he wanted them and I questioned whether this would be viable with the lifestyle I led.

~

The week after Dad and Chris left, I hosted a party at my house. I decorated my balcony with colourful cushions and carpets I hired for the evening, fairy lights all around and incense burning. A *shisha* pipe in the corner and curry on the stove.

By 11 p.m. my lounge had turned into a dance floor and about 30 guests wandered from the kitchen to the dance floor to the chill-out balcony. In the kitchen a small group of us had gathered for tequila shots, although I had never had tequila this way before.

'Right,' asserted Sven the Norwegian. 'First you get a partner . . . Emma, if you please . . . Then you place the salt on your part-ner's shoulder, or neck . . . or wherever you want. You place the lemon in your partner's mouth facing outwards like so . . . then you lick.' Emma squealed as he licked the salt off her shoulder. 'Sip!' He downed the tequila in one go. 'And le pièce de résistance . . . suck!' He sucked the lemon from Emma's mouth. Everyone squealed with a mixture of delight and 'oh my God—am I really going to do this?' and started choosing their partners.

The night got very messy and the 'sucks' ended up extending to sloppy yet sensual kisses, everyone swapping partners for the chance of another shot.

'That's hilarious!' I screamed over Michael Jackson's 'Beat it'. 'I love it!' I looked up at Zakir after a prolonged 'suck'. Mind you, I had also watched him 'suck' with three other girls by then!

BEEP! 'Whose phone, turn it off!' yelled someone from the back of the room.

BEEP! Another phone rang across the room.

BEEP! Another. 'What the . . .'

BEEP! Another.

'Shit—a bomb's just gone off at the Marriott,' yelled Tim, the guy from the Australian Embassy.

'Oh no . . . turn the music down.' Sven turned the stereo off and everyone checked their phone.

'What happened?' I asked, sobering up pretty quickly.

'Thank God, no one seems to be hurt, but who knows, it only just happened.' There was silence in the room as everyone looked around at each other.

'Oh my God, I was only there with my parents last week,' I whispered to Zakir, who draped his arm around me.

A few people responsible for security left the party to alert their staff; they had to investigate further. Sections of the city would be in lockdown again tomorrow. But as there were no fatalities that we knew of and we had become accustomed to the odd bombing, Michael Jackson was turned up and the party continued, even if in a somewhat more sombre mood.

At four in the morning, when all the guests had left, Zakir and I sat facing each other, cross-legged on the floor with a cup of peppermint tea each. We took turns massaging each other's hands as we finished off the last joint.

Zakir started to sing my favourite Qawwali song. He would sing to me and then translate the words.

Saaraa jahaaN mast, jahaaN kaa nizaam mast din mast, raat mast, saher mast, shaam mast mast shiisha, mast subuu, mast jaam mast hai terii chashm-e-mast se har Khaas-o-aam mast.

The whole world is ecstatic, the order of the world is ecstatic. The day is ecstatic, so is dawn and so is evening. The glass, cup and wine are all ecstatic. Because of your intoxicating eyes, everyone and everything is ecstatic.

He closed his eyes to sing in Urdu, and looked in my eyes as he translated the words to English.

Sab samajhtaa huuN terii ish nazar ai saaqii kaam kartii hai nazar, naam hai paimaane kaa.

I understand your alluring glances that cause intoxication, instead of wine.

Keep going, don't stop. I was in heaven. I closed my eyes and felt the heat rise between us, his singing becoming more passionate.

Na namaaz aatii hai mujhko na vuzuu aataa hai sajdaa kar letaa huuN jab saamne tuu aataa hai merii bandagii hai vo bandagii jo ba-qa-id-e-dair-o-haram nahiiN mera ek nazar tumheN dekhnaa baa-Khudaa namaaz se kam nahiiN.

Neither I know prayers nor ablutions, I prostrate whenever you come in front of me. My devotion is such devotion that it is not bound by the mosque and the temple. When I see you once by God, it is no less than a prayer.

I listened dreamily. Captivated. Floating.

I had never told Zakir how I felt. But the attraction was strong, thick like Arabic coffee. We felt connected emotionally, intellectually and, that night, it became physical too.

In the bedroom, I looked deeply into his eyes and somewhere, lost within each other's rhythm, it was as if I went into a trance.

'What's wrong?' he asked.

I shook myself out of it. 'Sorry, I don't know.' I kissed him. I didn't tell him what I had seen. In his eyes I had seen flashes of our future together. Falling in love, having children, living together—the images were captivating and so clear in my head that it brought me to a standstill. It was probably the mix of tequila and weed but it was powerful nevertheless. I wonder if he saw it too and if it is what scared him.

Something must have scared him, because after that night, any signs of kissing, let alone sex, came to a halt. *What the . . . !?!* He didn't want to 'go there' again, said he couldn't explain but he just wanted to be friends. I was confused. I assumed he just wasn't interested, yet he continued his visits every night and our connection was still strong. We swapped massages, talked deeply and the mutual attraction was still palpable—but for some reason he didn't want to take it further and pushed away my advances. I didn't understand why he would continue to stay with me, often until the 5 a.m. call to prayer, talking, playing with my hands, singing—but the sexual wall had been put up.

⌒

Six months in Pakistan had come and gone and it was time for me to leave. I didn't want to go home. Professionally, I'd really started understanding and seeing the impact of my work in the organisation. A new and confident human resources officer had started, the leadership team had more skills to deal with management issues, new systems were in place and full reports and recommendations for the future had been submitted.

'Krissy, we are often dubious about "outsiders" coming to help, but you have been a great asset to the Pakistan program. In six months you have not only raised the bar of the way we work, but

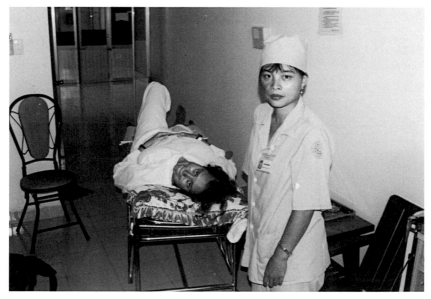

It's amazing how dangerous a dance floor can be. Dislocated knee in Nha Trang hospital, Vietnam, 2001.

With my step-brother Cameron in Angkor Temples, Cambodia, 2001 (before the accident).

Family visit to Sygiriya rock, Sri Lanka, for my 30th birthday, 2005.

Grandma and me in Sri Lanka. I am wearing the 'Jewel of the Nile' that she and Mum gave me for my 30th birthday.

With my brothers Paul and Cameron at a nightclub in Colombo, 2005.

'You started all of this Jim'.
My great grandfather, Dr Jim Cairns,
was greeted by marchers as we
joined mass protests against the
Iraq War, 2003.

A warm welcome from a small community in Sindh province, Pakistan, 2004.

Speaking with the community in Sindh province, Pakistan, about the impact of hygiene promotion and new water systems in their village, 2004.

Women washing clothes at the newly installed water pumps, saving them hours of walking. Balouchistan, Pakistan, 2004.

It is frequently children's responsibility to collect water for their families—often keeping them out of school. Bolouchistan, Pakistan, 2004.

Young boy drags jerry can across the stark desert to collect water. Bolouchistan, Pakistan, 2004.

Ruins at the epicenter of the Pakistan Earthquake, Balicot, 2005.

Pakistan Earthquake. This was a three-storey building, 2005.

The women I spoke with in Peshawar, Pakistan, 2005.

Dad wondering how there could be so much gold on this street when there is so much poverty surrounding us, Peshawar, Pakistan, 2004.

Friends playing Twister at a weekend escape from work in Pakistan, 2004.

A big night out in Colombo with Larissa, my partner in crime while I lived in Sri Lanka, 2005.

One of the many expatriate parties. Halloween in Islamabad, Pakistan, 2004.

you have managed to touch all of us with your smile and friendship. For this we want to thank you.' The staff held a farewell party for me and presented me with a beautiful gold and jade bracelet. I tearfully hugged them all goodbye, except for the more conservative men, where a hand on the heart and warm handshake expressed the sentiment.

Personally, I had made a great group of friends and connections I wanted to continue. But my role at Oxfam in Melbourne was still there and I needed to return to it. On my last night Zakir stayed, once again until daybreak. We breathed in sync for many long moments as we hugged goodbye. He said he would explain his behaviour in an email.

CHAPTER 8

LIMBO LAND

MELBOURNE 2004

The soft, velvet cushions cradled me in the old couch. The red walls reflected the luminous glow of flickering candles. Stephanie was radiant on stage, playing evocative melodies on her violin with her five-piece band. I looked around at my beautiful friends. Sipping red wine, chatting quietly, warmly. Glowing as the sounds wafted gently over us in the bohemian bar on Gertrude Street, Fitzroy. I was surrounded by love, but I couldn't get rid of that tight feeling in my chest. The one where you feel like you have a big knot right over your heart and it's hard to breathe. I sipped my wine, struggling to swallow. Everything was blurry as the tears struggled to stay within my eyes. But then I blinked, and there was no point trying to hold them back.

It didn't make sense. I was home with people I loved. In the kind of funky bar that I missed when I was away. Yet I felt empty and disconnected. *Krissy, get a grip. What's wrong with you?* I pinched myself. My body was there, but my heart and mind were in some sort of limbo land. As if balancing on a tightrope stretched precariously between Pakistan and the velvet seats of the bar. I thought it might be jet lag but it was more than that. After Stephanie's first set, I made my excuses and left. I'm not one who can pretend. 'I'll be fine,' I responded to the concerned looks of my friends.

I tottered slowly down Brunswick Street on my way home. Live music drifting out of the cool bars. Restaurant-goers spilling on to the streets. Wafts of garlic and cigarette smoke. The clinking of glasses. Life. The same busker who had been there for years played beats on his makeshift drums. Car lights shone contemptuously in my face and the rumbling of the trams assaulted my ears. Snippets of excited conversation as people passed dressed in eccentric and uniquely Melbourne styles. 'Oh my God, you won't believe what he said to me', 'I love your new shoes', 'Which restaurant do you want to go to', 'Nah, that bar's crap, let's go to the next one'. The bare shoulders and miniskirts of the girls shocked me. So much skin! Glaring fluorescent lights in supermarkets were blinding. Everything felt superficial. The roads were too straight and organised. The lights too bright and the shops too many. The choice and affluence made me sick to the stomach.

When I got home, I poured myself a glass of water from the tap, turned on my bedside lamp with the flick of a switch, lay on my comfortable bed and stared at the ceiling.

I had debriefed aid workers on 're-entry syndrome' several times and now heard my own voice in my head. 'Also known as reverse culture shock, it's quite common for returning aid workers. Symptoms include: headaches, lethargy, nightmares, sleeplessness and depression. But don't worry, it will pass and there are ways to deal with it that I'll go through with you. It's quite normal.' If I had been debriefing myself right now I would have told myself to 'fuck off'. Nothing about this felt 'normal'!

On Monday morning, I burst into Lucy's office. 'I NEED A DEBRIEF!' I wailed. Over time the feelings of disconnection dissipated. I started to realise how oppressive Pakistan had actually been. I could breathe more easily. I hadn't noticed it so much while living there, but there had been many limitations. What I could wear, how I could act, where I could go, what women should and shouldn't do. Bomb threats in my local shopping centre. Back home and with time to reflect, I realised that all these restrictions had taken their toll. Despite this, I still missed the adventure. The chance to work with amazing people, the local communities, the continual discovery of such a fascinating country, culture and religion.

I checked my emails daily and besides the odd 'Hi, how are you, we're missing you here' I never really got an explanation as to why Zakir suddenly went cold. I guess it didn't matter now. Pakistan was another world away and what had been such a strong bond started to unravel, like a stitch coming undone, slowly pulling away the shape from a well-worn dress.

Back in my job on the Humanitarian Relief Register, I found it no longer challenged me as it used to. I was unmotivated and completely over it. The places I had seen, the new skills I had gained and the rewarding experiences I had enjoyed overseas saw me bored and wanting more. Yes, I now had the kudos and benefit of experience to talk with more authority when deploying people to the field. But it wasn't enough. I wanted to be out there again. I started looking for jobs in Africa in an effort to satiate the unexplained pull I felt towards the continent.

Lucy could see I was getting bored and sent me off to another RedR emergency management course. It was an intensive five-day residential training course on Sphere humanitarian standards. Based in country Victoria, it was a residential course, set up with accommodation, training rooms and even a small bar. This is where I met Rob and the prospects of being back home seemed brighter.

Ten-hour days of practical learning about core technical sectors required to save lives during an emergency. 15 litres of water per person per day as a minimum requirement. *He has such a cute cheeky smile.* 3.5 square metres living space required per person. *Mmm . . . he keeps making excuses to turn around and look at me.* Latrines should be built no closer than 500 metres from living dwellings . . . *I wonder if he is usually so tactile . . .*

Each night the course participants gathered in the bar to swap stories and philosophise on the state of the world and what needs to be done about it. It was an eclectic group of people. Some had been in aid work for twenty years, others were straight out of university, some in private business wanting a change and others from military backgrounds. Rob was an ex-soldier. A logician who served in Timor leading up to Independence. After serving for over ten years he decided to jump the fence and join the humanitarian sector. I never imagined I would be attracted to an army type, as anything to do with the military is a turn off for me, however, Rob's shift to aid work seemed more aligned to his true values.

I don't know what it was about Rob. Sure, he was handsome in a rugged Aussie kind of way. He was shorter than my usual type but his shirt fitted his toned, muscular body perfectly. Those arms had me swooning. The more time I spent with him (usually in the company of big groups), the more I wanted to know. We were always among the last ones up, making use of the bar and flirting over the wonky pool table.

We talked for hours about our hopes and dreams. I told him about my time in Pakistan and my dreams of working in Africa. He told me about his time in Timor, and how he now wanted to work from a different angle. I told him how I'd been having vivid dreams and my interpretations of them in regards to real life. He told me he never remembered his dreams and wondered why. He believed in a god that was more about the earth, universe and humanity rather than the god of institutionalised religions. So did I. Each night after long days learning new skills on how to design a refugee camp, we would continue where we had left off our conversation. Philosophy, religion, travel, life, death, the cosmos. I don't think there is a topic we didn't cover.

We moved a little closer as the days and nights went on. Sitting close but rarely touching besides the accidental brush of the back of his hand as he lifted his drink, or leaning in close enough to inhale his scent as I got up. Other participants drifted in and out of our conversations, often not staying long, as they must have sensed our connection.

By day I could feel Rob wherever I was. Sitting in front of him in the training room, I could feel his eyes on me. My chest felt tight. Butterflies deliciously pirouetted in my belly. Casually we would make our way to each other during breaks. Joking around, laughing. Our eyes would meet briefly across the room while talking to other colleagues. Eyes lingering that little bit too long. Evenings were filled with lively conversations and debates, fuelled by alcohol. While I conversed with others on the course, I always felt him close.

'Standards are bullshit. Most countries we work in don't meet these in their daily lives, let alone in an emergency,' argued a 50-something-year-old man who had spent years in the field.

'Yeah, but we have to have some standards to work to. Look what happened in Bosnia,' said another, younger woman.

'Rubbish, it's unrealistic. I tried it in Somalia and people came from miles to be in the camp because the conditions were better than their own living conditions. It just sets people up for unrealistic norms that can't be sustained,' his voice got louder.

'I can see that, but without them, more conflict could be caused by agencies delivering different things . . . more fighting . . . we don't want . . .'

'Yeah, whatever.' The man went to refill his glass as the others continued.

'What do you think about Afghanistan? Can you believe the United States is dropping peanut butter in food packs . . . I mean, HELLO!'

'Well, we shouldn't be there in the first place. It's all a part of Bush's grand plan to . . .'

I loved these kind of conversations but decided to find Rob and challenge him at another game of pool instead. He was one game ahead of me and I wanted to get even. The flirting was fun and light, yet thick and deep at the same time. We danced playfully with our words. He penetrated me with his eyes.

Intense simulations of setting up refugee camps by day, with three hours sleep and hangovers. The nights were never long enough. We would always make an excuse for just one more drink. One more topic of conversation. Is there life after death? What do you think of the war in the Congo? What's your favourite food? If you had to have dinner with anybody, who would it be and why? What is Howard's immigration policy? We explored each other's minds yet barely dared to touch.

Under a blanket of stars, I stood in a nearby clearing contemplating my glass of sauvignon blanc and the universe.

'Can you see Scorpio?' I caught my breath as I felt him breathe against my neck. My heart was beating so loudly I was sure he could hear it. I could feel the warmth of his body behind me as he stood close, arm outstretched into the night's sky, trying to direct my attention to the constellation. I could hardly breathe.

'No, where is it?' I could barely speak. He stood closer.

'If you look directly right of that small cluster of stars. See that really bright twinkling star . . . and if you follow it around you will see the two claws of the Scorpion . . . see?' I followed his fingers and felt our cheeks close together to ensure we were focused on the same star out of a million on this starry night.

'Oh, yeah, kind of . . .'

'And then see how the tail curls around right to the horizon . . .'

'Wow, yes, I see it. That's amazing, I can't believe I've never seen that before.'

Among a million stars on this still night, the Scorpion appeared like one of those '3D magic eye' pictures that appear if you stare long enough. It was magnificent. I should have stalled for longer, as once I had it in view he moved away. There was no longer the excuse of having to be close enough to follow his direction. We spent the night pointing out constellations, discussing the possibility of life on other planets, our thoughts about astrology and seeing auras.

'If you were told you could go to the moon tomorrow, would you go?'

⌒

'Oh my God, Stephanie, I have met the most amazing man. There is something really special about this one, I know it . . .'

'Oh my God, did anything happen?' she screamed down the phone.

'No, we didn't even kiss. That's the beautiful thing.'

'Tell me more . . .'

'It was so strong, though, so real that I feel like we didn't need to. Oh, I would love to kiss him.'

'Why didn't you just . . .'

'No, it was a work training program so we were probably just being professional . . .'

'So are you going to see him again?'

CHAPTER 9

EVE'S TEMPTATION

MELBOURNE 2004

Not even a day had gone by before I got the first phone call from Rob. He rang to ask more about the Humanitarian Relief Register and how he could join. Whatever! I knew he was just calling to speak to me. Not once did we talk about our feelings but the connection was clear. He called me every few days over the next couple of weeks. Just to talk. Because he was bored at work. Or he had some random idea he wanted to discuss.

Rob was based in Sydney. I was in Melbourne. So it was only ever phone calls. I sent him a stone I found on a beach one day, with a letter attached. I said it was a dream stone so he could start to remember his dreams again.

After a few glasses of wine late one evening I decided to call him for a change. He was on one of his night shifts in the army barracks, and I could tell he was glad to hear my voice.

'I wish you were here,' I said bravely.

'I wish I was anywhere but work.'

We chatted small talk for a bit longer.

'So, do you have a girlfriend?' I knew he wouldn't, considering our intensifying relationship. I felt a bit stupid asking but I needed to—just in case.

'Yes, I do, Krissy.'

I was stunned into silence. Body weak and heart shattered into pieces on the ground.

'Excuse me, what did you say?'

Silence. Uncomfortable silence.

'Did you just say that you have a girlfriend?' I continued.

More silence.

'Yes, I'm . . .'

'But, but . . . WHAT . . . ? Why didn't you tell me?'

'Krissy, I . . .'

'Why have you been calling me? How can you have led me on like this?'

'I haven't been leading you on. We are just friends. You didn't ask. I wasn't keeping anything from you.'

'That's bullshit, Rob, and you know it. What about all the phone calls, the flirting?'

'What flirting? I never flirted with you.'

'Excuse me!!!' I couldn't believe my ears. 'Well, I'm not sure of your definition of flirting, but I must be living in a state of complete delusion.'

'No, it's just that . . .'

'Are you fucking serious? I can't speak to you now!' I slammed the phone down.

Sitting on the floor in the middle of my bedroom, the walls closed in around me. Shock, disbelief and rage whirled inside me like a tornado, uprooting all that had seemed safe and sure. I burst into tears. *No, how can this be? Not again.* His intentions seemed so real, our connection so strong. Did I really not have the insight to know a lie when I heard it? But it wasn't a lie. I knew it wasn't. I felt it. It WAS real. I replayed every look, every flirtatious comment, every 'accidental' touch. He was the one who had been calling me—I just didn't get it.

Over the next week Rob called a few more times. He finally conceded that I could have 'misinterpreted' his actions as flirting, but he never meant to lead me on.

'But didn't you feel a connection?' he contradicted himself. 'I mean, a really strong connection?'

'Of course I did.'

'So did I, Krissy. I don't think I have felt such a strong connection with anyone before.' *Oh my God—is this guy serious?*

'For God's sake, Rob, what am I meant to say to that? You have a fucking girlfriend!'

Holy shit—I just don't get men. Was he deliberately messing with my head? Rob had sent me a poem in the mail with a crystal meaning 'logical thinking and friendship'—what man writes poems to his 'friends', whatever the intent or topic?

A month later, after a lull in communication, I visited my family in Sydney. *Whatever you do, don't contact him, don't contact him.* But guess what? I contacted him. I had to know once and for all if there was any chance in the world that this was something special or a figment of my imagination. Maybe he and his girlfriend were breaking up anyway. Maybe they weren't happy. Well, I could only hope. We met in a bar at The Rocks. I had organised to meet some other friends that night so I would have an excuse to leave. Nerves subsided after the first glass of wine and we cut straight to the chase. There was no point in small talk.

'I admit that I am very attracted to you and if I was single I would definitely be pursuing you.' *Why is he sweating so much? He looks like he ran here!*

'And . . .'

'But I'm not single. I have a partner who I am pretty happy with.' *Pretty happy with . . .*

He went on. 'I would really like to be friends with you, as I think you are a really special woman.' He handed me a letter. 'It's not finished yet but I was going to send it to you when you called.' The letter was thirteen pages long! 'You can read it later.'

After another glass of wine, I decided that I'd try to be friends with Rob. But as the night continued, my decision became more and more blurry. Once again we found ourselves dancing with our words and reading way too much into each other's eyes.

'Let's go.' He jumped up suddenly. 'I want to take you somewhere.'

He led me through paved alley ways and then up an old grey staircase. A lonely red apple sat on a small pillar of the stairwell to the Sydney Harbour Bridge. Rob picked it up and was contemplating eating it.

'Yuck, you don't know where that's been.'

But as he placed it back on the pillar, I wondered if the apple was a symbol of that age old temptation from the bible. I was Eve—and there was the juicy red apple, ready for me to take a bite. How apt. Maybe I should have given in to temptation. What's the worst that could've happened? Apparently the world was already cursed with original sin.

On top of the Bridge, right in the middle, under the majestic arches, we looked over the edge. A gentle breeze and the reflecting lights of the floodlit Opera House further inflamed the night. I avoided Rob's eyes, as I knew he would be able to read my mind.

'You know you have enhanced my life, Krissy.' *Oh please, what are you doing to me?*

'I hope that I continue to know you until you are 90 but if not, I am so thankful for the time we've spent together.' I noticed a small freckle on his neck I hadn't seen before. *Cute.*

'Through knowing you, I've discovered things about myself that I never realised.' *You have to be joking! Just don't say anything, Krissy, just keep quiet and smile.* I gritted my teeth.

Waves of emotion swept over me. We were standing in the middle of the Bridge, overlooking one of the most spectacular views in the world. Warm air, starry night. If we were in a movie, this is when the boy would kiss the girl. But he didn't kiss me. He just kept on telling me how wonderful I was and that he had never met anyone like me before. I kept breathing slowly and telling myself that it was ok, and that we could just be friends.

Later, sitting in an upmarket Chinese restaurant overlooking the harbour, we continued to talk in the easy way that we did. We each talked about our family and upbringing and shared our adventure stories. I had to look away when the lingering stares over the table became too intense. And then he talked of Simone. Yes, that was her name. I needed to hear it. To picture an actual woman. Not some idea that I pushed away. Simone, Simone, Simone. It hurt each time I heard her name. We changed the topic and relaxed again.

'You know you don't need to wear glitter,' he said, referring to my eye make-up. 'You sparkle already.' He reached forward and touched my eyelid.

'Ok, that's enough!' I burst into tears.

'What?'

'You know what, Rob, I can't do this.'

'Krissy, I . . .'

'No, Rob—don't do this any more. You say you want to be friends and then you take me to the most romantic place in Sydney and . . .'

'It's not romantic . . .'

'Stop it, Rob, who the hell do you think you're kidding? You can't play with my emotions like this . . .'

'I just thought it would be a nice . . .'

'As if you would take a "friend" here . . . look at this—' The Bridge towered above us, the Opera House reflected the moonlight and the fine silver cutlery shone against the crisp white tablecloth.

'But we can . . .'

'No, WE cannot do anything. WE cannot be friends. WE cannot ever see each other again.' I was still crying but I was past the stage of caring about being polite. 'I'm sorry, but I just can't. I tried. I wanted to be friends with you. It's so sad we have to let go of such a strong connection, but I just like you too much. And despite your denial, I know you feel the same.'

My phone beeped. A text message. I had told my friends two hours ago that I would be half an hour late and they wanted to know if I was still coming.

'Shit, I have to go, Rob. It's probably good timing anyway.' I dried my tears and he got the bill.

We walked to the pub where I was meeting my friends and stood opposite each other at the entrance. Silent and uncomfortable.

'Goodbye, Rob.'

For the first time we embraced and I didn't want to let go. He held both my shoulders and kissed me on the lips. Not a passionate kiss but with all the passion in the world.

I watched him walk away and burst into tears again. He looked back three times before I walked into the pub. Fifteen minutes later I got a phone call. It was Rob telling me to walk down to the busker playing the saxophone on the foreshore. He had left a note for me. Thrust into a Jane Austen novel, the girls came with me, keen to follow the romance I had just relayed in tears over a cocktail. The busker thought it was some sort of practical joke as I asked to look through his coins. Maybe it was a different busker.

'I can't find the note, Rob.' I called him back on my mobile.

'It must have blown away, I just put it in with some change.'

'What did it say?'

'Your eyes are as deep and mysterious as the ocean. Thank you for a beautiful night.'

Is this guy for real? I couldn't say anything.

'Are you there?'

'Yes, I'm here . . . Goodbye, Rob.'

I turned off my phone and went to the next bar with the girls. But I couldn't take my mind off Rob and was shocking company. I had to excuse myself. I was in no mood to socialise. I missed the last ferry to Manly from Circular Quay. I watched as it pulled away from the dock. Feeling despondent, I slowly walked around to the Opera House, settling myself on a wooden bench under a street lamp. I looked over to the Bridge, trying to find the exact spot where we had stood just a few hours before. Exhausted from the tears, groggy from the wine, I opened his letter. It was thirteen pages of beautiful musings about life and love. I sent him a text message—'sweet dreams xx'. Not even a minute later my phone rang and once again we talked of our magical night, how comfortable we felt together. He told me how he wished that I could be with him now but knew it wouldn't be right. 'The night was almost too perfect,' were his final words before we said goodbye.

I hung up the phone and started to cry again. As if the universe was listening, the sky opened and it started pouring with rain. Tears washing away. Sadness and longing rushing in torrents into the lonely harbour. My life was a bloody cliché.

I really thought Rob was a potential Mr Right. Back in Melbourne, I revisited my list. I obviously wasn't putting the right messages out to the universe.

Mr Right will be (not in order):

Tall (6ft) *Ok, now 5ft 10″ (Rob was shorter than that but I still like tall. But seeing such amazing connection with a shorter than 6ft man, I should reduce this)*
Broad shoulders
Handsome (*to me*)
Confident
Successful in what he does
Intelligent
Good sense of humour
Wants children
~~Likes animals~~ (*desirable*)
Similar values to mine
~~Musical~~ (*ok, maybe this is too much to ask*)
~~Gives great massages~~ (*get a grip, Krissy*)
Open-minded
Good in bed (*well, I didn't get to test that one out. He was probably crap though—leave this on definitely!*)
~~Kind~~ (*covered later as similar to generous*)
Romantic
~~Good cook~~
~~Believes in feminist values, for example, helps around the house, women's rights~~ (*we can get a housekeeper! And the sentiment is covered in Similar values*)

Generous

Good manners (puts knife and fork together at the end of a meal) (*yes, still essential. A girl has to have some obsessive compulsive elements*)

Gets along with my friends and family (*not sure, but he told me how much his family would love me! Anyway, it's not about him. It's about the man of my dreams. Focus, Krissy . . .*)

Honest (*definitely*)

Loyal (*definitely*)

And there was one major missing ingredient. I didn't realise I had to spell these things out to the universe, but nevertheless let me add it now to avoid confusion:

SINGLE!!

⌐

It was New Year's Eve and I was dancing by a fire at my favourite festival—Confest, a big alternative living hippie festival on a tributary of the Murray River. Away from civilisation, television, materialism—not a care in the world. But amidst the frivolities, news of the growing devastation of the Indian Ocean Boxing Day tsunami was spreading like wildfire. When I started to hear the seriousness of the tragedy, with reports of over tens of thousands dead in Indonesia, Sri Lanka, Thailand and beyond and the toll growing, I went into the closest town to call the office. Like many Oxfam staff, I cut short my holidays and rushed back to start emergency preparation of staff for deployment.

A few weeks later, Pritha, the HR manager I had worked with in Bangladesh, was on the phone.

'Krissy, we need you in Sri Lanka for the tsunami response.' But my heart was set on Africa and in the previous months I had already started searching for a position.

'Thanks, Pritha, but I'm looking for jobs in Africa at the moment.'

'Please, Krissy, this is one of the biggest emergencies of the century. It will be a fantastic experience for you. You can always go to Africa later.'

Pritha was right. This was an incredible opportunity and I felt pride in the fact that after seeing my work in Bangladesh and Pakistan, she had the confidence in me to do the job. But this role was in a league of its own. It was one of the biggest and deadliest natural disasters recorded in history. I wanted to work to save the lives of others and to overcome poverty. I wanted action and adventure—and I wanted to get back into the field. Well, here it was. This was the kind of emergency I had been training for. If I wanted to make a difference—now was the time.

'You would be crazy to miss this opportunity, Krissy, go get 'em, girl.' Lucy gave her blessing. She knew this was the chance of a lifetime to boost my career as an aid worker. She was such a supportive manager and a great friend.

'But I tell you what, if you miss my wedding I'll kill you!' she said.

I quit my Register job and started packing my bags to head off to tsunami-hit Sri Lanka, where around 35,000 people had died, and more than half a million people were homeless and at risk of further disease and death. I had signed a one-year contract as human resources adviser.

Before leaving, however, I kept my promise and attended Lucy's wedding. It was beautiful, even if I was one of the only single people there. Set in a beautiful Peninsula winery, the vows were exchanged at sunset under an ancient oak tree. Of course I met someone lovely at the reception. A friend of the groom. We danced, drank and laughed through the night.

'Can I have your number?'

'That would be great but I'm leaving next week.'

'That's ok, can we catch up when you get back?'

'I'm away for a year.'

'Oh.'

Great. What if he was Mr Right!?

Meeting this guy at the wedding was a reminder of my life choices. By fulfilling one dream, was I compromising the other? Aid work was a known breaker of relationships. But would it mean that I wouldn't meet Mr Right in the first place?

How am I going to meet someone if I keep leaving? Maybe Mr Right would be overseas? I always thought of Africa as being that 'dusty far away place' the clairvoyant had told of, but I guess that could be Asia too? While lots of my friends were hooking up into long-term relationships, I still had single friends so I didn't feel like too much of a freak. I wasn't even 30 yet. I figured that after 30 was when I would have to start worrying.

Checking in with baggage 20 kilos overweight packed with everything from a year's worth of tampons, my *shalwar kameezs* from Bangladesh and Pakistan and, of course, my bible—the trusty Lonely Planet guide—I was on my way. I had no comprehension of the challenges that lay ahead of me. I read the latest headline about the tsunami on the plane: 'the death toll is now over 200,000 across fourteen countries'. *Oh shit, what am I getting myself into?*

CHAPTER 10

'THIS WAS MY HOME'

SRI LANKA 2005

The fan whirled slowly above my mosquito net as I pulled myself out of my reminiscing. The dance floor in Vietnam seemed like forever ago, as the reality of where I was sank in once more. The rain continued to fall and dogs howled in the distance. The white flags that had fluttered lightly in the wind earlier would be limp and waterlogged. After what seemed like hours, I slowly drifted into a deep sleep.

The next morning I woke in a panic. I dreamt a massive wave swept me out of bed and carried me up above the buildings. I held a tiny, wet kitten above me, struggling to keep my head above water, trying to swim and save us both. I was desperate to save the kitten but I didn't know how and I was losing my grip. As the wave was about to crash I woke, my heart beating quickly and my body sweating in the humidity. No prizes to interpret the meaning of that dream. I had a cold shower, which brought temporary relief. It was really hot. The type of oppressive heat that makes you feel like you need another shower just after you get out of one. Where the air is so thick that it's hard to breathe and your clothes stick to you.

Despite the heat, and the enormity of the task ahead of me, I knew I was in the right place. As soon as I walked onto the warm, sticky tarmac and breathed in the midnight air in Colombo the week before, it felt right. I was here as human resources (HR) adviser for a whole year, and although I had some experience up my sleeve, this was my biggest job yet. I was terrified and hoped I would meet the high expectations of Oxfam. They had faith in me. I just needed faith in myself.

Barely touching the ground in Colombo, where I was to be based, and with little understanding of the situation, I was sent straight over to the field offices to help recruit staff, advise managers on workforce issues and run an induction program. I had to get up to speed quickly. Oxfam's program had been running in Sri Lanka for about seventeen years and already had 70 staff in place. In only a few months it was my task to work with managers to increase this to over 350 staff to meet the extreme demands of the emergency. This included opening new offices. I would also assess the need for trauma counselling for our staff.

It's only recently that HR as a profession has been valued within the aid sector. On the Relief Register, we would focus on engineers, health workers, program managers and logistics specialists. But with the growing realisation that having experienced human resource staff was essential to a large-scale emergency response, I knew that I would never be out of a job. Increasing a workplace by 400 per cent and expecting effective and efficient staff to hit the ground running within a couple of months, including the start up of several new offices, is quite a challenge. Let alone the complexities of mixing extremely busy, stressed people from twenty different nationalities and backgrounds, whose focus is to work fast to reduce the risk of disease and save lives.

After a quick breakfast an Oxfam car took me to my second day in the Batticaloa field office, where the program manager briefed me on Oxfam's work so far. The key areas included providing emergency and transitional shelter, making sure there was clean water to drink, wash and cook with, building toilets and providing hygiene education to stop the spread of disease, and a livelihood program to help the thousands of families who had lost their source of income. The office was one of seven across Sri Lanka working with hundreds of thousands of people.

I walked around the internally displaced people's (IDP) camp, white tents scattered around palm trees providing much needed shade. The shiny Oxfam buckets, hygiene kits and cooking sets were held proudly by their new owners. It was an impressive operation and there had been no major outbreaks of disease, which is one of the biggest threats in the aftermath of such a massive disaster, particularly with everyone living in close proximity. At least everyone here had the bare essentials.

The young children looked up at me with their wide, brown eyes. Big, shy smiles. The resilience of people always amazes me. Despite losing so much, people were just getting on with it. Rebuilding their lives. Children made do with pebbles to play with. The trauma and pain was still strong, but the hope and hard work of the community was evident. In some areas, even the long-standing civil conflict between the LTTE and the government army had subsided and everyone was helping each other.

The LTTE—Liberation Tigers of Tamil Eelam (otherwise known as the Tamil Tigers)—were a separatist militant group that fought for an independent state for the Tamil people in the north and east of Sri Lanka. At the time they held a large majority of the land up north, which was run as a separate mini-state. The tsunami temporarily softened the growing tensions as many worked to recover what was left of their lives.

I watched two young girls picking up bits and pieces from debris near the edge of the camp—a heart-shaped plastic wall clock; a silver Christmas decoration. Through my interpreter, the girls told us their story.

'My sister and I woke up early and went to watch TV at our neighbour's house,' said Niroshini, the older of the two. She must have been about thirteen, her sister Hansani, a few years younger.

'The big waves took everything.' She looked down at the heart-shaped clock in her hand. 'The water filled the house and my sister and I floated to the ceiling in here.' She pointed at a single faded, yellow brick wall with a door frame in it. Chunks of the wall hanging off twisted metal. The wall was standing on its own—the roof and three other walls had been washed away.

'This one?' I pointed in disbelief at the remains of the house that had saved them.

'Yes,' she paused, 'and I watched my cousin outside holding on to a palm tree,' she looked towards the ocean, 'but he couldn't hold on and was taken away.'

'I'm so sorry.'

'We were taken to hospital because we swallowed lots of water, but luckily we are ok,' she smiled. 'This was my home.' She walked to some concrete foundations only five metres from the yellow wall. 'My mother was in here. But now there is nothing.'

The slightly bigger, stronger house with the TV was what saved them. It was the only wall left standing among a beach full of rubble.

I can only imagine what else they saw that morning. It was a miracle the girls were still alive to tell their story. I didn't ask about their mother, but looking at the concrete foundations, I already knew her fate.

Back in the office, I met with some of the staff who had been there since day one and I listened to their stories. In the immediate days after the waves hit, they had the distressing yet honourable task of transporting thousands of dead bodies to makeshift morgues and delivering essential items—food, water, blankets and plastic sheeting for shelter—to those who were still alive. The staff had assisted as distraught families studied face after face of the dead bodies, trying to identify their relatives. Skeletons with skin ripped away. Red raw, shrivelled and waterlogged. The water and the ferocity of the tsunami stripping them beyond recognition. Families desperate to find their loved ones, yet at the same time desperately hoping they were not one of the bodies lying in a rotting row, and that by some miracle they would swim to shore any moment.

Listening to the stories was heart-wrenching, but seeing the photos on the office computer sent me into shock. There were dead bodies everywhere. I watched as the photos flicked over. A half-buried naked woman in sand. What looked like a man's legs coming out from under a grey slab of heavy concrete. Rows and rows of bodies in the morgue, mainly women and children, laid out for identification. Bodies wrapped in white sheaths and being laid into mass graves. Grief-stricken, shocked faces of survivors.

I struggled to even look at the screen, but this was the reality. From a human resources perspective I needed to understand as much as possible the trauma that staff were suffering and to see what they had already worked with. Many of the local staff had lost family themselves and were working in their own communities. It was their houses, their families—yet they worked with barely a break through it all to save the lives of others.

﹏

Hundreds of aid agencies inundated Sri Lanka, making it an uncoordinated mess. All had their own agendas and differing time lengths to be there. There were some professional long-established aid agencies like Oxfam, and other people who just wanted to help— but often had limited ability to do so. All had good intentions, but sometimes caused more work for the professional agencies. We had to pull down and rebuild some latrines built by well-meaning but inexperienced do-gooders, as they were dangerous and built near natural water sources that would get contaminated. Tents designed for the Antarctic were donated for people to sleep in, but it was 30 degrees Celsius at night time, and people couldn't sleep in them.

Aid is much more complicated than I ever imagined, and it becomes apparent in large-scale responses such as this. There are so many layers of bureaucracy to get through, with government, United Nations and other non-government organisations (NGOs) all fighting for their part of the humanitarian pie, all wanting to fly their flag higher and paste their logos on the water tank or shelter.

Of course, Oxfam was a part of this game too and it's a part of donor funding, relationships and accountability. But sometimes it's annoying and time wasting when it's people's lives we are dealing with. We were all there for the same reason: to save lives and prevent further suffering. As if young Niroshini and Hansani, or the mother of three who had to let go of a child to survive, or the man who lost his entire family and belongings care which country donated money for their new house or community well. They were busy grieving for their loved ones and the life they once had. Working to survive and rebuild their lives.

CHAPTER 11

WORK HARD, PLAY HARDER

SRI LANKA 2005

A month later I was back at home in Colombo. The sixteen-hour average working day, seven days a week and travelling thousands of kilometres between our field sites were taking their toll. I was already feeling emotionally and physically exhausted. Some days I felt I was going to crack and I would run to the toilet and burst into tears. My phone was on around the clock. 'Krissy, what's the policy on poor performance? Krissy, I need ten adverts in tomorrow's newspaper. Krissy, how do we recruit more women to the positions? Krissy, can you run another induction training. Krissy, our staff are being poached, what should we do? Krissy, someone was shot outside our office today and Veronica witnessed it . . . can you please organise a debrief.' In addition, I built my team to be based across our seven field offices and received daily briefs, along with fire fighting of constant issues. And I had to report back to our regional and international headquarters, who made unrealistic demands of our time. The sky-high piles of CVs in our office was surely an occupational health and safety issue.

Our policy was to recruit local staff where possible, but this was the largest emergency the country, if not the world, had seen for many years, so external aid workers from all over the globe were bought in as team leaders and technical specialists. Initially, this caused some tensions with local staff, who had been working in a long-term development capacity for Oxfam for twenty years. 'Who are these strangers coming in taking over our jobs and telling us what to do?' was a common feeling. Fair enough, too, and where possible we tried to retain local staff in management positions. However, coordinating fifteen staff in a long-term development program was quite different to 50 staff, a new mandate, and managing the complexities of brand new emergency programs. Most international staff were sensitive to the dynamic their presence would create with local staff, but tensions would arise nevertheless.

Considering the extreme stress the staff were under and the rapid growth of the organisation, I only had to manage a few disciplinary or poor performance issues. The patience, tolerance and support that staff offered each other in this time, despite their different cultural backgrounds, was impressive. Particularly as many of the local staff had lost family, friends and their own houses as a result of the tsunami.

Managing my team and having to advise so many staff, I couldn't show my own stress. I was the one supporting others to work well together and manage their high workloads. It was only a month on, but it was so intense and I had never worked so hard in my life.

'Mum, I can't do this,' I cried down the phone.

'Yes, you can, baby girl.' Even though I was the oldest child, I would always be my mum's baby.

'I'm so tired. There's too much to do and not enough people or time to do it all.'

'Krissy, you always say this and you can always do it. They are so lucky to have you, my darling.'

All I could do was blubber down the phone.

'It's ok, have a good cry, you are so tired, darling.'

'Muuuummmmm . . .' I launched into more blubbering.

'Can you see the moon from where you are?'

'Yes.' From my bedroom balcony I looked over the ocean at the half crescent moon.

'Well, I'm sending you all my love, darling.'

Since I started travelling at 21, Mum and I always sent our love via the moon. It meant that wherever I was in the world, I had Mum with me. It was always a comfort.

'Thanks,' I sniffled.

'Just take it one day at a time. I promise you'll be fine.'

I hung up, feeling better. I was nearly 30 years old but Mum always did the trick.

Take it day by day, she said—but in reality I was taking it hour by hour. Juggling constant demands and trying to meet the needs of seven different field offices. I never let the people at work see this side. They only met with the efficient, professional manager who while slightly stressed was usually on top of it all and supportive of others.

◡

Three months later the program grew from 70 (as expected), to 350 people, including 50 expatriates arriving intermittently from different parts of the globe. I was their first point of contact and my phone was on 24/7. I grew my HR team from two to eight to support the field offices. An HR manager was brought in to oversee the bigger picture and the strategic direction of the program. Originally, I wanted this job and thought I could do it all, but with hindsight, this was the biggest gig I had ever managed. Carrie, an astute and personable blonde English woman with years of humanitarian experience, was a great support to me and the team. At least now I could run ideas past her and share the overwhelming workload.

Despite my personal insecurities, we were actually achieving a lot and the hard work was paying off. But after a while the lack of sleep, the stress and bearing witness to such destruction and trauma had to be expressed somehow and for me it was in the form of tears.

It's not like a 'normal' job back home, where if you miss a deadline or have a day off money might be lost or a customer not satisfied. Here, if we didn't get staff in place to run the program it meant people didn't have clean water to drink, no shelter to sleep in and increased risk of getting sick or even dying. There had already been so much death here—we didn't want to see more.

Each week, we would sift through literally thousands of CVs. Recruiting skilled people was hard. With so many agencies on the ground poaching staff and inflating salaries, the task became more difficult. In the remote areas where the majority of our offices were situated, poor education and employment infrastructure, particularly for women, meant that human resources were really limited. Sometimes we would have to recruit anyone with just the basic skills. We'd intensively train them at the same time as delivering the programs. On the job training at its best. I had to be flexible with Oxfam's human resources policy yet still ensure quality and good practice was being maintained by managers and that minimum standards were followed. A challenging task during chaos.

One of the best supports I could ask for was Larisa. Larisa was a lively white Zambian woman with Russian blood. A volatile mix! We shared a modern apartment in Colombo. Larisa was 29, the same age as me. A single mother, she was working hard to send money back to Zambia, where her parents looked after her five-year-old son. Larisa was hard-core: she smoked, drank, swore and didn't seem to give a shit what other people thought. She didn't suffer fools gladly and was quite comfortable to say it how it was. Tough luck to anyone who disagreed with her. Despite this she knew what she was doing and got things done.

Under her tough exterior, Larisa was a softy. An incredibly strong woman with a kind heart. She was a loyal friend and we became inseparable. She kept me sane and pulled me up when I would be uncharacteristically short with people.

'Krissy, you are becoming a bitch,' she said one day.

What?!? . . . ME, A BITCH? I'm not a bitch! I was always known as a caring and understanding people's person. But the stress and workload were obviously getting to me. That was the slap in the face I needed to take a few steps back, a few deep breaths and learn how to manage my emotions and stress levels.

After the first three months, the manic phase of the emergency was subsiding, which meant a reduced workload, fewer hours and less stress. We started to get our weekends off.

Larisa and I were able to relax a bit more and quickly discovered an active social scene. While she was the tougher 'who cares, fuck 'em' girl and I was the softer, 'it'll be ok, how can I help' girl, we did share things in common.

One: We were both party girls.

Two: We were both a little (or a lot) wild.

Three: We were both single.

What a combination. A combination that soon had us dubbed 'The Queens of Colombo'. 'Here comes Krissy and Larisa!' announced the DJs, as we danced our way into the trendy new clubs heaving with well-to-do Sri Lankans.

Clubs, beach parties, drinking, speeding down the highway from one club to the next. Our newfound Sri Lankan friend, Imran, at the wheel with alcohol pumping through his veins. I would NEVER get in a car with someone who had been drinking in Australia, but when you are overseas, caution often goes out the window. I guess when surrounded by such poverty and destruction it was also a way to escape. Life seems shorter and you've got to really live it—and we certainly did.

We knew all the people to be known in the club scene, the managers kissed us on arrival and we drew the attention of all the hot Sri Lankan men. Dirty dancing to R & B music, pumping and grinding on the dance floor, dancing with one, then another . . . the attention was intoxicating. We were frivolous, careless, and with our Sri Lankan friends, we formed a close knit crew and felt glad that we were outside the usual expatriate scene.

Except when we were on field trips, Larisa and I were out most nights after work. In the morning we would don our dark sunglasses, hale a tuk tuk and pick up a fresh coconut for sale for ten cents on the side of the street. And begin another day of serious work and responsibility. I don't know how I juggled the two. The most challenging, stressful and rewarding job of my life coinciding with the most active and haphazard social life I have ever had. I think I must have been running constantly on adrenalin.

Larisa and I shared regular hangovers, but we also shared a strong work ethic. At the office, we worked hard getting into action with drive and efficiency during the day. That drive and efficiency would then take us to the Colombo dance floors in the evenings. And it would start all over again the next day. Work hard, play hard, play hard, work hard—my dad's mantra living strongly in me.

Our party crew, predominantly men, became protective of us but also increasingly jealous. They wouldn't like it when we talked to other men. We were 'their girls'. Despite this, we all became good friends who were inseparable. Over time, we found out that they led double lives. One of our friends had a family and children that we didn't know about for months. Another talked up his connections in the hood but actually came from a strict Muslim family, still lived at home and lied to his mother about where he was. Middle-class Sri Lankan society was all about who knew who. Larisa and I didn't care about any of this. We just wanted good times and honest friend-ships, so discovering the truth hurt. But we were already too close, so we forgave them and ordered another shot.

Larisa and I flirted shamelessly with different men at various times, revelling in the attention. One of the guys I liked was a well built Sinhalese man. The first time I saw him I knew I wanted him and I could see from the look in his eyes that the feeling was mutual. His English was average but we didn't need verbal communication. Back in my bedroom, we were giving my bed a good work out.

'I'm going . . .' he said breathlessly.

'Where're you going?' *Where the hell is he going?* It was three o'clock in the morning and we were in the throes of passion . . . *at least finish the job, matey!*

'I'm going, I'm going . . .' his pace quickened with his breath. *What!?*

'Ah, Krissy, I'm going . . .' *Oh, he means he's coming! . . . Don't laugh, Krissy, don't laugh . . .*

'Ohhhhh, I'm going . . .'

Well, there was no chance of me 'going' at all, as I held back hysterical laughter. The story gave Larisa and me hours of amuse-ment for days to come.

⌒

'Krissy, can you hear yourself?' Stephanie spoke seriously to me on the phone.

'What are you talking about? I'm just having fun. Big deal!' I laughed.

'The way you talk about men. This isn't you.'

'Of course it's me. It's me having fun.' I continued to laugh.

'Krissy, you just don't sound like the woman I know.' Her tone was serious.

'Whatever, Stephanie. Thanks for the concern, but I'm fine.'

'Well, just be careful.'

Getting off the phone to Stephanie, I knew I'd changed. I had lost my once strong values. I had always been the life of the party, but I was also known as a bit of a hippie and had a strong sense of spirituality. Now I was so busy going between work and partying that I didn't stop to think about my spiritual side and I was losing touch with it. It was hard to put my finger on and it was not one action or another. It was just my sense of being. But I pushed this notion to the side. I was having fun and rationalised that I was working hard and achieving ambitious goals with Oxfam to rebuild Sri Lanka, so what did it matter. I never let my partying get in the way of my work. A girl's got to have balance, right? If it was all stress and business without any fun I'd go crazy. What I didn't realise was that my idea of balance was completely out of kilter.

⌒

I was heading to our Ampara field office, thinking how fast time goes by. It had already been six months and I was halfway into my deployment. A big night out and a little hungover was making it a woozy ride. Embarrassed, I asked the driver to stop and vomited on the side of the road. 'I'm a bit car sick, must be all the windy roads,' I apologised.

'So, how are things going here?' I was in a meeting with my newest HR officer. *I can't believe I was sick, I didn't drink that much!*

'Good. We hired three engineers this week.' *Hold on, when was my last period?*

'Great! Any females?' *27th of July—or was it the 20th?*

'No, but there're some in the next round.' *I think it was the 20th. Oh shit, what's the date today?*

'Sounds good . . .' *Nah, it will be fine. It's probably just alcohol. I'm sure it's that.*

'And what about the performance management training? When can you . . .'

'Oh yes, thanks for the reminder. Let me just check my diary.' I thumbed through the well-worn pages. *One week, two weeks, three weeks . . .*

'Krissy, it's August, you're looking in July.' *Four weeks, five weeks, six . . .*

'Krissy?' *Shit!*

'Sorry, yes, where were we . . . training . . . yes . . . um . . . how about September 15th?'

CHAPTER 12

SECRETS

SRI LANKA 2005

The following week, pushing my fears to one side, I travelled to the Trincomalee office to help out with some interviews and visit our programs. Life had started to look a little more normal in the communities. Fishermen had received new boats as part of our livelihood program, and the initial fear of being back in the ocean and of eating fish, due to the belief that it might be poisonous, had now subsided.

It was encouraging to see the strong new wooden houses that the shelter program had been working on. All the emergency tarps that had been used in the beginning were now being used for shade outside the new houses, or over rooftops for extra protection from any leakage if it rained. There had been major issues regarding shelters. Land ownership was a big issue. All documentation (for those who had any in the first place) had been swept away to sea. The government was looking at implementing a 'buffer zone', which meant that people who had houses originally right on the beach were no longer able to use the land for rebuilding. Supposedly, this policy was in the interest of 'safety', yet there were suspicions about plans to build tourist resorts in prime positions. In addition, all the agencies were building to different standards, and competition between communities was rife.

Stopping in Habarana, the halfway point in the seven-hour journey back to Colombo, I met up with Larisa, who was on her way out there. This was a usual lunch spot to break up the long journey. Larisa had been on leave in Zambia for two weeks and I was bursting to see her.

'What's wrong?' she said without a hello. I looked around to check we were alone.

'I'm late . . .'

'What do you mean, we have plenty of time to . . . YOU'RE WHAT?'

'Larisa . . .' my voice quavered.

'No, you'll be fine . . . how late?'

'Two weeks. Oh no, Larisa . . . what if . . . ?'

'Don't think about that now, it's probably nothing.'

We ate in silence. She looked up occasionally with a worried if not slightly amused expression on her face. What if I was pregnant? I couldn't even fathom the idea.

'Larisa, what am I going to . . .'

'DON'T think about it . . . it's probably just stress. Go home and I'll see you tomorrow. I'm only in Trinco for one night. Seriously, Krissy, it will be ok.'

'Shit.'

Thoughts and questions whirled around my mind like a vicious hurricane. Oh my God. A baby? This wasn't in my plan. It's not meant to happen like this. I was meant to have a loving partner by my side. It couldn't be true. Not now. Not here. *Please no . . . please no.* What would I do if I was pregnant? Would I give up my humanitarian career and go home? Have a baby and become a single mother? Would I have a termination? If so, where and how? I don't even think it's legal in this country. Maybe it's nothing. Maybe I don't have to worry at all. *Please let it be stress, please let it be stress.*

The next day, back in Colombo, Larisa walked into my room without knocking, sat on my bed and handed me a handful of pregnancy tests.

⌒

Larisa and I sat together in shock, next to a mountain of tissues. I could hardly see the red line on the strip through my tears.

'Give me another one.'

'Krissy, you have already used four. I think it's pretty certain. Don't worry, you'll be . . .'

'I will NOT be ok, Larisa. What am I going to do? I can't believe it!' I burst into tears again. Larisa handed me a toilet paper roll as I had emptied the box of tissues.

You stupid, stupid, stupid girl. How could you be so irresponsible? You idiot. What are you going to do now? But I already knew. I was absolutely terrified but there was one thing for sure. I wasn't ready to have a baby. I was devastated. I was turning 30 in a few months and if I had Mr Right by my side, then it wouldn't be a question. I was born to be a mother—but this wasn't the right time. It wasn't the right man. And it certainly wasn't the right place.

After crying down the phone to Stephanie, desperate for a solution, she sent me daily emails with all the research she could find. I read them from my desk at work, hoping I could disguise the looks of horror on my face. She never imposed her own judgement or opinions on me and only talked me through my decision to make sure I was sure. But with the information she sent through, I wasn't sure of anything.

'Termination of pregnancy is illegal in all parts of Sri Lanka and is punishable by jail.'

'Sorry, darling, I can't get the "termination pill" because you need a prescription from a doctor.'

'What about going to India—it should be easier there?' she wrote.

'It's a sin, it's a sin,' I heard my dad speaking as I contemplated a termination. But this was one of the reasons I denounced Catholicism. I believe in pro-choice and that it is a woman's right to choose and control her own body. It seemed that the Sri Lankan government didn't have the same idea.

Before this happened to me everything I knew about terminating pregnancies was purely theoretical. Sure, I had friends who had been through the same thing but this time it was me. I could easily recite the health, philosophical and human rights reasons for 'pro-choice'. Unsafe termination is a major cause of maternal deaths. Globally, women have limited access to information and services and little control over their reproductive rights. Most women around the world can't choose to use contraception let alone terminate unwanted pregnancies. One woman dies every minute due to complications in pregnancy and childbirth, and unsafe termination is one of the main reasons for this. Thank God I had safe options.

For me, it was no longer about theory, ethics or principles—it was the fact that I was not ready to bring a child into the world. Yes, it was irresponsible of me, yes, I should have been more careful, and yes, I made a mistake. But there I was, pregnant, scared and in a country where I could go to jail if I had a termination.

My other choice was to go home, cut my humanitarian career short, have the baby and bring it up as a single mother. This was not an option for me, therefore my decision was easy. What wasn't so easy was how to go about it in Sri Lanka.

⤙

'Congratulations, you're six weeks pregnant!' The doctor in the hospital confirmed the worst with a blood test. I burst into tears— again. Now it was for real.

'Where's your husband?'

'I'm single.' I started to cry. 'I am just here for the tsunami and I made a terrible mistake.' I couldn't look the doctor in the eye—all I could do was cry. I didn't know how the medical establishment felt, let alone this doctor. What if he called the police!

'So I take it this wasn't planned?'

'No.' I looked down at his shiny black shoes.

'It's ok, there is a doctor you can speak to in the hospital.'

The next day I found myself in yet another waiting room. I sat between a Sinhalese woman in her beautiful sari and a Muslim woman in full black hijab, her eyes the only part of her body exposed. I avoided eye contact with both women, instead focusing on the doctor's office door. It was grey with a muted silver number 3. I stared at it blankly and wondered how on earth I had got myself here.

A single girl. Pregnant. In the middle of a tsunami response. My head was fuzzy, my eyes were red, and I had no idea of my options. I hoped the doctor behind door number 3 could help.

'Nicholson,' the nurse called my name. I froze. I couldn't move.

'Nicholson,' she said louder, shaking me out of my daze.

'Yes.' I stood up, averting my gaze.

'Please, the doctor is waiting,' she said kindly, as she opened door number 3.

Dr Jayasuria, a middle-aged man with greying hair, sat behind a small, cluttered desk. He looked at me with kind, understanding eyes.

'It's ok, don't cry. You're breaking my heart.'

I sobbed my way through the telling of my situation.

'It's ok, sweetie, there is a chance that your pregnancy is benign.'

'What do you mean benign?' I looked him straight in the eyes.

'Well, it's not likely to be a viable pregnancy therefore I would advise termination.'

'You mean . . .'

'Krissy, it would not be healthy for you to continue this pregnancy.'

Through my tears I realised he was trying to tell me in some sort of medical code language that this was the way that we would be able to terminate legally. I hoped and prayed that I was reading into this correctly. I jumped up and hugged the man, nearly knocking him off his seat.

Unlike at home where I would book in and have the procedure under anaesthetic, I had to get an ultrasound and pretend to the nurse that I was happy when she showed me the image of the baby growing inside me. Back in the office and among my friends, I pretended that everything was fine when, really, nothing was fine. I wondered if they noticed me eating more than usual. Having snacks throughout the day to stop the nausea. I didn't allow myself to think of it as a baby. It was a bunch of cells. It meant nothing. Yet any time I thought of it, I teared up. The waning moon shone through my window and I felt Mum's love rush in.

'Krissy, what's wrong?' said Mum's comforting voice on the other end of the line, as I cried loudly down the phone.

'Mum, I'm so sorry, I . . . I . . .' The ultrasound images were clutched tightly in my hand.

'Kris, it's ok, stop crying, what's happened? Take a deep breath . . .'

Originally, I had decided not to tell her. I didn't want her to worry. But I couldn't go through such a big thing without her.

'Please don't tell Dad, he would be so disappointed in me.'

'He'd understand, Krissy, he . . .'

'No Mum . . . please . . . I don't want anyone to know.'

'Can you see the moon?'

'I'm looking at it now.'

'I'm with you, my darling.'

The day of the operation, I called in sick. I organised it for a Friday so I'd have the weekend to rest and would be back at work on Monday, as if nothing had happened. By chance, Dad called while I was in hospital, dressed in a white gown and waiting for the operating theatre.

'Are you ok, Krissy?' He must have heard something in my voice.

'Yeah, Dad, I'm just at home having the day off. Feeling a bit sick, that's all.'

I hadn't lied to my father since I was fourteen years old, when I lied about going out drinking with the twenty-year-old-boys up the road. But I couldn't disappoint him. I was his little girl. Dad once studied to be a Catholic priest and had stopped taking holy communion at church since the divorce with Mum. This sin would be much worse.

'Ok, darling, get better soon. I love you.'

'I love you too, Dad.'

Half an hour later I was on the operating table. I had no more tears to cry. I grimaced as the needle pierced the back of my hand, the smell of the alcohol swab stinging my nose.

'You'll be ok, Krissy. Nothing to worry about.' Dr Jayasuria held my hand.

'Ok.' I could hardly hear my own voice.

I felt like I was on the outside looking down at another poor woman in a white gown, bright lights in her eyes and the backdrop of shiny white floors.

'Now count down from ten for me . . .'

'10 . . . 9 . . . 8 . . . 7 . . . 6 . . .'

I would be forever grateful to that doctor.

⤳

It was less than a week after the termination that I was up in Kilinochchi, the LTTE—Tamil Tiger—controlled north of Sri Lanka. It was known to be dangerous and most people did not have access to the area. I eyed off the automatic machine guns slung over the young woman's shoulder as she scrutinised my passport and our driver explained Oxfam's work to an older Tamil soldier with an even bigger gun. I thought back to the security training I went through when I first started with Oxfam. It was hard to believe I now worked in a country filled with conflict and I hoped that I did not have to put into practice what I learnt in the hostage scenario!

Although listed in many countries as a terrorist organisation, I sympathised with the Tamil cause for sovereignty. While I didn't agree with the violent tactics, use of child soldiers and suicide bombings that reeked havoc, it was clear to me the disadvantaged position the Tamils held in Sri Lankan society. The government retaliations didn't give me faith either and there were human rights abuses and deliberate targeting of civilians on both sides. There were no straightforward answers and the conflict was fraught with politics and emotion. Complex history and relationships that I could never begin to understand.

Kilinochchi was a different world to the rest of the country. The roads were worse, houses were sparse, there was limited electricity and most buildings had bullet holes. It was hot, dry and the mood was never really relaxed. As always, the staff and communities we met with were open and friendly, however, their disadvantage was obvious. We drove carefully on much used roads, steering clear of the millions of landmines which continued to kill and maim farmers working their land, women collecting water or children simply playing in the fields. In a second, a life lost or a leg or an arm gone. The scary thing about landmines is that they remain long after wars, and innocent people may be victims of them years later. Thousands of people are killed or maimed by landmines around the world every year, with the majority of victims being children.

It had been nine months since the tsunami and we were starting to plan for longer-term development work. Many contracts were coming to an end as they had been intended just for the initial emergency. The long-term program looked different now so we needed to set priorities for what work was to continue and create a new staffing structure to accommodate the program needs. In the areas in which Oxfam worked, people seemed comfortable in transitional shelters, water wells were clean and being used, and water supply and storage systems were being put to good use.

My room in the compound in Kilinochchi was simple. A mattress on a concrete floor, an overhanging mosquito net and a small window with floral cotton curtains a few centimetres too short, and allowing the light in. An old, stained toilet outside that was shared with other staff as well as the local frogs. On my first night, I woke up with crippling cramps in my abdomen. I felt around me—it was warm, sticky. The mattress was soaked. I couldn't tell whether it was blood, sweat or urine. With no electricity, I struggled to reach for my torch. *Oh my God, it's blood. What the hell is happening to me?*

I practically crawled on hands and knees to the outside toilet, stopping to steady myself against the cold concrete wall. I felt like I was haemorrhaging. *Stay calm, Krissy, stay calm.* I slid down the wall, squatting, and tried to regain my balance. Focusing on the black stain on the wall opposite, I steadied myself and made it to the toilet. I didn't want to faint out here in the middle of nowhere. There was a male colleague asleep in the adjoining room, but I knew it was something to do with the termination and I didn't want to explain. Next thing, there was a bright light shining in my face. Had I fainted? It was the guard. His English was limited but somehow I communicated my need for a sanitary pad. He must have (somehow) figured I had my period and returned promptly with a pad and a glass of water.

Five hours later it was only just light as I desperately tried to call Dr Jayasuria on the land line. *Bloody phones.* There was no connection and no mobile coverage out here either. Thank God I felt better and the terror of the night before had subsided. I stopped bleeding and the cramps disappeared. I felt the worst had passed and I just had to face the embarrassment of showing the cleaner the blood-stained mattress and my failed attempts to clean it. As a woman she understood it was 'just a very heavy period'. I figured I must have had some sort of miscarriage of an 'unfinished' job, but I couldn't be sure. No time to think about it as the jeep pulled up with the public health team. I pushed the incident to the back of my mind, donned dark sunglasses and put on a smile.

Driving to the camps, my palms sweated and I couldn't sit still. I didn't know if it was fear of the few dozen Tamil Tigers training with guns we passed, or nerves from the previous night. Whatever it was, I felt sick to the stomach.

In the camp I was shown the massive Oxfam water tanks that provided for thousands of people here. I watched as a group of women showed me hygiene promotion drawings that they were using to educate their communities. A pair of hands washing with soap. Squatting on a latrine. Using nail clippers. They proudly showed me a 3D map they had produced to facilitate clean up camp day to get rid of rubbish and deter the rats. They were the volunteers we trained to educate their fellow communities, and talked of positive stories as a result of their work.

A toddler stumbled up to me and handed me a leaf.

'Thank you, sweetheart.' I picked up the child and looked into her big charcoaled eyes.

I smiled at the young mother. *That could have been me in a couple of years. That could have been me.*

CHAPTER 13

A FUNCTIONAL DYSFUNCTIONAL FAMILY

SRI LANKA, OCTOBER 2005

A month later, I beamed at my family and friends as they stood around Larisa and me at our party, all singing in unison. The sand was coarse between our toes, and the lights of the beach hut reflected softly off the ocean. 'Happy birthday to you, Happy birthday dear Krissy and Larisa . . .' Our birthdays were a month apart and we had organised a shared party with all the usual suspects.

Thirty years old . . . another decade gone by. Still single, but having the time of my life.

Dad, my stepmum Christine, Mum, my brothers Paul and Cameron, and my best friend Stephanie were all there. Even 81-year-old Grandma had made a special effort to come over. My Sri Lankan friends had Grandma up on the makeshift beachside dance floor for much of the night and she loved it. Luckily, this time there were no dislocated knees.

117

The following evening I took Paul, Cam and Steph out clubbing. The night was fun but Cam ended up sick, as he was unused to the copious amounts of alcohol and was on strong antibiotics recovering from a flu. It was Stephanie who took him home while I stayed out partying, unaware of the irresponsibility of my actions. It was my best friend who had just arrived in the country who took my sick brother home while I continued partying.

Lying on the beach one day, at the fifteenth beep of my text messages within the hour, Steph cracked it.

'I'm going to throw that bloody phone in the ocean if it doesn't stop . . .'

'Sorry, I'll just respond to this one . . .'

'Shit, Krissy, we have come all the way from Melbourne to see you and all you do is text your friends here. What's going on?'

I knew it was bad but I couldn't help it. Larisa, the boys and I had become inseparable over the past year and I missed them. It was like an addiction. I had also started something with one of my close friends, Imran. He had pursued me all this time, but it wasn't until he started flirting with Stephanie on arrival that I realised how jealous I was and that I must have had feelings for him after all. That shows you how lost I was. Besides our love of partying, Imran and I shared few other values. Stephanie and Mum both commented that I was different. I'd lost perspective. I had a hardness about me that wasn't there before. Maybe I had but I reasoned to myself yet again that I was still having fun and working with drive and passion, contributing to Oxfam's program.

I took two weeks leave for a family road trip. It was a relief to have a break from work, but also to get away from the party scene in Colombo that I was so entwined with. I planned our trip meticulously, organising a minibus to take us around the main sites. My brothers playing guitar and sing-alongs ringing out of the bus window in between the many tourist attractions. I took them to the elephant orphanage near Kandy, the Buddhist temple of Dambulla, the rock fortress of Sigiriya and the beaches of Hikkaduwa. I pointed out the tsunami-affected areas we passed on the road south but avoided the worst. I wanted this to be a happy holiday for them and it was a good opportunity for me to see parts of the country that were still intact.

One evening I sat up with Grandma after an elaborate Sri Lankan buffet dinner.

'Grandma, Mum and Steph are saying I've changed. Do you think I've changed?'

'It's ok, darling. You're a smart girl. You know what's right, and you will do what you need to do.'

Grandma was an amazing woman. She never imposed her own views or made judgements and was only ever supportive. I could tell her anything. Her wisdom was beyond time or space. She was progressive beyond her generation and we shared a special relationship. She was even one of the first people I told when I lost my virginity (besides Steph, of course). I was going to tell her about the termination as it was such a big thing for me; I knew she would understand and be supportive but the right time never came.

It was lovely to have three generations of women who were so close and spiritually aligned. My grandma, my mother and myself. We seemed to share a certain quality that drew people to us, we were all the 'counsellor', the one people came to, and I felt an inexplicable bond between the three of us. Our connection transcended that of daughter, mother and grandmother. It was as if our souls were one.

In fact, our family is quite unique considering it is a broken family. It's amazing that we all get along. People always get confused as Mum and my stepmum Christine even socialise together sometimes.

Mum's partner, Wayne, didn't make it over to Sri Lanka, but it is not unusual back home for us all to share a family birthday or Christmas and other random occasions. Of course, we endure our share of family dramas, but in general we are the most functional dysfunctional family that I know.

We all sat around the pool at our hotel in Hikkaduwa. Paul and Cam performed one of their usual improvised comedy skits, which had us in fits of laughter.

'Dad, you should see Krissy and her entourage of men and trails of friends that she always has,' teased Paul.

'Pumpin and grindin on the dance floor . . . you like the big black fellas don't you, Krissy?' Cameron stood up, gyrating his hips in exaggerated movements as he danced stupidly around the family. He put on a Sri Lankan accent and wobbled his head from side to side, singing 'Hey, Sexy Lady, wanna dance with me . . .'

'If you have Black, you never look Back. Right, Sister . . .' continued Paul.

'SHUT UP, boys . . .' I slapped Paul on the leg and held back my laughter.

'Krissy!' Dad said sternly, as he finished his third glass of wine. 'I hope you're being sensible.'

Mum looked at me. It was only a fleeting look but I knew what she was thinking. We hadn't had time alone to talk about the termination.

'Whatever, Dad, have another drink!' I refilled his glass. 'Anyway, who's the one who taught me to work hard, play hard?'

'You got me there, go out and have fun! Cheers everyone!' The clinking of our raised glasses rang into the night, while the orange sunset glow lit our faces.

I remember when I was a teenager, if ever I stayed home to have a quiet night and a video with friends, Dad used to jeer at us for being boring, saying 'why aren't you out partying?' My 'party bones' were definitely from him. At the same time, no matter how big a night I had, Dad would always insist that I get up early the next day and go to uni or work or wherever it was I should be. He was just as serious about the work hard as the play hard.

It's funny that I didn't talk much about my work. I told them a little about Oxfam's programs and some of my experiences, but for some reason I didn't want the holiday to be about the tsunami. I think it was a welcome relief for me not to think about it too much. It was all-consuming during my day-to-day work life and I needed the break.

Besides a few stolen moments alone with Mum and Steph to tell them about the miscarriage (or whatever it was) in Kilinochchi after the termination, I didn't talk about that much either. We had a cry together and there were lots of hugs, but we didn't really need more words.

A couple of weeks came and went and we had a great time. I was sad to see them go. Before they left, Grandma pulled me aside.

'Kris, you are such a special girl, I wanted to get you something for your 30th birthday.' She pulled out a black velvet pouch.

'Grandma, you didn't have to . . .' I hugged her.

'I wanted to, Kris. I love you so much and I want you to have something that you'll always remember me by.'

I slowly undid the gold ribbon of the pouch and pulled out a stunning crystal blue pendant. I had a sudden intake of breath. The pendant was one of the most beautiful pieces of jewellery I had ever seen. Set in white gold, it was a uniquely shaped, three-sided setting with a light blue topaz sparkling in the middle. The crystal was as clear and brilliant as a tropical island sea. It reminded me of the *Titanic* movie that I loved so much and we called it 'the jewel of the ocean'.

'Here, let me help you put it on.' Grandma's old hands struggled with the tiny clasp, as she patiently placed the pendant around my neck.

'Oh, Grandma, thank you. I adore it and I adore you . . .' We hugged, our eyes glistening, and said our goodbyes.

It wasn't long after their departure that I got a phone call to go to Pakistan. There had been a colossal earthquake killing 80,000 people and they needed an interim HR person immediately. Sri Lanka was still busy but no longer in emergency phase so I agreed to go for three weeks while they waited for a full-timer to arrive.

Off to Pakistan again, I thought of Zakir and the old gang. I wondered if any of them were still there. Imran made me promise not to be with any other men, although I didn't know if I could resist Zakir if I saw him. The reality that I was about to dive into another large-scale disaster also hit me. I hoped I would cope and braced myself to bear witness to more death and destruction.

CHAPTER 14

BEYOND RECOGNITION

PAKISTAN EARTHQUAKE, OCTOBER 2005

Perusing the perfume section at Dubai Airport en route to Islamabad, I couldn't believe I was travelling to my second large-scale disaster. By now I had worked in three other countries with Oxfam, travelling through many others and I was feeling more confident in my professional abilities. I thought back to the moment of realisation in Peru when I knew I wanted to become an aid worker. Now I was able to give beyond that dollar or lolly to a begging child on the street. This had become my life.

I had travelled so far yet I felt my journey was really just beginning.

Driving through the ruins in Balicot, close to the epicentre of the earthquake, I didn't realise that this was the same town where I had stopped to get some snacks with Faiza on our girl's weekend over a year ago. *OH MY GOD*. I remembered the street. Once bustling with life, beeping horns, clattering cars and the odd donkey cart. The call of prayer had rung out its magic over the whole city as we parked on the roadside to stock up.

Now it was as if a giant had stomped its heavy boots on the whole town, taking care to leave nothing intact. The pile of rubble barely resembled the town where I'd stopped with the girls. The only way I recognised it was driving back to base and passing a coffee shop where we'd been in a nearby town. I couldn't believe it.

The trees on the mountains surrounding the city remained ominously still and the snow-capped peaks in the distance reminded us of the cold nights ahead. Broken bricks, shattered concrete and wiring were mangled together. The occasional protruding window frame or lopsided wall told us that this mess of rubble was once a functioning city.

The air was hazy and a thick layer of dust lay on everything. The city looked like a demolition site on the largest scale I had ever seen. People wandered the streets. Men sorted perishable wood into piles by the side of the street. Boys walked with their prized surviving goats. Children stared as we passed tents that had popped up on any piece of clear, available ground.

It was a couple of weeks after the earthquake in Pakistan, which measured 7.6 on the Richter scale and took over 80,000 lives, leaving 3.5 million people homeless. Most of the bodies had been cleared and the cold air reduced the stench of decomposing corpses yet to be recovered from the rubble. As with Sri Lanka, I was rather glad not to have witnessed the first few days of the emergency, where clearing bodies was a primary task. Thousands of people were still missing, more than likely trapped in tombs of dust and rubble. Winter was fast approaching and the surrounding mountains were closing in. The feeling of loss was thick in the air.

Unlike the tsunami, where most villages were washed into the ocean, everything here remained, but was now a chaotic pile of debris. Bewildered, in awe at the power of nature and in wonderment at how on earth reconstruction could even begin, we made our way through the city. How could people fathom such loss? As with the tsunami, everyone here had lost loved ones. Fathers, mothers, children, sisters, brothers, uncles, aunts, teachers, priests, local shopkeepers . . . everything . . . gone. Entire communities had been wiped out.

Water, crops, mosques, electricity, livestock, roads, bridges, hospitals, schools. It's hard to imagine your whole life, belongings, social systems collapsing around you in a matter of minutes. The few structures left standing were dangerous and could collapse with the next gust of wind. Aftershocks rattled the ground. I slept with an emergency pack and shoes nearby, ready to run out the door.

I was based in one of Oxfam's outposts near the epicentre of the earthquake, in Mansehra district. I shared a room with a colleague and we had it lucky. The public health team were camped in tents up north, and others shared with twenty in one room. But at least we had shelter. There were just not enough buildings left standing to house the hundreds of aid agencies that came rushing in, let alone the survivors of the disaster. The earth moved a few times while I was there and unfortunately it was not due to meeting that hot doctor.

A couple of days in, I was reviewing a pile of CVs when suddenly the office shook violently. We dropped everything and ran outside. Suddenly, there was a loud cracking and rumbling noise. *What's happening?* The house next door crumbled to the ground. Ten seconds and it was down, tumbling like a tower of children's blocks. Thank God there was no one inside. After that I often worked outside in fear that our office would be next. Life could be so short. You never know when it's your time. Seeing life taken so quickly made me appreciate every minute.

'Zakir . . . it's Krissy . . . I'm in Pakistan.' My voice wavered. I didn't know how he would react. It had been a year since we last made contact and I never did get that email to explain why he withdrew all those months ago.

'Hey, Krissy! What a surprise.' Zakir's deep soulful voice on the phone got my heart pumping again.

'I'm here for the earthquake response.'

'Right, so are you coming by Islamabad?'

'Yes, but I leave in a couple of days. I'd love to catch up for a drink or something . . . for old time's sake.'

'Great. That would be great.'

'It's good to hear your voice, Zakir.'

'You too, Krissy.'

Hanging up the phone made me realise how much I missed a real, deep conversation. All my conversations with friends in Colombo seemed superficial. How many bottles of vodka we got through, who looks hot tonight, what's the latest goss. I wondered whether it was pure escapism from the serious conversations at work and from witnessing such tragedy, but actually I think we were reliving our delinquent years. I craved that depth I had with Zakir. I reminisced about the many hours we had spent talking when I lived here. I hoped our connection would still be there.

In only a couple of weeks, my role was to get human resources systems in place, assist with recruitment and issue contracts. It wasn't uncommon for me to hold meetings at 10 p.m. when managers were back from the field to brief them on recruitment protocol and hand them some promising new CVs from the slush pile. I was that annoying person who had to make sure minimum standards were met. That all new staff who came on board were interviewed and had their references checked. Understandably, the managers were frustrated at following such a process, when as far as they were concerned they just needed people out there doing the work to save lives at such a crucial time. Stuff the references! I felt the same but also knew the detrimental effects of getting the wrong person into a job, which could mean less efficient and quality aid, and ultimately people were thankful for my guidance.

As always, women were difficult to recruit. Particularly in this conservative region where women were barely allowed out of their houses (or what was left of them), let alone to go to school, therefore the skills we required were hard to find. Much of our hygiene promotion work required female staff, because women needed to speak to other women. It was culturally inappropriate for men outside immediate families to talk to women, let alone educate them on hygiene issues and toilets.

Many Mullahs in the area made it more difficult for us, preaching that women should not be influenced by western non-government organisations, some even threatening western women for working in the area, saying we should be expelled from the country. I never felt threatened. It just made me more admiring of the local women who did want to work, as I knew the social pressures they were under. I wondered if we would have to resort to the strategy we used in our Afghanistan program: in order to hire some women we had to pay one of their male family members to chaperone them in their work. If that was the only way we could have women on our staff it might be something we would need to consider. Luckily, when I was there, we had some competent women apply for the key health posts. What strong women they were. Passionate about helping, despite the fact they had social and cultural pressures working against them.

Another issue was that just like in Sri Lanka, our staff were being poached left, right and centre. As with all big emergencies, the NGOs rushing in with lots of money to spend was overwhelming and they would often offer twice the salaries. Oxfam already paid above average in the sector, but sometimes the counter offer was too attractive for our staff. They did not always consider the fact that these organisations would be in and out within six months, whereas Oxfam would be staying for the long term. I had to put in place retention strategies that included salary increases for the duration of the first phase of the emergency.

After a few weeks of relentless work, there were some things I realised on returning to Pakistan.

One. I was over HR. I loved working with people and enjoyed the training side, but rules and procedures go against my core. And so much of my role consisted of insisting that the rules were followed. And if I looked at another CV I would be sick.

Two. I could never be an emergency junkie. A person who flies from one emergency to the next on three-month contracts. I found being back in the throes of a full-scale disaster so soon after the last one just too stressful. Every now and then would be fine. You see immediate results and it certainly gets the adrenalin pumping, but I liked the fact that I was staying in Sri Lanka for a year and saw beyond the initial emergency phase to being a part of the long-term development. Being witness to people getting their lives back— slowly, but surely—was rewarding.

Three. A public health career was what I wanted now. I assisted with a public health emergency needs assessment with a public health specialist from Ghana. This had us walking among the ruins talking to people to find out their water, sanitation and hygiene needs. Did they have a functional toilet? Where was the nearest clean water source and could they access it? Did they have soap and what were their handwashing practices? Was there anyone who was sick? Working on the ground where I could see the direct results my work could have on a community rather than behind the scenes was inspiring.

I'd sent off my application to do a Master's degree to Monash University in Melbourne a few months before and was just waiting for an answer. I couldn't believe I actually wanted to go back to school, but it was the only way to break into public health.

~

Sifting through the billionth CV on the grass outside the office, the ringing phone was a welcome distraction.

'Krissy, is that you?'

'Stephanie? . . . Oh my God, are you ok?' Steph rarely called; we usually corresponded via email.

'Yes, I'm great.'

'Steph, you won't believe where I am now, I'm literally sitting in the hills of Pakistan surrounded by mountains of . . .'

'I'm pregnant!'

'What?'

'I'm pregnant!'

'Arghhhhhhhhhhhhhhhhhh . . . oh my God, wow . . . that's amazing. Congratulations, darling!' We were both in tears.

'I wanted to hear your reaction. I wish you were here.'

I was so happy for Stephanie, but I felt further away from her now than ever. I looked up at the sun shining through the trees, then slowly disappearing behind the mountains beyond. I looked at the pile of CVs in front of me and the list of 25 new positions we needed to fill yesterday. I loved my life. I loved the adventure of it all. The discovering of new places and cultures. Being at the forefront of major disasters and working with incredible teams. I felt good about my work and loved seeing lives change as a result of it. But it took me away from people I loved. Important birthdays, events and weddings. I wanted to see Stephanie's tummy grow, I wanted to know every detail of morning sickness, pictures of the ultrasound. I would be home for the birth but I would miss most of my best friend's pregnancy.

And then it dawned on me. We would have been pregnant together—only a few months apart. It had always been our dream—to have babies together and live on the same street. I got rid of any chance of that happening a few months ago. I was still sure that I made the right decision, but the idea of being pregnant at the same time as Steph was . . . well . . . there was no point thinking about it really.

⟶

Three weeks of CVs, interviews, salary reviews, systems development and contract management en masse, I handed over to the Bangladeshi HR adviser who would be here for the next six months. I felt for the other workers. Stress and exhaustion due to long hours and limited resources was already showing in their tired eyes, yet it was only the beginning. It was a familiar scene to that in Sri Lanka and I knew that it would be a couple more months before the staff would be able to slow down and take a break. In the meantime, I had to get back to Sri Lanka to a less urgent, yet still busy and stressful job.

Before that, however, I had one night in Islamabad and took the opportunity to catch up with Zakir.

He sang passionately to me once again, with his guitar in hand

and his eyes on fire. When he finished playing, we just smiled at each other. We'd been singing and chatting, catching up on old times for the past few hours.

'It's so good to see you,' he smiled. 'Come here.' I moved in for a hug. It was as if no time had passed and was just like one of the nights we used to have. Except this time the tables were turned. Zakir's hands felt warm and strong as he massaged my shoulders. Bliss. I relaxed back into him and his arms wrapped around me.

Shit. Shit. Shit. Shit. Shit. Stop now, Krissy. Stop now. Shit.

I remembered my promise to Imran and I sat up. I wasn't even in love with Imran. I really cared for him and loved him as a friend, but I shouldn't be with him romantically. Zakir leaned in to kiss me.

I moaned in frustration. 'Oh, Zakir . . . I'm so sorry but I . . .'

'What's wrong?'

'It's just that I . . . I've kind of got a boyfriend.' *Shit. Shit. Shit.*

'It's ok, let's just . . .'

'No. You don't know how much I want to but I really can't.'

Damn my stupid morals. I couldn't believe I even made that promise. There I was with the man I had wanted for so long and I couldn't have him. Finally, he is throwing himself at me and I am refusing. *YOU IDIOT, KRISSY.*

'Now you know how it feels?' I jeered.

'What do you mean?' His tone changed.

'Nothing . . .'

I couldn't believe he had forgotten the evenings we had spent together, with him refusing my advances. How could he not know? But I wasn't going to explain it to him.

'Can we just cuddle up?'

So we snuggled up against the cushions on the ground, both feeling frustrated and denying the depth of our feelings. Qawwali music played in the background, I cursed myself for committing to someone who I'm not even into, and then finally I let go and enjoyed the moment for what it was. Unfortunately, my time with Zakir had long passed.

Flying back to Sri Lanka, I read the latest news headline: 'Seventeen aid workers shot dead at point blank.' Oh no, I prayed it was no one I knew.

CHAPTER 15

THE MONK IN THE RAIN

SRI LANKA 2005–06

Sri Lanka was growing increasingly volatile. Tensions between the LTTE (Tamil Tigers) and government soldiers were on the rise and movement between field offices was becoming increasingly difficult. The peace-building efforts that had come naturally with locals working together to survive the tsunami were now being undermined. A man shot dead in front of Oxfam's office and the sounds of bombs going off in the distance unsettled me. Accompanying water engineers on a field trip to check the water quality of the new wells, we had to find alternative routes as we came upon barricades made of burning tyres, and armed men in the streets were becoming commonplace.

Each time we passed through a checkpoint, I was nervous. Generally, a foreigner in the car meant an easy passage, so I smiled and waved to dark scrutinising eyes while holding my breath. We got through with no problems. Each day there was a new security incident and tensions were high. The most shocking was the news of the seventeen Tamil aid workers from the NGO next door to the Oxfam offices who were murdered. Shot dead at point-blank range. I was glad that it was no one I knew, but it shook up the whole team because it could easily have been our local Oxfam staff. It was upsetting for all and we had to adopt more stringent security guidelines. The murders were rumoured to have been carried out by the military, but who knows what the truth was. I couldn't believe anyone would kill those who were trying to provide aid to communities. Of course, this claim was denied, but the Sri Lankan human rights record was not exactly clean. Hadn't these people been through enough? Working for Oxfam, my job was to remain neutral and focus on giving aid to those who needed it, despite their political or religious affiliation. The principle of neutrality was essential for our work as an organisation, however, as an individual it was often difficult to uphold.

Feeling on edge and continually anxious, I knew I was definitely not suited to working in a full-scale conflict zone like so many of my colleagues. Iraq and Afghanistan—not for me. Not now, anyway.

Larisa took me for a short break to Zambia and Botswana for Christmas and New Year. Although I had travelled to most continents in the world, Africa was the one that always called me, the one I dreamt of the most. But for some reason I'd never been and I couldn't wait.

Much of our time there was consumed with family activities, so we didn't get a chance to visit rural communities. We did, however, manage to tour some of the big game parks, escaping stampeding elephants and silently watching lions and their baby cubs play by a water hole.

For me it was more about the feeling in the air. The cities were unorganised and chaotic but rich with colour and life. The raw, sweet smell permeating from the earth at sunset was intoxicating. The craziness of the traffic juxtaposed with the somewhat calm slowness of life.

The trip renewed my passion to work in Africa. So when I was asked to sign up for another year in Sri Lanka, I declined. I had been accepted to do my Master of Public Health and was anxious to complete this and satiate my longing to work in Africa.

The tsunami response was winding down to move into longer-term development work. International staff started to go home, which meant I was busy debriefing stressed and tired staff who had often seen too much. I am sure images of bodies piled up on trucks, or finding a body shot in front of their office, were memories they would take back to their respective countries. But as well as talking about traumatic events and ensuring they knew professional counselling was available, we also discussed the positives, the progress and the difference that the program they were responsible for had made to the lives of thousands of people who had survived. And that's what it's all about.

The scale up of an emergency response of this size was challenging, but scaling down again had its own issues. While there was less sense of stress and urgency to save lives, the change of organisational scale and structure moving from emergency response to long-term development brought its own challenges. It was my role to lead the change process, a finicky and detailed role that involved workforce planning, deciding which programs (and offices) would remain open and continue into long-term work, and which would close. The review of each and every job description in the organisation, every office, every management line. I hated the gruelling process of interviewing five staff for only two jobs. Although many of the newer staff had been hired on a short-term contract, the organisational needs had changed so much that we even had to make several 'old time' staff redundant. It was heart-wrenching to watch the face of a man who had managed a program for fifteen years when we told him that his job no longer existed due to the growth of the organisation. I made sure that everyone was clear on their options, provided career counselling and ensured everyone had a fair go as much as I could. Difficult decisions and uncomfortable conversations; it was a painful and necessary process.

Visiting communities over the year, it was heartening to see so much had changed in the areas in which Oxfam worked. People were getting back on track to lead 'normal' lives. They were no longer living in makeshift tents and had solid houses in which to live, some with advanced solar power panels. Water wells were in safe use again. Many children were back in schools. Fishermen with shiny new boats were out at sea and women had opportunities to start their own business and feel more empowered with the gender equality programs we were running. Disasters like this don't just go away, and the aftermath of the tsunami would be felt for many future generations. The poverty apparent before the tsunami was still there, yet some communities ended up with better houses and water sources than ever before. By and large, despite criticism it was a successful response to a horrific situation and Oxfam made a difference to the lives of hundreds of thousands of people in that first year.

Unfortunately, the political situation in Sri Lanka continued to worsen, with a rising incidence of conflict and violence. The peace agreement between the government and LTTE was flailing, and I was scared of what the future held.

Larisa was also leaving in a few months, and I couldn't imagine life there without her. Imran was caught out by several lies in trying to pick up other women. As much as he denied it and then apologised, it really just illustrated the lies with which he lived much of his life. Honesty was such an important value for me, and I wondered how we had ever got so close. I only had myself to blame for being in a relationship that was not at all reflective of who I was and what I wanted. Saying this, we were all filled with so much love and were like peas in a pod about to be separated.

Driving to the airport, Larisa, Imran and the rest of our gang squeezed in for my farewell. The car stopped to let an old monk pass in front of us. It was dark outside, and the rain reflected against our headlights, which shone on the monk's bright yellow umbrella. His burnt orange robe draped over his body as he shuffled slowly across the street. It was a fleeting moment but to me he seemed to walk in slow motion.

I stared at the monk and burst into tears. The tears were different to those I shed for leaving Sri Lanka and my friends. They were for the realisation of the opportunity I had missed. Living in such a spiritual country for so long, I had got lost in spirits of another kind . . . namely vodka and gin! My values had dropped and I had certainly lost my spiritual, hippie self somewhere along the way. As we stopped at our favourite club for our final shot of tequila, I brushed these thoughts to one side.

A year in Sri Lanka had come and gone. It had been the most challenging work experience of my life, mixed with the most avid social life and close-knit friendships. My friends had supported me through so much over the year, and despite our ups and downs they saw me right to the international departure gate. Larisa in particular, but all the boys in general had held my hand when I was sick, got me through a distressing termination, given me wake-up calls when I was overstressed at work, danced with me through the night and entertained me endlessly. Despite my feelings of being out of kilter with my true self, I would really miss them.

As I boarded the plane, I knew it was time for the next chapter of my life. My dreams of Africa were very much still intact. Imaginings of myself working on health programs with women and children in remote villages full of thatched houses in rich and diverse cultures were as clear as day. My family and friends were waiting at home and my acceptance letter to begin my Master's was fresh in my mind.

Little was I to know the painful barriers I would encounter ahead.

CHAPTER 16

SHATTERED DREAMS

MELBOURNE 2006-07

Coming home was easier this time, probably because my goal of achieving my Master's and working in Africa was still fresh. It had been over ten years since I had formally studied anything. The new study would be a far cry from my Bachelor of Arts degree, where I learnt just as much about the use of megaphones on the streets, protesting about everything from student fees to women's rights as I did about Plato's theory of Love and Hate, postmodern feminist thought on capitalism and whether a table has feelings.

This time, I was a mature age student who thrived on learning new theories, asked lots of questions and actually did my homework. It was fascinating and while I felt inadequate, being one of the few students who didn't have a medical background, I found my emergency experience gave me a greater depth of understanding than many.

Although biostatistics and epidemiology nearly killed me, I relished subjects relating to refugee health, training and communications

139

for illiterate communities and managing HIV/AIDS programs in developing countries. I drank in the knowledge and felt so much closer to achieving my dream of becoming a public health professional in Africa.

Despite being home, the intense contact with Larisa, Imran and the gang in Sri Lanka continued via phone and email. But I knew I needed to let go in order to move on. I realised my relationships, particularly with the men in Sri Lanka, my friends and my lovers, were quite toxic. They were not honest or true to my values. I saw how much I had hardened emotionally and I felt a deep sorrow for the part of myself I had lost that year. My spiritual, sensitive side had been left unnourished. I needed time to process and analyse my feelings and behaviour. I hadn't realised how far I had drifted until I came home. Slowly, I began to unravel myself from what I realised were verging on co-dependent relationships.

I couldn't get the image of the monk in orange robes crossing the street as I left Colombo, out of my head. I was sure it was a sign to wake me out of my spiritual complacency. I began to read Buddhist texts again and felt my energy shift. I looked within and started to chip away the hardness I had developed. Stephanie was well versed in Buddhism and passed on many books and pearls of wisdom that helped me analyse myself, who I wanted to be and how I wanted to live within the world.

I didn't discuss any of this with Larisa and I'm sure she must have felt the gradual walls I was putting up. I knew it wasn't fair as it was a projection of my own feelings and inadequacies. It was nobody's fault but my own, yet I couldn't help connect my loss of self with my friendships in Sri Lanka.

I felt guilty, but I didn't know how else to behave and instead I focused on my studies and friendships at home. As usual, my life became ridiculously busy and I knew I needed to slow down. Every single night was full of social engagements. Dinners, coffees, drinks, parties. During the day I was either studying or working part time at Oxfam. I was burning the candle at both ends. My back started to give me trouble but nothing that a strong painkiller couldn't appease.

After a hard year of study and an active social life I decided to reward myself with a backpacking trip to India. I carried a 15-kilo backpack, rode on camels, travelled on bumpy buses and slept on beds with no springs, with a bad back. Nothing would stop me.

~

'I'm sorry, young lady, but you need back surgery.' *Back surgery!!!*

In a medical specialist's office in Melbourne, Mum, who had driven her once again invalid daughter for treatment, squeezed my hand. My back got worse while I was in India, making it painful to even walk. I don't even know what set it off in the first place, but sitting in the doctor's office, I wished that I had done something about it earlier.

Back surgery?? 'No, I can't. I have to finish my Master's degree this year and then I'm off to Africa.'

I stared at the MRI image of what he called 'one of the worst cases of a herniated disc he'd seen'. My disc was clearly sticking three-quarters of the way into my spinal canal.

'Not possible. In your condition you'll have to postpone your studies, stop any type of work and there will be no travelling for at least a year. It's a wonder you can even walk.'

The specialist may as well have hit me over the head with a cricket bat, tied my hands behind my back, bound and gagged me.

Tears started welling in my eyes and he tightened the ropes by adding, 'Oh, and I think you need anti-depressants, the pain you're going through is obviously getting you down.'

That was the last straw.

HOW DARE YOU! You have known me for a two-minute consultation, you have asked me NOTHING about my mental health history and you are prescribing anti-depressants!

I started balling my eyes out. No holding back, it all just came in deep loud sobs that could be heard down the hospital corridors.

'I am the happiest person I know,' I sobbed. 'Nothing can get me down. I am the life of the party.'

I could hardly breathe between my sobbing and was way past knowing how ridiculous I sounded.

'I don't NEED any drugs for depression, thank you very much!' *You arrogant, drug pushing bastard!*

As I continued to wail (and I mean seriously wail like I had just been told I was going to die), my whole life and dreams slipped away. Just like that, out the window and carried away like a plastic wrapper caught up among leaves, whirling around and around on a wind gust and floating away to nothingness. Delay my Master's degree! Stop work! And worst of all, end my dream of going to work in Africa. What was this man saying? Why was this happening to me?

Stubborn as I was, I pulled myself together and thanked the doctor for his time, ignoring his advice of surgery and anti-depressants. I don't need any biomedical model to fix me. I'll get a second opinion. I'll try alternative therapies. I'll do anything. Back surgery just sounded too severe. I hobbled out the door in excruciating pain.

I spent the next six months seeking intensive physio and reiki treatments, visiting osteopaths and delving into Chinese medicine. I was vigilant about doing my core strength exercises, and things did seem to get better, slowly, but I was still living in constant pain and taking painkillers as if they were smarties.

I was forced to postpone a few subjects, but I was determined to finish my Master's, although I had to go part time. Self-consciously, I'd enter lectures and lie down on the floor up the front of the class room. I was unable to sit in a chair. I could only lie down or stand up. During one lecture I was in so much pain I hobbled out in tears. Fellow students found me on the hallway floor in spasms, teeth chattering and in shock. Despite all this, I completed all my assignments from bed, lying horizontal with my laptop on bent knees.

To make matters worse, I developed corneal erosion in one eye. As for why, I had no idea . . . this was the year of bad health for me! The outer layer of my eyeball would rip away and I felt like I was being stabbed in the eye with a hot needle made of sandpaper. So not only was I a cripple, but I couldn't see out of one eye for a few weeks. *Thank you, universe . . . for WHAT!!!??*

My eye recovered after a while but my back just got worse. There were months upon end that I was confined to home and couldn't do anything except contemplate and reflect. I was like a caged butterfly. I couldn't drive my car, I couldn't go out to restaurants or bars, I missed friend's parties and important celebrations. Much of my time was spent on my back.

As with most things in my life, I always try to think of the 'why', the 'this must be happening for a reason'. With close to a year in pain and much of that confined to my bed, I really did learn a lot. For someone who has struggled with solitude for so long it was probably an enforced year of rest. Even before my back injury I remember talking to friends about feeling the need to slow down. I was burning the candle at both ends; work hard and play hard was getting to me. I think my back injury was the universe actually forcing me to slow down.

143

If I had broken a leg or an arm I would have continued, I would have kept going out, working, studying, partying. But my back was so debilitating it meant that I *had* to slow down. That I had to become comfortable with solitude. It gave me time to read more Buddhist texts and a myriad of philosophies on quietening the mind, on living in the now. My back forced me to live in the moment as I couldn't really think beyond my next movement. Turning over. Getting up to go the bathroom. Even putting one foot in front of the other was a considered, deliberate movement. There was no such thing as the future. It was day by day, minute by minute.

One day I suddenly lost most of the feeling in my leg and could hardly walk. I had to use my arms to help lift my leg to make the next step. *Holy shit!* I took myself (somehow) to the emergency unit, where the doctors were incredulous as to how I had lived so long in such a severe condition. Not only did I live with it, I completed a Master's degree with it!

A few days later I was on the operating table.

Of course, I developed a crush on my surgeon, who I felt saved my life. Maybe this was the doctor the clairvoyant had talked about? I fantasised about him asking me on a date, flirted with him every visit. Although I'm not sure how appealing I was in an unattractive hospital gown that gaped at the back, or the fact that I couldn't go to the bathroom without a nurse's aid, or that delightful green colour I would turn as I nearly fainted each time I tried to walk in the first few days after surgery. I mean, I don't really know how he resisted me.

Back at Mum's again after surgery, my recovery was quick and I returned to Oxfam six weeks later. Surely nothing else could go wrong this year.

But then Grandma died. My dear, darling Grandma. It was brain cancer, and despite a strong fight to the end she was ready to go. I made her promise that she would work from Heaven to send me Mr Right. I wore the 'jewel of the ocean' pendant she had given me all the time. Grandma was still very much with me and always would be.

A few weeks later my share house was robbed. *You have to be joking, universe!!* My laptop with my work and travel pictures and, worst of all, my jewellery which had been handed down to me including Grandma's pendant was stolen. Having focused intently on Buddhism, I told myself that they were just material possessions and that it didn't matter. But I tell you what, it sure did test me. I mean, this year had to be a bad joke.

My career meant that I was surrounded by disasters and tragedy, but when it enters your own life so personally it hits you on a whole other level.

There are not many times in my life that I can look back and think 'what a shit year'. In general I have fun and one or two adventures up my sleeve. I have always lived a great life. That is up until 2007. The year that if anything else went wrong I think I would have handed back my ticket.

I thought of the suffering, resilience and courage of all the people who had lived through the tsunami and earthquake and in the other disasters where I had worked. How they continued with strength and pride and hope despite all they had suffered I don't know. I hadn't experienced half of what they had, and it certainly put things into perspective for me.

As I became physically stronger and got back into everyday life, I felt back on track emotionally and spiritually. I was more in tune with who I was, who I wanted to be and how I wanted to live my life. I would always have fun and be a party girl, but I recognised the need for balance in all aspects of my life—physically, emotionally and spiritually. Despite maintaining a strong work ethic in Sri Lanka I felt the other parts of me had weakened, and although 2007 was challenging, I grew so much stronger as a result of it.

～

Early in the new year, I was on a crowded tram on the way to work when it hit me with ferocity. A new realisation. I didn't know where it came from but it was crystal clear. I no longer wanted Africa. My bright dream full of colour had faded to grey. Maybe Grandma's death and my bad health year had taught me that life was short and I wanted to be close to my friends and family. Maybe it was that I finally had my health and wanted to count my blessings at being in Australia. I didn't know. My aspirations of a public health job in Africa seemed a faraway memory. I had been living moment to moment for so long, and after everything that had gone wrong the previous year I couldn't afford to dream into the future.

I was happy in Melbourne and resumed my learning and organ-isational development job at Oxfam. Comfortable in my life, Africa drifted into the shadows. Holding on to the railing as the tram wobbled along Swanston Street, I wiped away a tear. With it went my dream of Africa. I had already been an aid worker in some of the biggest emergencies the world had seen. Surely that was enough?

CHAPTER 17

IS THAT A GUN IN YOUR POCKET?

MELBOURNE 2008

It was 2008. 33 years old and still single. Each year I heard myself saying it. 'Still single . . . still single . . .' The phrase was getting tired. I'd reason with myself that I wouldn't have had the incredible experiences if I had already met Mr Right . . . ! But I was sick of that rationale. It was time to focus. The Africa dream was out the window—aid work was obviously getting in the way of meeting Mr Right. What did it matter that I didn't make it to Africa and that the freshly printed Master's degree was not going to be used. If I was going to find Mr Right, it needed all my energy. My prediction of meeting the love of my life by 30 obviously hadn't happened. I was three years past that. I needed a new goal.

The 14th of February came rolling along.

'Happy Valentine's Day, darling.'

The words every single girl longs to hear.

'Thanks, Dad.'

Every year my Dad calls. Once he even gave me a chocolate heart. Sweet . . . but slightly depressing. Each year rushes by as fast and direct as cupid's arrow, but always seems to slow leading up to 14 February. *Who's bloody St Valentine anyway?*

I find myself teary eyed and eating chocolate in bed as I snuggled closer to my teddy. Whitney Houston's 'I will always love you' rings out as I tune into 'love songs and dedications' on my bedside radio! A glutton for punishment. Well, at least the chocolate is dark (less calories) and fair trade (less guilt).

But it was time I found my own Valentine. It's not that I have had a shortage of men. They just happen to be Mr Unavailable, Mr Emotionally Inept, Mr One Night Stand, Mr Married but Failed to Mention It, Mr Lives on the Other Side of the World, Mr I Want You for Your Visa, Mr Flirt, Mr Right at the Time, or Mr ALWAYS Right— all equating to MR WRONG!

I thought back to Rob and Zakir and the random men who were oh so wrong. Beautiful men . . . but essentially unavailable.

So my new goal was this: To meet Mr Right and be pregnant with our first child by the age of 35. I figured that was a reasonable age in these progressive times. We are living longer now and middle age is no longer 40. Well, that is what I tried to tell myself anyway. I had two more years up my sleeve to find Mr Right, get to know him, have a couple of adventures and then pop out some kids. Simple. I had written enough strategic plans and achieved many work goals, so why not have a plan for this.

One overcast afternoon, Stephanie came over for an emergency planning meeting. With a bottle of sav blanc disappearing as fast as our ideas onto paper, we started our list.

1. Get fit and healthy.

With my back on the mend, it was still precarious and I needed to make sure I was strong. Plus, I needed to lose the weight I'd always carried.

'No point finding Mr Right if you ain't going to be able to have a good work out with him,' teased Stephanie—'if you know what I mean . . .' She exaggerated embarrassing pelvic thrusts.

After being flat on my back for a year and unable to have *any* action in that regard, I definitely knew what she meant.

2. Review list of Mr Right.

Maybe my expectations were too high!? Maybe I was putting the wrong thing out to the universe.

'Ok, now focus,' encouraged Steph. 'What are the qualities you really want?'

I put on a serious voice. 'Mmmm . . . yes, I have been giving this a lot of thought and I have the solution . . .' I picked up a pen and wrote on the page in big, clear letters.

Mr Right is:

—Male
—With penis
—Breathing

Steph nearly spat wine over the page as we burst out laughing and re-filled our glasses.

'Ok, ok, no, seriously . . . I wrote a list last night. Here it is.'

Mr Right will be (not in order):

Single
Handsome (to me)

Successful in life
Intelligent (emotionally and intellectually)
Good sense of humour
Family oriented
Similar values to mine
Open-minded
Good in bed
Romantic
Generous
Good manners

'Great, now do you really need "good manners"? Remember, we want the essentials.'

'Definitely, you know how psycho I am about the knife and fork being placed together at the end of a meal! . . . Ok, so are you ready?'

'Ready!'

'Mr Right is . . .' and I proceeded to read the list out loud.

'Say it like you mean it,' encouraged Steph.

I read it again.

'Not good enough. You've got to believe it. Stand up. Back straight. Chest out . . . now . . .'

I took a big gulp of wine, put down the glass and stepped up onto the chair. After I got my balance I shouted . . . no, I sang, the words with all my might, one hand outstretched and one clutching my heart. 'Mr Right is . . .'

We collapsed in laughter again but the list was made.

3. Stay in one place long enough to develop and maintain a relationship.

'Good, tick, you've done that,' said Steph.

'Did they survive?' Waterlogged photo album among the debris in Batticoloa, Tsunami affected Sri Lanka, 2005.

It is hard to believe a whole village used to be here. The aftermath of the Tsunami, Batticoloa, Sri Lanka, 2005.

Niroshini, standing in front of her neighbour's house that she was sheltering in when the Tsunami hit. This strong wall saved her life. Sri Lanka, 2005.

Danger sign warning for landmines. Who knew where the mines were after the Tsunami? Killinochchi, in LTTE controlled Sri Lanka, 2005.

Hansani, Niroshini's sister, salvaging Christmas decorations from her demolished village after the Tsumami, Batticaloa Sri Lanka, 2005.

Makeshift graves on the side of the road, Sri Lanka, 2005.

Transitional shelters for Tsunami affected communities. Residents were relocated there after living in emergency tents, Sri Lanka, 2005.

Oxfam hygiene kits distributed to communities living in emergency tents in the immediate aftermath of the Tsunami, Sri Lanka, 2005.

Community health workers, displaying hygiene messages to promote a clean camp, Killinochi, Sri Lanka, 2005.

From large 4WDs to small tuk-tuks. Transport for Oxfam staff as we carried out our work in Tsunami-affected Sri Lanka, 2005.

Gender discrimination was actively addressed in Oxfam's aid work in Sri Lanka. Water pump with messages to prevent violence against women, 2005.

Camels are like gold in Somali region, Ethiopia. An entire house and belongings were packed on the back of this camel, searching for greener pastures, 2009.

Woman leading a camel down the main street of Jijiga in Somali region of Ethiopia, 2009.

Curious girl in Ethiopian village, 2009.

The girl with the blue sarong… scared of the camera but finally came around. Ethiopia, 2009.

Standing in front of Oxfam office, in a remote village in Somali region, Ethiopia, 2009.

Injeera, the sour pancake, a staple food in Ethiopia. Tasty with an assortment of curries, yet it sits in your stomach like a brick.

Vegetation and water is scarce in drought affected Somali region. Pastoralists moving their flocks to find better land, Ethiopia 2009.

Bierkat, water storage pool built as a part of the drought response program. Somali region, Ethiopia, 2009.

I'd just moved into a new apartment by myself. The first time ever that I wasn't in a share house. For me it was about becoming more of an adult. Having my own space and stability. And I had signed a contract with Oxfam and committed to stay for at least a year. The job was with the learning and organisational development team. Still human resources but at least it was the training and organisational change side that I loved. It wasn't public health, but I was responsible for exciting initiatives crossing over our thirteen global field offices. It was challenging and exciting but also kept me in Melbourne.

4. Get out more. Actually go out and meet men.
'No no no . . . you've got it all wrong. You . . .'
  'Hello . . . what else am I meant to . . .'
  'Internet dating. It's the . . .'
  'No way in the world, Steph. There is no way I'm . . .'
  'Krissy, the man you want is not in the pubs getting pissed and picking up any more. He's at private barbecues with his married friends, working during the day and at his holiday house during the weekend.'
  'Holiday house!?'
  'Well, if you're gonna dream . . . !'
  'No way!'
  'Krissy. This is the way people meet these days . . . and I've taken the liberty of making you a profile.'
  She turned on her laptop and staring back at me was my photo and a short profile. She hadn't made it 'live' yet. All I had to do was say the word and my profile would be out in the world!
  'STEPHANIE!!!'
  I resisted internet dating for a while. I always thought it was for desperate people. For people with no other options. But Stephanie

was right. I was 33 now and if I was going to achieve my dream, I should try all the available options. Lots of people were on-line now. It was a normal option to meet people. At least that's what I tried to tell myself. I tentatively dipped my toe into cyberspace, feeling like I was Armstrong and it was my first step on the moon.

The first couple of months I was inundated with 'kisses' from a range of men. It gave me and my friends hours of entertainment. Is that guy for real! Does 'tongue4U' who claims to enjoy 'using his tongue' really care for an 'intelligent, down to earth woman'? It's not like a clitoris has an IQ! Does 'YoungAtHeart', who is 52 years old, really not want anyone over the age of 25? Is 'Bigboy' really just hiding the fact he is actually 'small'? And if I read another profile that says their favourite movie is *The Shawshank Redemption*, or that 'I like going out but enjoy quiet nights in too' and 'I'm even handy in the kitchen' . . . Isn't there anyone original on this site?!

I used my human resources experience to shortlist and interview potential 'candidates'. I worked up the courage to meet a couple of guys for a drink or three. 'I'll be the one wearing a red scarf.' I would text them an hour before I arrived. It was so nerve-racking meeting at a random bar. Oh God, what if they think I am a fat ugly pig? What if they don't like me? What if I don't like them? What if we have nothing to say to each other? What if, what if, what if? But generally after the initial awkward kiss on the cheek hello and first drink consumed, the dates were good. Really nice guys—but not Mr Right.

I wondered if my standards were too high. I didn't think so. Advertising myself on the internet never sat well with me. It just didn't feel natural. But I figured that all these guys were in the same boat, so we could be embarrassed together.

There was one thing for sure—I wasn't going to settle for second best. I had seen so many women over the years hooking up with the first man who wants them in a desperate attempt to beat their ticking clock. I would prefer to be single than with someone who I didn't think was right for me. But that was a fleeting thought I hoped I would never have to revisit. I had to maintain my confidence and continued on my search with various men from the net . . .

Like Bradley the osteopath. Walking up to him, my nerves dissipated slightly as I saw a tall, handsome man sitting with a beer. I just about jumped him until he looked up at me and smiled. Teeth came out of his gums in all directions like a mutant cob of corn. More gaps and crevices than Kings Canyon. I don't think I am a shallow person but I just couldn't imagine kissing that mouth. I focused on his eyes and brow, thinking how handsome he was. But as my eyes slipped to see him talk, I lost all concentration. *Come on, Krissy, don't be ridiculous, don't be so shallow . . . what's the big deal . . . he can get work done.* But when he talked about working in healf care, I realised that his teef would be an issue. NEXT . . .

Like Barry the electrician—mmmm . . . Now, this guy was cute. Dark hair, cheeky blue eyes and sexy. We had a great date full of flirtatious banter, and although I was not so keen on his constant brags about how much money he earned I was keen to see him again. The fact that he paid for the meal, took me out for after dinner drinks and kissed me at the end of the date, meant I was sure that he was interested. But no. Despite my follow up 'thank you for a lovely night, it would be great to catch up again' text message, he never replied . . . *What the!?* NEXT . . .

Like Rodrigo. A hot-blooded Latino man who wooed me with romantic emails and long phone calls before we even met. Upon meeting he looked deep into my eyes, grabbed my guitar and serenaded me with passionate flamenco solos. After a few romantic dates, he told me he was going back to his old girlfriend. NEXT . . .

Like Anil, my Nepalese toy boy. Seven years younger and full of energy and charisma. This was purely fun as he frequented my bedroom and entertained me endlessly with his youthful energy and new moves that saw me in positions requiring more flexibility than an Iyengar yoga class. Never going to be 'the one', so it was ok when Anil's student visa ran out and he returned to his homeland. NEXT . . .

And then I met Sergeant Steve.

On web chat Sergeant Steve was articulate, engaging and funny. It wasn't until a few days of online chatting that he told me he was a policeman. *Oh no . . . a policeman!* Stereotypical images of right-wing, racist, small-minded, conservative coppers came into my head. He lived in a country town in the middle of nowhere. We talked on the phone and despite his Aussie ocker country drawl and use of classic lines such as 'flat out like a lizard drinking' *(yes, I'm serious)*, I decided to keep an open mind and organised a date.

We met at a local bar. A beautiful big bear of a man with kind eyes and a gentle face, Sergeant Steve was a sweetheart. Even if he did wear the synthetic version of my dad's shirts and a 1980s leather jacket. I could manage his wardrobe later. He was open-minded and analytical. Loving and kind-hearted. He'd moved to the country years ago for a change of scenery and to spend more time with his family. He had two kids and was going through a messy divorce.

On the second date he told me he was a 'shooter'. Yep, he liked to hunt. *Oh my God—what am I doing!* I didn't hide my shock and dismay very well and proceeded to question him on his enjoyment in killing animals. Mind you, I wasn't a vegetarian, so who was I to judge? Although I didn't eat much red meat, when I did it was bought in neatly packaged white containers from the supermarket. Packaging hiding the reality that animals had died for my food. I had several philosophical conversations with him concerning the ethics of hunting.

Sergeant Steve, who I referred to as 'SS' to my friends, always ate his kill, which I guess made it a bit easier for me, and in fact he argued he was quite the environmentalist. His argument stood ground as it is certainly more green to kill and eat your own meat using every part of the animal, rather than eat meat bred for consumption in unethical conditions. I was always impressed with his well thought through and intelligent arguments on the practice. But whether it was a more sustainable, ethical and environmentally friendly way of consuming meat, I just couldn't get over the fact the man I was dating actually enjoyed the kill.

He also belonged to a shooters' club. Clay pigeons. Despite many invitations, I blatantly refused to go along. I was secretly afraid I would enjoy it. Not killing animals, I'd never like that, but target shooting actually sounded fun (not that I *ever* admitted that to him). I was relieved that his ute didn't brandish an 'I shoot therefore I vote' bumper sticker. But he did have a ute . . . and he did shoot.

'I brought you a gift.' SS walked through the door of my apartment and stood proudly with a big smile on his face. It was our third date. He held out some beautiful hand-picked wild flowers.

'Oh, how beautiful, thank you.' I walked towards him for an embrace.

'And this . . .' He proudly held up a massive slab of bloody flesh in the other hand.

'Aghhhhh . . .' I couldn't hide my horror . . . 'Ummm . . . thank you . . . can you just put it away in the freezer . . . ummmm . . . thanks . . .' I tried to stay calm, as I basically shooed him with one hand and backed away. I did not kiss him hello until the bloody corpse was completely out of sight.

'Got the butcher to make some snags out of that beauty too.' If he was fazed by my less than graceful acceptance of his gift, it didn't show.

'Did you . . . ahhh . . . shoot that?'

'Sure did, gorgeous, it's deer. Was drivin' in the cop car and saw it crossing the road. Jeez, the opportunity was too good to let go so I shot it with me work gun and hauled it back into town. I'd get in strife for that but this beauty will last me a year!'

Oh my God, it's Bambi! Images of 'Me Tarzan, you Jane' rushed through my head. I felt like I was back in the hunter-gatherer days, where the man brought back the kill. Some of my girlfriends tried to tell me that it was masculine, sexy . . . but I couldn't help but squirm.

I couldn't get the image of my new lover shooting poor little Bambi while dressed in full police uniform. *Oh dear, what am I doing?* My friends and family were taken aback and highly amused with the thought of me—a Greens-voting aid worker who hardly eats meat—dating a National Party voting shooter policeman. Well, it amused and perplexed me too. I must say that the relationship opened my mind and I learnt a lot. I relaxed the stereotypes I had of hunters and the police and faced my own left-wing prejudices. SS was a really decent, salt of the earth guy.

SS lived a six-hour drive out of Melbourne, so we only saw each other a couple of times a month, but we spoke on the phone daily. I grew really fond of SS. It was so lovely to cuddle up to him in bed, to have romantic dinners, to go on spontaneous picnics, but there was something always amiss. Despite his declarations of love for me, it just didn't feel right. I really gave it a good go. I wanted to be sure. But sometimes I was scared that I wanted to find Mr Right so much that I was deluding myself with someone who was lovely. In the six months that we dated, I grew to love SS as a beautiful, caring man. But I was never 'in love' with him.

So when Pritha, the HR manager, contacted me from her new post in Nairobi and offered me a short secondment to Ethiopia, I knew what I would do.

Africa was back on the cards. I actually think it had always been in the background waiting for that ace of spades to be pulled from the pack, but I had been sitting quietly waiting for the right hand. My surgery and awful year had disheartened me, diminishing my dream of Africa. Plus, I was comfortable in a job I loved—but that all too familiar craving for travel and adventure took hold of me once again.

Although I knew SS wasn't the 'one', I was in turmoil about leaving. So many questions bombarded my thoughts. But what if I *do* fall in love with him? I think I could. He is such a lovely man. He loves me. I could be happy with him. What if I never find anyone else? What if, what if . . . what if . . . ? But I already knew.

CHAPTER 18

AFRICA–ARMS WIDE OPEN

ETHIOPIA 2008-09

So here I was. In the middle of nowhere. Hot, dusty and single again. Surely the perfect conditions predicted by the clairvoyant to meet my doctor! I wondered whether I had made the right decision, as I adjusted my seatbelt on the Ethiopian Airlines flight.

I had left my great apartment, friends, family, job and summer in Melbourne. I had left Sergeant Steve too. I missed him, and he continued to send the most loving emails telling me how much he missed me but that he wanted me to follow my dreams. Did I let go of Mr Right? Could it have worked in the long term? Was I just incapable of holding down a long-term relationship? All these questions swirled around in my head like the sandy whirlwinds outside the plane window. I felt dizzy, but I knew I would find my feet. Well, I hoped so anyway.

The greenery of Ethiopia's capital, Addis Ababa, seemed far away as the plane flew low over the desert. The scorched land showed little sign of nourishment. Diminutive vegetation and the veins of dried up river beds pulsed weakly through the country. The big 'talk' Dad had given before putting me onto yet another plane at Melbourne Airport reverberated in my head like the clang of a cymbal.

'Krissy, I'd like to tell you a story.' He sat me down on the couch. 'I want to tell you about a documentary that I saw.' *Oh oh, he looks serious.* 'It was about a woman, just like you, who had been doing humanitarian work for many years.' Dad paused and looked at me intently.

'Go on . . .'

'She always wanted to find the right man, get married and have children,' he spoke slowly, deliberately, 'but because she was always travelling and doing things for other people, she never found anyone. As she grew older, past the age of having her own children, she decided to open an orphanage in Indonesia and is now looking after about twenty children who otherwise would be destitute.'

'Oh, how lovely, what a beautiful story. It sounds like . . . hold on a minute . . .' The real moral of Dad's story dawned on me. 'Do you mean . . . DAD! I can't believe you . . .'

'Well?' he looked at me, part joking and part serious.

What he really wanted to say was, 'Krissy, if you don't stop now, you'll never meet anyone and end up like this woman. And, more importantly, I won't have the grandchildren that I've always dreamt of.'

Ok, so he didn't say this directly, but he has before, and this is exactly what he meant. When I realised I started to laugh.

'DAD!!! You're unbelievable!'

Now, don't get me wrong. Dad is extremely proud and support-ive of me. Why else would he make the effort to come to Pakistan and Sri Lanka? But a big part of him wants me to have a 'normal' corporate job and settle down and provide him with grandchildren, rather than living and working in the middle of natural disasters or conflict zones, where disease is rife and bombings are commonplace. He wants me to be happy, but he always misses me when I go away, and he longs for grandchildren. Well, at least I felt loved!

Looking at the desert beneath me, I shivered. Dad had tapped into my own fears. I think that the woman in the documentary is doing an amazing job, but is it where I want to be? No way in the world! I still dreamt of meeting Mr Right and having my fairytale wedding, two children and a golden retriever! I looked around at the humanitarian aid industry and saw so many beautiful, talented, intelligent women who were still single. I never understood why, but I guess the lifestyle of running off to the next emergency is not conducive to meeting the man of your dreams and settling down with children, is it?

The seatbelt sign pinged, interrupting my thoughts. My ears started to pop with the descent.

Did the attainment of one of my dreams mean the other wasn't possible? Could I be an aid worker and find Mr Right too? Should I stop doing what I love to find love? Or, should I trust that I'd find the right man doing what I love?

There was one thing that I was sure of. Whether or not I was in Pakistan, Sri Lanka or Melbourne, I wasn't finding the right man. You'd think that in the 50 countries in which I had travelled, I would bump into him somewhere. Maybe in Ethiopia . . . ?

I thought about some of the men who had entered my life. I fell for Rob, the army man, and now Sergeant Steve the policeman. I wondered why I was attracting these men in uniform, their work and mandate so against my own values. Who would be next? There was certainly no sign of that doctor, but at this stage the illiterate farmer in the nearby Ethiopian village was looking pretty good to me.

Don't get me wrong. The aim of my travels and work has not been to find Mr Right—it's just one of those things that I hoped would happen on the way. In fact, if I had found Mr Right all those years ago, I wouldn't have been able to do the work that I've done.

〜

Landing on a small tarmac in the middle of the desert, a lonely tin shed the airport, I knew I must be somewhere pretty remote. Feeling slightly uneasy at the imposed 8 p.m. curfew, I told myself it was safe. It was months since the last bombing.

'I don't like coming here,' said Haset. 'It's not safe.'

'Really? Well, I'm excited. It's very important to get out of head office and see the programs every now and then.'

Maybe I should have been scared too. Haset was born and bred in Ethiopia after all and knew better than this newbie, who was just happy to explore more of our programs. Addis Ababa had been my home for a few weeks now. Haset was the HR manager, and as a part of her performance development plan I had been brought in as her management coach. Basically, it was a capacity building role to build her skills and confidence to a more strategic level.

My initial concerns about not being accepted by Haset melted away as we developed a strong relationship. I was worried she'd see me as a young white woman telling her what to do in her own country. That it may have been an 'improving performance measure' that was being imposed on her, but she embraced the opportunity and we worked well together. Plus, my approach was never to tell her what to do, and we worked together on her strengths and set goals that worked for her and the organisation. One of the issues identified was that she required a stronger understanding of the issues in the field offices. So this was one of the purposes of our visit:

to run performance management training for all staff. To give staff an opportunity to air any concerns they had. And to visit some of the programs to understand their working conditions.

We were in Jijiga, the heart of the Ethiopian Somaliland region, where Oxfam's pastoralist program had been operating for ten years. Setting off in the white 4WD with Oxfam logo, flag flying and 'no guns' symbol stamped on the windows, I felt a familiar feeling in my gut. That sense of adventure, sense of being in the thick of it. Elation to be a part of the humanitarian world again after giving it all up with my back injury. I was like the prodigal daughter returning home. And Africa's arms were wide open.

I thought of Larisa. It was three years since Sri Lanka and although we were still in touch occasionally, our relationship was a lot more distant. I still felt guilty about putting my walls up. She knew I was in Africa but I didn't have time to see her. Besides the airfares to Zambia being astronomical, it was more than that.

We had been such good friends and Larisa was there for me during one of the most challenging years of my life. But I couldn't help but associate her with the boys, the lies, and with my hardened spirit. Really, the only person I could hold responsible was myself, and I knew it. But Zambia seemed like a world away from Ethiopia and I still didn't feel ready to see her. The feelings of guilt sat in the bottom of my stomach like the brick of *injeera* I had eaten for lunch. Despite my usual policy of honesty and openness, I couldn't bring myself to talk to her about how I felt. I knew I'd have to one day but now wasn't the time.

I let the *injeera* digest and threw myself into my work. Ethiopia: the quintessential aid work context. The popular poverty campaign of the 80s had shown images of dying children with distended stomachs and flies in their eyes. But to me, it was another fascinating culture that offered abundant beauty and richness.

CHAPTER 19

THE GIRL WITH THE BLUE SARONG

ETHIOPIA 2009

Mahdi, the Oxfam driver whose white hair and beard suggested he was well into his sixties, had learnt English through BBC radio. He had a wide smile, two wives and nine children. Mahdi told me of the fascinating ways of the pastoralist communities and clan tribal culture. He explained that these communities lived for their animals and followed weather patterns to ensure they were fed and watered, an increasingly challenging feat considering the drought that had stripped the once fertile lands. These communities were some of the most marginalised in the country, with poor basic services, recurring droughts and conflict making them particularly vulnerable.

We drove through the harsh desert landscape on what looked like a road to nowhere. Women and children stared as we passed by, leading their herd of goats to hopefully greener pastures. We were right near the border of Somaliland. Women wore brightly coloured Islamic headdresses that flapped in the wind. Bright greens, reds and pinks offset their beautiful, black weathered features; a stunning contrast to the blue sky and dry and dusty desert terrain. The few more affluent groups led camels—the most prized commodities in this land.

'Camels are like gold,' Mahdi explained, as we stopped to speak to a woman guiding a heavily loaded camel in the middle of the desert. Families with camels meant they had access to money, transport, food, milk, dowry for brides and high status within a community. I couldn't believe the materials loaded on the camel's back would build a whole traditional hut. Easily packed up and transported. Like a Toyota Cruiser with a built in, flip out trailer tent! The region was experiencing another long drought, therefore people and animals were scarce. This woman was heading towards the Somaliland border, where most communities had already moved due to talk of more rain and better pastures.

A couple more hours drive towards Oxfam's remote outpost, we stopped to visit the *bierkats* (large water storage pools) that Oxfam was restoring as part of a disaster preparedness program. The community told us this work would make it easier for them to stay in one place for longer and have access to clean water. But that was if the rain came at all.

Oxfam is the only non-government organisation working out here. 'Oxfam is like God,' said an elderly woman we spoke to on our journey. She was a beneficiary of our water program. Powerful words that reflected the life-saving qualities of water.

The drought meant that the water dams were quickly drying up. Livestock were beginning to die and communities that had been in this region for hundreds of years were exploring other options, which were few. Another 'in your face' impact of climate change.

In one of the small towns, we were shown into the local pharmacy. A white, windowless room, its walls were lined with medications. I wondered whether they were even within their use by date. A young woman with a brown head scarf and a shy smile looked up when we entered.

'This is Shyla. She was a part of our maternal health program.'

'Great.' Maternal health always fascinated me. It was hard to fathom that every single day, 1000 women die of preventable causes related to pregnancy and childbirth; 99 per cent of these deaths were in developing countries.

'Can you tell me about the program?' I asked her.

'Yes, well, I used to be a traditional birth attendant which was ok but still many women died.' Shyla talked enthusiastically as an Oxfam staff member translated. 'Now I have learnt how to know the signs of a problem delivery and send the woman to hospital early.'

'That's fantastic, what an important role you play in your community,' I said encouragingly.

'Yes, and I manage this pharmacy, give babies vaccinations and do outreach work.'

'Wow, it's a big job!'

'The other day I delivered a baby right here.' She motioned to the floor of the pharmacy where we were standing. I wondered whether I understood her correctly. Haset was from a different region and didn't understand the language either and shrugged.

'But the problem is fuel.'

'Fuel?'

'Yes. Even if I tell them they need to go to a hospital, there is no fuel for the one car in the village and a donkey is not fast enough. Sometimes they die in labour on the way to hospital.' Women were known to walk for days to reach hospitals but many weren't lucky enough to make it.

Transport was a common issue for health programs. Even if you have trained health workers, if the nearest hospital is more than a day's walk away then it can be too late. While the Oxfam program provided fuel during the program, invariably it would be used up by people with other needs. Particularly, more powerful elders of the village who could easily override the young, female birth attendants.

We said our goodbyes and stopped for lunch in a small mud brick hut. It was the only place in the village that served food. We sat under the shade of an uneven wooden veranda. At least it was out of the searing heat. Lunch was *injeera* served on a large white plate with various curry concoctions slopped on top. In Addis I had quickly overdosed on the slightly sour, spongy pancake staple which is made out of teff or corn flour. It expands to feel like a rock in your stomach after eating it, but there wasn't exactly fresh salad out here. The first few times I had eaten it it was an exciting and exotic culinary delight, but I soon grew tired of my stomach expanding like a balloon after every meal. After washing our hands with the precious water out of a plastic container, we ate with our hands as the goat sharing our shade stared at us. The food tasted ok, but I must admit I was a bit nervous seeing the hygiene standards in the area. I just hoped the hand-washing hygiene program had reached the cook in this little hut.

As we ate, a rosy cheeked girl with big brown eyes and a blue tie-dyed sarong poked her head around the corner. She retracted her head just as quickly when we noticed her. The girl looked about ten.

'Hello, cutie,' I cooed. She was adorable.

I tried to converse without a translator and after a while motioned to my camera.

'Photo?' She looked at the camera with a mixture of awe and fear. I lifted it to my eye and adjusted the lens in her direction, but before I could 'click', she screamed and ran off.

Returning quickly, she again poked her little head around the corner.

'I don't think she's seen a camera before,' said Haset, amused.

Making sure the little girl was watching, I took a photo of the goat and held up the screen so she could see.

'No problem,' I said, knowing full well that she would not under-stand English, but hopefully my expressions and voice would put her at ease.

She laughed, looking from the goat to the screen and back again. She looked at me with a 'how is that possible' expression on her face.

I took a picture of the chicken outside and showed her the image. She spoke excitedly. Thinking she must understand the context now, I held the camera up to take a picture of her.

'Argh . . .' She ran away again. Haset and I laughed as we each scooped up another handful of *injeera* and goo curry.

Two minutes later the girl returned with three friends. They all looked into the veranda shyly, giggling. She motioned to the camera and then pushed her friends in front of me. As if wanting to test the technology that she was so afraid of on them before she dared to do it herself.

I raised the camera again and they all ran off squealing. They returned and once again the girl with the blue sarong pushed her friends towards me. Click. I got a quick photo in and showed them. They tiptoed towards me and peered at their image. There were screams of delight, as they pointed at their image. I took some more pictures, each time accompanied by infectious explosions of laughter. I don't think they had ever seen a photo let alone a photo of themselves. They caught on quickly and started posing. Changing their expressions with each shot. Pretending to fight in one shot. Serious in another.

The girl with the blue sarong stood to one side watching. Still unsure if the camera would harm her. But watching her friends have so much fun and laughing at their images, she finally conceded. I motioned to her and the camera and she took a step forward. *Click. Click. Click.* Her blue sarong gleamed in the sun.

Soon every man and his dog wanted to be a part of the action. A toothless man with his hoe returning from the field; a tall teenage boy with a head full of curls; another group of barefoot kids.

Visits to villages often saw me with children hanging off my every limb and squealing in delight as I showed them photos of themselves. I regularly had to literally drag myself away. The adults always looked on amused, striking their own poses. Besides the odd woman who didn't want a bar of it, photography was a good icebreaker. But I'd never experienced someone being scared. It was a beautiful moment and the girl with the blue sarong will be with me forever.

No matter how many places I visited, I was still shocked by the lack of resources and poverty that many communities live with. No vegetation, no clean water, the odd health post with no health worker, and if there was a school there were usually few teachers. It was amazing the effect of a simple program that trained up health workers who were already within a community, or building water systems so that women would not have to walk across the desert for hours in the hot sun. It is the type of thing that we take for granted at home.

With each new village and each new conversation, the niggling tugging that drove me to complete my Master of Public Health a few years ago started to tighten its grip. While my job in human resources and working with local staff was satisfying, I came alive when speaking directly to communities. My desire to put my public health skills into practice became stronger.

~

'Krissy, we need a decision. Are you coming back to your role in Melbourne or not?'

I racked my brain thinking of the pros and cons of returning to my role as a learning and organisational development adviser in Melbourne. I was loving the recent work with change management and training, and hoped to further develop my coaching skills. I was told that the change management framework I had designed for Oxfam Australia had now been approved to go global, and my opportunities if I decided to go down this path would be endless. But it was still in the vein of human resources, and while using the framework was important for organisational change and in the long run would improve the quality of our programs, I wanted to work more directly with changes within the communities.

Bushfires had just ravaged Victoria, taking close to 200 lives and destroying a couple of thousand houses. Australia is no stranger to bushfires, but this was the biggest loss of life due to fires encountered in Australia's history and the country was in mourning. I have never felt so far away from my family, knowing they were vulnerable to their own emergency, as Mum lived close to where the fires were headed. Maybe the best decision was to go home to be with them. I had a great career to return to.

Plus, more than ever, all I wanted was to have a baby! My biological clock was ticking as loudly and repetitively as a drummer in a heavy metal band. The chances of finding someone in outback Africa were slim. Once confident about the clairvoyant's prediction, I had been to so many outback, dusty places that the fantasy had started to dissipate.

On the other hand, I was finally in Africa with a public health degree in my hand. Was this the opportunity to live my dream, or should I take a different path and return to my family and friends? Pursue my dream of a family? I tossed and turned all night, hoping the decision would be handed to me on a platter.

CHAPTER 20

THE KARAMOJONG

UGANDA 2009

I decided to quit my Melbourne job and put my trust in the universe once again. I was going to try my luck at finally achieving my dream of public health work in Africa. I felt a strong pull towards Uganda. I don't know why Uganda, I didn't know anything about the country. Maybe it's because Mum used to tell me her childhood dream of hiking there with the gorillas.

I sent my CV off to different organisations and informed Pritha, the HR manager in Nairobi, who had seen me through from my very first deployment in Bangladesh. Two weeks later, as my contract in Ethiopia was about to end, I received an email.

'There's a two-month change manager role with Oxfam Uganda—are you interested?'

Is this for real!? I didn't even mention my interest in Uganda to Pritha. It was still a human resources role, but I accepted the assignment on the condition that I could work with the public health team

171

for a few weeks at the end of the contract. Plus, the fact that it was in Uganda seemed to be too good to be true. Pritha agreed on the public health work at the end under the condition that it would be on a voluntary basis only, as they didn't have the funds for a new role. It would be the foot in the door that I needed to get a step closer to my dream of a public health role in Africa.

YIPPEEEEEEE! Sometimes my luck with work surprises me. It's like I just send my wishes into the universe and someone is listening. Why can't that happen with my wish for Mr Right? However, with this luck, I felt the universe was working in my favour. And maybe this time Mr Right would be in Uganda!! That clairvoyant could be right after all.

❱

'Gain Hips and Bums' was the first sign I saw on the drive from Kampala Airport. For those ladies who want to develop the much desired African curves and big bottom. *HELLO MAMMA, me and my curves are in the right place! Halleluiah!* I smiled as my western influenced self-esteem preferred this concept than the usual 'lose 10 kilos in 2 weeks' signs I'd see at home. My booty would fit right in here!

Kampala, with its disorderly, potholed streets, felt right. Surrounded by lush, green and muddy vegetation, lying close to the Equator, the smell of tropics was ripe and welcoming. No time for me and my big bottom to relax, however, as I realised the enormity of my role here (not of my backside). A change manager is one of those new, fancy job titles where people look at you blankly and nod their head when you tell them what you do. Basically, as change manager, I had exactly eight weeks to finalise the ongoing changes in the organisation that had been causing grief and uncertainty among the staff. Restructure, redundancies, interviews were all on the agenda. Nobody likes change and if managed badly, particularly in an organisation where there is so much at stake, it can really affect staff performance, and thus the quality of programs. It was an important and challenging role and while I enjoyed aspects such as running leadership and change management training, I found the detailed restructuring and redeveloping job descriptions, etc. increasingly tedious. At least now I was in a country I wanted to be in and my dream of moving into public health work was finally within reach.

On arrival in Kampala I was given a half-hour brief, half an hour to freshen up and then I was ushered straight into the uncomfortable 4WD for a nine-hour journey to the wilds of Karamoja. After a few days of management training, difficult conversations about redundancies and team-building workshops, I was assigned a Sunday field trip to see our programs. Heading off with a journalist who was reporting on Oxfam's work to decrease the effects of climate change, I was briefed about the region.

Karamoja is one of Uganda's toughest, indigenous minority areas. A place of deep ritual and tradition that would be incomprehensible to most. A place where cattle rustling (tribes stealing one another's cows, often leading to violent conflict and death) is rewarded. A place where witch doctors are held in high esteem and animistic practices are still carried out. It is also a place which has some of the poorest people in Uganda—where a common meal consists of mixing the blood and milk of a cow and drinking it. A place where it is not uncommon for cars to be ambushed and all passengers shot dead and looted. The driver pointed out crosses on the side of the road where visiting missionaries had been attacked. I felt nervous but better knowing the violence had now decreased significantly, due to a stronger army presence and the disarmament program in place.

The effects of climate change had hit hard and there were signs of a major food crisis occurring across the whole region. Oxfam's response was to implement safe water, hygiene and livelihood programs. Digging water holes, dams, building toilets and health centres and developing seed banks to increase women's access and ownership of agricultural activities, were among a few of the many projects Oxfam was working on. The resilience of the women we spoke to was humbling.

A group of women had gathered in a dry river bed. They were standing in the sun, taking it in turns to scoop the little water left in a one-metre-wide hole in the ground, using old buckets to dig further down. Much of the water they collected was sandy and it had to be carried back on their heads to their family huts up to two hours walk away. The drought had hit hard in this area and it was obvious looking at the distended bellies and gaunt faces of the children that they were suffering from malnutrition.

Up the road we spoke to another woman who was working for the seed bank. There was little use sowing the seeds as there had been no rain. It was heart-breaking seeing the women and children digging at the hard, dry land with rudimentary tools in the hope that it would rain to soften the soil enough to plant seeds. Dry dust blew into their faces, a thin layer of it etched into their clothes, skin and hair . . . they could be waiting for a long time.

As we left, the woman told us to be careful on the roads as a young girl had recently been shot due to the tribal warfare. Despite the police crackdown and disarmament campaign, the deep-seated conflict was still strong.

One of the reasons I was here was to downscale the public health program. But seeing the way these people lived, it didn't make sense to me. Why can't we get more money to ensure the basic needs of people are met? Water is essential but it was a luxury in many places here. Again, the reality of aid hit hard. If international governments pull out their funding, there is little other option for large-scale programs such as these. Karamoja was not on the 'sexy aid funding lists', it was not popular at the moment. One of the forgotten emergencies in the world. If there is no foreign interest in an area, there will be no money. These people will continue in the cycle of poverty. And as climate change worsens, it is only a matter of time that the dried up river with only limited water access will disappear altogether.

On our way home through semi-arid landscapes, travelling on dirt tracks, we saw a frenzy of colour and activity off on the road side. There was a group of people near a decrepit church and a handful of leafless trees. Getting closer, a melodic chanting cut through the heat. The frenzy started to take shape and revealed 60 or so men and women jumping up and down. Singing. Men chanting lyrics to a deep natural beat. Women intermittently crying out in a high pitch, 'Yy Yy Yy Yy Yy . . .'

We got out of the car to take a closer look. It felt surreal, as if I had just walked into the middle of one of those documentary films. But this was for real. The energy was vibrant. Feet lifting high off the ground as if they were jumping to the clouds. Bright colours—men in hats with feathers, and wearing sarongs, women heavily adorned with red, green, blue, yellow beads around their necks and wrists, worn over the top of western t-shirts. Hair twined in elaborately designed tiny plaits, framing the deliberately scarred faces of the women, the scarring forming patterns, symbolising beauty.

I tried to be inconspicuous so that I could witness this cultural ceremony without disturbing them, but of course as I approached some stopped to stare at the only white person around. This area was not on the tourist track. It was not a show. What I was witnessing was a part of Karamoja everyday culture. I was awestruck, mesmerised.

As I reached out to shake the hands of a group of women staring at me on the outskirts of the group, they launched back as if I was going to hit them. *Oh no, I don't want to frighten them!* Giggling, and in turn, they each approached me to shake my hand. Forcing myself to leave such a beautiful scene, I felt elated on the journey back. Even though I didn't understand what was going on, the experience blew me away. I couldn't get the smile off my face and my heart filled with a deep sense of joy at having experienced such a culturally rich, joyful interplay of life here. I wanted to stay but the sun was lowering into the mountains beyond. Our driver was getting nervous as the security protocol meant we had to be back before dark. So we got back into our 4WD and the chanting and colour disappeared gradually as we drove away.

The sadness at the extreme conditions I had witnessed that day was still there, but I was touched and overwhelmed by what I had seen. And once again I was reminded of the power of the human spirit. Children continued to play, even if it was in the one set of dirty, ripped clothing they owned and with stones as their toys. Men and women still danced, practising their customs that gave them hope and a sense of community. No matter where I go—the resilience of people never ceases to amaze me. Even in some of the harshest conditions such as Karamoja. I pushed the possibilities of drought and a worsening situation to the recess of my mind and enjoyed the lingering air of celebration.

CHAPTER 21

THE AFTERMATH OF KONY

UGANDA 2009

I wrapped up my work in Karamoja and a week later found myself flying into Gulu, an hour and a half from the Kitgum office where I would be based for the next few months. The old twelve-seater plane was enough to raise the heartbeat. Aid workers from the United Nations, Red Cross, International Rescue Committee (IRC) and various other NGOs clambered into the small cabin with an air of self-importance, faces down in reports. Most aid agencies had left the area years ago, when the funding dried up as the large conglomeration of Internally Displaced People's (IDP) camps were phased out.

I read my notes on Kitgum. Close to the Sudanese border, Kitgum had been the stomping ground of Joseph Kony and his Lord's Resistance Army (LRA). There had been twenty years of terror, rape, murder, boys being abducted to be child soldiers and forced to kill their own families, girls taken as young wives/sex slaves, whole villages burnt to the ground and countless other atrocities. The majority of soldiers in its army were stolen, brainwashed children. The conflict had seen two million people displaced, with a vast majority forced to live in overcrowded camps.

Kitgum was a small town with some basic amenities: a second-hand market, a couple of primary schools, shops, a bank, a run down but functioning hospital and a smattering of bars and cafés. Thousands of children, known as the 'night commuters', used to walk hours every night to sleep on people's porches, in alley ways, in shop windows, anywhere to prevent the LRA kidnapping them. In response to the growing number of children on the streets, Oxfam started up a night centre for the kids, providing them with a place to sleep, food and some basic education.

It was only a couple of years prior to my arrival that people started to feel safe to move back and start to rebuild their old villages, as Kony spread his army into the Democratic Republic of Congo and South Sudan. Kony is a crazy man who claimed he spoke to the Holy Spirit and dreamt that he should institute the Ten Commandments into Uganda's constitution. Listed as number one on the International Criminal Court's 'Wanted' files, there has never been enough international attention on his activities, and Kony's jungle tactics are elusive. In addition, there were stories of the Ugandan military blurring the lines between those who were helping and those who were attacking. These situations are always more complex than they seem. Although Kony was long gone from the villages here, the scars, both physical and emotional, remained. Even when I was there years later, child soldiers and sex slaves were still escaping and returning from the jungle.

Oxfam's work was now focused on moving from the humanitarian response, where most people lived in camps, to longer-term development initiatives, such as providing safe, accessible water and sanitation, hygiene promotion and agricultural activities, including providing tools, seeds and training to help communities get back on their feet. My briefing had been that there was a lot of organisational change taking place in Kitgum and there was some resistance from staff. They were looking to scale down some programs, which would mean several staff would not have a job after the process was complete. I had the change management framework I designed in Australia in hand and would run training that week on how to manage change effectively, including understanding people's normal reactions to change and how that can affect performance and morale.

Rattling loudly, the plane started its descent. Looking out the window, I wondered where we would land. Long, brushy grass as far as the eye could see. No buildings in sight. And then a short, red strip of earth no longer than a cricket pitch appeared. The familiar white 4WD branded with various agency logos waited patiently for pick up. Approaching the car with the Oxfam flag, I pinched myself. I felt like one of those aid workers you see in the movies. I guess I was. I often felt like this. Aid work was always such a dream to me, such a fantasy that when I found myself in quintessential aid work contexts, I never quite believed it was me. A far cry from the office set-up in Melbourne—or Kampala for that matter.

Aid workers are a certain breed of people. After years in the industry I now understood the lingo and the importance of gaining 'field cred' by throwing those TLAs (three letter acronyms) around: Disaster Risk Management (DRM), Emergency Needs Assessment (ENA), Participatory Rural Approach (PRA) and the like. Although knowing the language to speak, I still had much to learn. Every situation is different and with each place came a whole new set of rules to play by.

You can never make generalisations about one place having worked in another, even within the same country. Intertwined with standardised program outcomes was a diverse history, politics, language, tribal issues, religion and hundreds of other variables. The age-old saying of 'the more you know, the more you know you don't know' definitely applied here. No matter how many books I read about the places in which I worked, I always wanted to know more and wished I was blessed with a better memory for facts and figures. I felt technically confident from a human resources perspective: I knew the lingo, the policies and procedures, behavioural interviewing techniques and participatory training tools. I was a strong communicator and able to work well with a range of people. However, I was still a novice in many areas with much to learn, and I spoke to as many people as possible to assess the lay of the land.

The beauty of being in this industry for a while was that I felt more comfortable to ask questions when I didn't know the answers. I asked for explanations of the histories and politics with which I was unfamiliar, or the latest catchphrase or popular 'aid worker speak' TLAs.

I felt more confident with my own style when working with staff or visiting communities. Of course, walking into any new situation I felt apprehensive, but this usually dissipated quickly. Shadowing several aid workers over the years, I felt I adapted my personality when meeting people to be 'professional'. Relating to people was my strength and I found it interesting that I curbed my 'comfortable' style to be what I thought was more professional. People reacted better to me when I was myself—when I played with the children in the communities, when I was more 'informal' and sat in the dirt with the women rather than sitting on the only chair they had provided (unless of course it would offend the community).

I had been told by some that as a human resources professional in a senior role, I needed to maintain my distance from staff so that I could make objective decisions. But I found that a limiting approach. I gained a lot more trust and the respect of the staff if I was down to earth and friendly, but still professional. I believe it is the personal relationships formed within teams that can ensure smooth change processes and better team work in general. As a result, staff were more willing to be honest and open up if they were experiencing problems, and trusted that I would take them seriously.

So, no, I wasn't good at quoting the date that the LRA took over, or who was in power at the time, or the exact number of people who were affected by the conflict, but I did have the ability to communicate with people across cultures, and the insights I got from just talking to people were profound.

Wheeling my luggage across the red earth towards the Oxfam flag, Okeny grabbed my bag and threw it in the back of the white 4WD as I hopped up in the front seat. My ears were still ringing from the small aircraft. It was good to see a familiar face. Okeny was one of the drivers who had worked with Oxfam for ten years. He drove me the nine hours to Kotido when I first arrived and he was my favourite driver. On a barren stretch of dirt road, Okeny seemed quieter than usual.

'Are you ok?' I asked. The lines on his black face reflected a life I couldn't even start to imagine.

'No problem.'

It was dry and hot. The air-conditioning in the car had broken years ago. The desert reminded me of Australia. Low, muted coloured brush that grew out of the harsh earth. So different to the south of the country.

Suddenly, Okeny spoke. 'It's just this stretch of road always reminds me of the old days,' he said.

'Do you feel like telling me about it?' I'd read the many accounts but it was stories of those who had experienced the war that really brought the reality home.

'See this scar?' He pulled down the collar of his shirt to reveal a thick scar a few centimetres long.

His other hand stayed on the wheel, his eyes remained fixed on the road. He continued.

'I was on my way to school in a pick-up truck and suddenly there were gunshots from every direction.'

The car groaned as it changed gear to negotiate another pothole.

'We couldn't see anyone . . . the shots were coming from the bushes . . . I jumped out and ran. I didn't know where I was going. I just ran and hid in the bushes. It wasn't until I stopped that I realised I'd been shot.'

I looked again at his scar. The bullet must have skimmed the side of his neck. One centimetre to the right and he would have been dead for sure.

'I was safe but some of my friends had been shot dead. Others were taken to be soldiers.'

'Okeny, that must have been so scary, how old were you?'

'Fifteen. I waited in the bushes for two days before someone found me.'

'I'm sorry.'

'But it only got worse. I remember one time, when I first started working with Oxfam. I had to drive over dead bodies to get staff from the office to the camps where people needed assistance.'

'What!?'

'It's true. If we stopped we would have been attacked too. Added to the bodies. We couldn't even stop to collect them.'

I looked out the window in silence. It was hard to imagine along this very road, a road that now looked so peaceful, that so many had been attacked and killed.

I thought back to Charles, the guard at my hotel in Kampala. He was from this area as well. One day as I returned from grocery shopping, he went beyond the usual polite greetings and told me his story. Stolen at the age of twelve to be a soldier, he was abducted in the middle of the night. Forced violently away from his family. He told stories of boys who tried to escape being rounded up. He was made to watch while they were hacked to death by other boys wielding machetes. A deliberate strategy to instil fear into the boys so that they wouldn't run away.

Charles described how the induction into the LRA was being whipped 100 times. If you cried, if you made a noise, they'd start again. Toughen you up. Brainwash you. Force you to attack your own villages, your own families.

After three years Charles escaped during an ambush by the Ugandan military. He was fifteen years old. He escaped with a bullet in the leg and was taken into the safety of an NGO. He was working in the hotel now to put himself through school.

Another time, a friend of a colleague came to pick up an old laptop donated for his studies. I tried hard not to stare in shock as I realised that his ears, nose, hands and lips were missing. Chopped off. I handed the laptop over to stubs that he had learnt to use efficiently, and the deep, hard scarring where his lips used to be stretched further into a grateful smile. Mutilations such as these were a signature of the LRA.

Although the stories were distressing, it was important for me to hear them. Otherwise I could have continued under the misapprehension that Kitgum was always just another rundown, remote country town. Despite its history, I really enjoyed living in Kitgum. It was great to be based out of a capital city for a change. No traffic, lively thunder storms and beautiful sunsets. The office was a five-minute walk from our guesthouse. Walking along the narrow dirt paths, I passed goats and barefoot kids with shaved heads on their way to school. It was so peaceful here. Not being much of a meat-eater, the main thing I missed was fresh vegetables and I always put my requests in for those travelling up from Kampala. Sometimes it's the simple things that you miss the most.

The Oxfam guesthouse that became my home was situated inside high, red-brick walls with a green, rusty metal door that creaked loudly when opened. Guards took it in shifts to man the door, which was standard practice in most places I had been in Africa. A couple of taps or an approaching car and the gates would be dutifully opened. Our comings and goings were tracked and each guest was signed in and out—reminiscent of the days when it was dangerous to walk the streets and a strict curfew was imposed. But those days were over now and it was safe enough to walk the streets.

It was a simple house with pink bougainvillea framing the entrance, giving it a touch of femininity. But that was it, as the house had obviously not had any feminine influence for years. The lounge contained a few pieces of cane furniture, and an old armchair facing a television, where the clearest channel showed the latest high quality Nigerian dramas. A scrabble set with half its pieces missing and a grubby pack of cards sat sadly on the bare shelf with other useless odds and ends collected over the years. Many aid workers had been in and out of this house before me. If only these walls could talk.

It's amazing what a bit of rearranging, a rug for the floor and coloured material could do. There wasn't a lot I could do for my own room though. It had a stained concrete floor and a flimsy bed draped with a blue mosquito net. We had a cook and cleaner who were lovely, but there was only so much goat curry and rice that I could handle, and it was one of those places that felt perpetually grotty.

There was an interesting mix of people living in our compound. All from different backgrounds and beliefs: Kenyan, Sudanese, English, American, Somali. I initiated a rule in the house of limited work speak, otherwise we would never escape from it. For me, home needed to provide rest and down time from stressful work days. It was not like the stress of a large-scale emergency response where adrenalin was always pumping and it was a race to save lives. It was just the general day to day stress of competing deadlines, frustrating and slow systems, and the added pressure of changes in staffing and structure. Everyone agreed that we could talk shop for an hour, and then we'd leave it. Of course, there were exceptions during particularly hard days or difficult times, but in general everyone respected the rule, and as a result we got to know each other beyond our work lives.

We shared stories of our lives back home, tested each other's cooking (and yes, most of them hated the taste of Vegemite), had discussions about our religious differences, but celebrated the fact that despite our differences we were all working for one cause. Of course, the inevitable conversations about relationships came up. All of us were single except for one married man who had been trying to get his wife pregnant for years. *Um . . . that requires being in the same country, right?* Besides the odd trip back home it's pretty hard to maintain a relationship, let alone impregnate someone if you are apart so often. To me it illustrated the sacrifices that people in aid work have to make.

I didn't have much hope of finding a relationship out here in the middle of nowhere. The place came closest to the description of 'dusty and far away somewhere in Africa' where my doctor was meant to be, so who knows—but I wasn't going to hold my breath. There were a handful of international agencies here. Little sign of much of a social life but there was potential. I'd just have to throw the parties. Liven this town up. I knew I was clutching at straws but I had to hold on to something.

CHAPTER 22

DON'T EAT YOUR OWN SHIT

UGANDA 2009

Six weeks of long days leading an intensive restructure, interviews, workshops and management training, it was time to say goodbye to my work as change manager. I submitted my final report, and made the switch to public health. Just like that.

It was the 'three week' volunteer role that I had negotiated while still in Ethiopia before taking on the change manager role, but after discussions with my new manager it seemed there was a lot more work for me and that I could stay for a few more months if I wanted to. I would continue in the Kitgum office and still had the same guesthouse accommodation and food covered as well as an allowance that was sufficient for other living costs.

The public health manager was a sprightly, 30-something-year-old American called Ramona, with brown curly hair and a smattering of freckles across her nose. Ramona was professional and fun, and it was great to join her team. My previous role had meant we worked closely together, so we already shared a strong relationship and being of a similar age we were already good friends.

Ramona ran self-taught yoga classes in her lounge room and we delved into several deep and meaningfuls about the trials and tribulations of being a single woman in this industry. She was in the midst of an email relationship with a man based in Afghanistan whom she'd never even met, while a colleague from another NGO read out the attributes of sperm donors she was shortlisting for her return to Canada. We joked about adding a new component to all aid work job descriptions:

WARNING: This job may be detrimental for single women.

It was Ramona who introduced me to the concept of 'Emergency Goggles', and we rolled around in fits of laughter one evening sharing stories about the men we had dated during our deployments who we would never even consider back home. Similar to 'Beer Goggles', where you find someone attractive after a few too many beers, I completely related to the phrase 'Emergency Goggles' and adopted it as my own.

Ramona introduced me to the only bar worth going to in town— Fuglys. A small guesthouse and bar run by a sarcastic but sweet South African couple, it was a second home to a motley crew. Mercenaries, missionaries and misfits: many aid workers and volunteers fitted snugly into the latter category. Fuglys was the only place that served good food and cold gin and tonics. It became quite a haven for the few expats who lived here. Fuglys even had a pool—it was only 8 metres long and 1 metre deep, but it added to the feeling of a grassy little oasis in the middle of nowhere.

Ramona was keen for me to start work with her team and had some great projects lined up for me to manage. She even promised a few extra months beyond the initial three weeks discussed.

Whether this was due to my high level of competency or because she didn't want to lose her yoga and socialising partner I didn't know. Probably a mixture of both, but I didn't mind as my dream of doing public health work in Africa started to become a reality. Having worked with the staff over the past couple of months as the change manager I was already familiar with the programs, and was excited about the transition.

And what a transition it was. You see, in my human resources world, OD stood for Organisational Development. In my public health world, OD stands for Open Defecation. Quite a shift, I can assure you. I used to run training sessions and coach people on team development and how to manage effective change processes. Now I started to teach people not to ingest their own shit. Yes. You heard right. Don't eat your own or other's shit. It was a part of Community Led Total Sanitation (CLTS) methodology that we were trialling in northern Uganda. Popular in Asia, it was quite a new approach here. CLTS empowers communities to build and use their own toilets, to become open defecation free (ODF). At the heart of CLTS is the recognition that providing toilets does not guarantee their use, or result in sustained sanitation and hygiene behaviour change. In layman's terms the message was: Don't shit in the bush as, eventually, due to flies, livestock, contaminated sources and not washing your hands, you will end up ingesting it, making yourself sick and you could die as a result.

The idea is that if people are motivated to change themselves and build their own toilets, the results will be more sustainable in the long term. The approach relies on behaviour change research showing that education, or simply knowing something, is not enough on its own for people to change. CLTS empowers communities to take their health into their own hands and support each other to do this instead of relying on aid agencies. While this may seem simple, the fact that these communities lived in camps and had been reliant on humanitarian aid for the last twenty years made it a challenging shift. Many of the younger people had grown up or been born in the camps, so in a way they were learning a new way of life.

We hoped this approach would ensure these communities no longer added to the distressing figure that over 2.4 billion people lacked hygienic sanitation. It was encouraging to see the increase in the number of toilets with every visit, and to know the program was working. Our CLTS program was run in conjunction with our water and agriculture program. It was a good example of providing a 'hand up rather than a hand out'.

~

Walking into a village on my first field visit as a public health worker, it was the singing I noticed first. I wasn't sure where it was coming from but it was what propelled me forward through the long green and brown grasses lining the dirt track. A splash of colour and movement appeared through the brush, the singing got louder and my heart began to beat faster.

'It's their traditional welcome,' whispered Patience, the young public health officer who was also interpreting for me. She was obviously amused by my excitement. Patience was about 25 years old and was a year into her contract with Oxfam. She knew the communities well. She had a slight build and, like many women in the more educated circles of Uganda, wore a wig of straight ironed hair. Some women at work changed their hair as much as they changed their underwear! In the beginning I would re-introduce myself to people I had met the week before as I did not recognise the new 'do'. Common in the middle classes, it is the only option for women who want a change in hair style from the coarse, tightly curly hair that grows naturally. The women in the villages who could not afford this luxury generally shaved their heads and it was the same with children.

Breaking through the long grasses into a clearing, I couldn't believe my eyes. About 80 villagers stood in the shade under a large overhanging tree. The refracted light from the sun danced through gaps in the branches and the singing grew in strength as we drew closer. Rhythmic soulful voices. A woman stood out to take the lead as the others followed her in both action and response. Hands were raised to the sky, and then they all shimmied down towards the earth. Call and response. Callused bare feet stepping to the beat. 'Yy Yy Yy Yy Yy Yy Yy'—I recognised the same high pitch celebratory call I had heard in Karamoja, despite the different style of song, dance and language.

This community may not have had many material goods but they certainly had the power and unity of music. It was an unexpected welcome that I grew to know and love on future visits to communities in northern Uganda.

'They're singing about you.'

'Really?'

'They are saying how happy they are that you are the first Muzungu to visit their village. And they sing of how they hope to rebuild their village now there is peace in their land.'

I was touched. Muzungu was their slang term for 'white person'. I always felt a bit uncomfortable being put on a pedestal just for being white, but if it helped to motivate the community to make change then I was happy.

I took time to study their faces as they sang—old, young, men, women. Women in long colourful dresses with puffy sleeves, many with babies tied to their backs by a piece of material. The men in sarongs or trouser pants. A baby suckled on her mother's breast as she played with her mother's wooden crucifix necklace. An elderly man with bare feet sat on a stool as he leant his chin on a walking stick. The men sat to one side, the women to the other. There were two newly built *tukals* (huts) in the clearing.

A little boy with a pudgy face waddled up to me. 'Are you a Muzungu?' he asked as the community roared with laughter. He had obviously heard about white people but I was the first one he had encountered in his short life. At least he had the courage to come up to me. Some younger babies burst into tears when they saw me, perhaps due to my ghostly white skin.

The village quietened as a village leader, obviously dressed for the occasion, came out in a white shirt tucked into dark western pants held up by a belt around his slim waist. He greeted Patience with familiarity. She had been working with this community for the past three months regarding the installation of a new well. Patience introduced the rest of the team. The leader shook each of our hands in turn, as wooden chairs were brought out and placed on the hard earth. Possibly the only chairs in the whole village. I felt uncomfortable in a chair considering everyone else was on the ground, but it was a token of their appreciation and I felt it would be rude to refuse. As we took our seats the singing came to an end; we applauded and everyone sat down as the formalities began.

No matter where I was in Uganda, the formalities at the beginning of any meeting, training session or community visit were always elaborate. Long welcomes from VIPs in the village: the leader, the deputy leader, the leader of the women's council, the village health workers. And, in turn, we introduced ourselves and said why we were there. As usual I received a few laughs of appreciation by trying out my Acholi (a local dialect) language skills but Patience took the lead.

'We will be coming over the next ten weeks to discuss hygiene and sanitation. To make sure that as you rebuild your communities, you have everything in place to be healthy.' Patience addressed the crowd with confidence and ease.

She asked a few warm up questions to ensure everyone felt comfortable and knew the importance of us being there. We never forced ourselves on communities and would only return if invited back. Patience asked about common illnesses and problems in the community, and discussed what we were able to address and what we were not able to address. She explained our focus would be on water and toilets and, no, we were not able to build health centres and schools for their children.

It is really important to ensure communities have clear expectations of what you are able to do, and to work with the government and other organisations that have mandates in other areas of need. Unfortunately, in this area, there was so much need and very few government resources to meet the needs. The village knew that having clean, accessible water was crucial. Although there was some resistance to toilets when there was a perfectly good bush to do your business in.

'The first thing we need to do is to develop a map of your village. How many people? Who lives where? Where are the water points? Where do people shit? Are there any latrines? Paths, fields and things like that.' Using the local word for 'shit' was a part of the CLTS strategy.

'But only a quarter of our people are back,' piped up an older man in the crowd. 'They are still moving from the camps over the next few months. We have come ahead to start the building and digging of crops in time for the rains.'

'That's ok, we can map out what is here now, and if there are any plans for where each family will live we can add them later.'

'So using any materials available—sticks, leaves, dirt—whatever you can find, I'd like you to develop a map on the ground, and a volunteer can then draw it on to this big piece of paper.' Patience held up some flip chart paper and markers. 'As there are so many of you, half go with Krissy and David, and half stay with me and Edward.' David and Edward were the other public health officers in the team.

The group divided in half and we began the community mapping process. It was a commonly used participatory technique I had learnt about in my Master's degree and I was thrilled to see it work in practice. A couple of people took the lead and directed other community members to collect the stones, while a small argument broke out as to whether the main path was more to the left or the right. I was impressed with their ingenuity.

Stones were used to depict the *tukals*, leaves were scattered in areas to depict their new fields for crops, sticks showed the roads and pathways, and then someone brought ash from an old fire to represent areas where people would commonly go to defecate. There were only two actual latrines that had been built in the entire village, shelter and crops being the building priority. The map was then transferred on to flip chart paper for safe keeping. The idea was that as new latrines and houses were built, they could be added to the map to show progress.

The community was enthusiastic and all got involved. They wanted more than anything to live in a secure, well-built village and many already understood the importance of good sanitation and how it prevents disease.

Over the next couple of weeks we moved into different villages trying to 'ignite' communities to inspire change. On our way to a village that was new to me, I was anxious to see the 'shit in the bottle' approach. I had learnt about it in the CLTS training, but felt pretty uncomfortable and yuck about it, although intrigued to see how it worked in practice.

'Is it ok if we have a walk through your village?' Patience requested.

About twenty men, women and children followed, while the rest stayed behind to talk with another colleague about how the new bore hole we had constructed a few months before was operating. Patience walked randomly up a path, passed a couple of *tukals*, down another path lined by thick grass with a random beautiful sunflower popping up every now and then. Unbeknown to the group, she was looking for human shit. She knew she was close as she started down one path.

'No, don't go down there,' suggested a young man in a red t-shirt.

But she continued and stopped in a small clearing with the group scattered around her. The smell assaulted my nostrils before I saw the evidence on the ground beside Patience's right foot. But Patience continued speaking, pretending not to notice.

'So how are the crops growing this year?' she asked the group. 'Hasn't been much rain lately, has there.'

I looked around to see the expressions on the group's faces as they shifted uncomfortably, and their faces contorted with the smell.

'Let's move away,' said an older woman with a pleated purple dress with puffy sleeves.

'Why, what's the problem?' replied Patience.

'It smells here, look—' the old woman pointed at the shit on the ground. 'Be careful you don't step in it!'

'Someone shat on the ground, what's the problem with that?'

'It stinks,' giggled a cheeky young boy about twelve years old.

'It's dirty,' added a woman in her twenties, looking embarrassed.

None of them looked at my eyes during the conversation, but I was intrigued watching the process unfold.

One of the village elders yelled at a young boy to 'quick, get something to cover it up'. He was obviously embarrassed at his guests having to witness it.

'Good idea,' said Patience, 'but instead of covering it, can someone pick it up and bring it back to the bigger group.' They looked at her as if she was mad.

The elder sent a young boy off to get a shovel and the group started talking about why all we wanted to do here was find their shit. They didn't understand what we were doing, and frankly I would not understand if my guests decided to have a conversation about my toilet either. Let alone pick up my shit and bring it to show everyone. Flies buzzed about the pile on the ground, as Patience continued to ask questions about why the shit was dirty . . . and what was the problem with it.

'Because it can make us sick if we are near it,' piped up a teenage boy in shorts and an oversized t-shirt falling off one shoulder.

The group again shifted uncomfortably as we stood around talking about the shit, and the relief was palpable when the boy with a shovel came to remove it.

The boy picked the shit up with the shovel, and led the group back to the centre where the rest of the community was waiting. What a sight we made. The community started talking and laughing slightly as we approached. Some seemed angry and disgraced at the spectacle as the boy led us back, shovel of shit in hand and a sour look on his face. Flies swarmed behind.

'Thanks for that,' Patience said to the little boy, and indicated for him to put the shit on a piece of paper we had placed on the ground in the middle of the wider group, who had been waiting in the shade under the tree. She put a piece of bread about 30 centimetres from the shit and then retrieved a bottle of water from her bag. We all watched in disgust as a swarm of flies landed on the shit and then flew to the food and back again.

'Who would like this water?' Patience held up her sealed bottle of water.

Most of the community put their hands up and Patience gave the bottle to an older man, leaning up against the tree. He unscrewed the lid and started drinking as everyone watched on with confused faces.

'Ok, can I have the water back now, please?' The man handed back the half empty bottle.

Patience found a long thin stick on the ground and ran it along the shit before putting it in the bottle of water. She shook it around and then took the stick out. The water didn't change colour and if you didn't see her put the dirty stick in, you wouldn't know the water was contaminated.

She held the bottle up again. 'Now, who would like to drink the water?'

The group stirred, looks of disgust on their faces. Some shouted out 'No way'.

'Why wouldn't you drink the water now, what's changed?'

'There's shit in it!' yelled out a woman in the crowd. 'I don't want to drink someone's shit!' she continued, as Patience put the open bottle of water next to the piece of bread. The flies continued to move from the shit to the bread and some rested on the mouth of the water bottle.

Patience facilitated a discussion about how ingesting shit can make you sick and how bad it is for you. She never told anyone the answers, she just asked a series of questions that led the community to their own solutions.

'So, what is the difference between having the shit right here next to the food, and over there in the bushes? It's not like the flies stay in the bushes either, is it?'

The community looked at the shit and the bread and the bottle of water and the flies flying from one to the next and sometimes landing on them and you could see the shift in their thinking as they realised that shitting in the bush meant that they were essentially eating their own shit. They talked about the animals that would walk through it and bring it through their village, and also drink from their water sources.

'We have to change this,' said a woman with a babe strapped to her back.

'How?' asked Patience.

'We need to build latrines, we need to stop shitting in the bush. I don't want to be eating your shit!' she said to the whole group. Many laughed with her. Some light relief in an uncomfortable situation. But others continued to look disgusted.

'Get it away!' yelled another older woman.

Patience nodded as the boy with the shovel picked it up and took it away.

For the next half hour Patience led a discussion as the community talked about how they could stop this problem. They committed to dig latrines for every household. They discussed the difficulties of having a transitional village, that people were still moving back from the camps, but that they would need to tell the newcomers as well. They invited us back in six weeks time with a commitment of having latrines in every household by then. They agreed that they wanted to be an 'Open Defecation Free' village.

We talked about how they would be a leading example for other communities and told them we would put their story in the paper. They posed for a photo with their hands held up in the air in solidarity. We will be ODF in six weeks time, they committed. 'Click'—I took the photo and later that day wrote an article for the local paper.

I was amazed at how quickly the community committed to action. I could not believe how well the process had worked. But the proof would be on our next visit to see whether they kept their promise. We were only in the village for a couple of hours and in that time such a significant shift in thinking had occurred. What a powerful approach this was, and I was hopeful that they would follow through on their commitment.

$$\backsim$$

Back at the office I was completing a report of the day's activities and hadn't realised the time. It was always exhausting going into the field. Hot, long bumpy hours in the car, struggling with language and interpretations, engaging whole communities and then back again to write up notes. Rewarding but tiring work that often saw us labouring on into the evening.

'Are you ready to leave?' Selma was waiting at the door.

'Yep, let's get out of here.' I sighed deeply, shutting down my computer.

It was already dark outside and although home was close, no electricity meant negotiating the dirt streets by torchlight, and Selma and I made it a ritual to go home together when we could.

Selma was a Somali woman in her late twenties. For a while, we were the only women in the Oxfam guesthouse and developed a lovely connection. Walking home that evening we talked women's business, complaining about getting our period in the field.

'The only toilets are holes in the ground and that's if you can find any in the first place.'

'I know, thank God for tampons,' I said. I had packed three months worth, knowing I wouldn't find any in Kitgum.

'Tampons?'

'Yeah, you know . . . tampons.'

But maybe she didn't know. Maybe there weren't tampons in Somalia. Here, most women used material or even leaves, unless they were in the city. Rags like our grandmothers would have used. Maybe Somalia was the same?

'They are little cotton things that you use, I'll give you some to try later.'

I figured it would be easier to show her than try to explain. We walked in silence down the dirt path, goats bleating as we walked by.

'I don't think I can use them, Krissy.'

'Why not, it's easy. It's ok, I'll explain. Once you . . .'

'No, I mean . . .' Selma looked at me shyly. 'I can't.' She looked at me to see if I understood.

'Oh, you mean . . .'

I had read a lot about female genital mutilation. It is a procedure practised widely in many countries across Africa to intentionally alter or cause injury to the female genital organs for non-medical reasons. It is often carried out with blunt instruments and can cause severe bleeding, infections, infertility and complications during childbirth, including the increased risk of newborn deaths. While there are arguments that it is an important cultural practice, I think it is a violation of the human rights of young girls. I always assumed it would have been carried out in rural, uneducated families. Not on someone like Selma!

'Yes, I've been sewn up.' *OH MY GOD. Poor Selma.*

'Oh, sorry, I didn't mean to . . . do you feel comfortable talking about it?'

'With you I do, Krissy.' I was slightly in shock, but I was intrigued to know more.

'So what's it like?'

'I was five when they did it. They cut it all away and sewed me up.' I tried to hide my dismay. 'It's ok, I know it must sound shocking to you.'

'Well . . . it's just . . .'

'They left a hole this big,' she held up her little finger, 'to let the blood come out.'

We arrived at the green gates of our compound and after a couple of knocks the guard let us in.

'It's just horrible,' she continued when we were out of the guards' earshot. But the boys were already in the house when we walked through the door.

'I'll talk to you about it later,' she said.

'I'd like that.'

It was a simple exchange between women. Two women who were from such different cultures. I shuddered at the thought of my genitals being cut and sewn up. I had so many questions and it sounded like she wanted to open up, but there was little privacy in the house and it would have been rude to lock ourselves away in one of our rooms.

I was only two weeks into my public health role with the focus on CLTS. I was getting good experience and was surprised how transferable my skills were and how much of my Master's degree knowledge I was directly applying in practice. I had a holiday planned but Ramona confirmed my contract extension for a couple of months upon my return. I couldn't wait to throw myself further into the public health world.

CHAPTER 23

OH MOTHER!

EAST AFRICA 2009

It was about eight months since I had left home and it was so good to see Mum walk through the arrival gates at Nairobi Airport. Already homesick, a 'mum fix' was exactly what I needed. We had a month full of adventures that saw us marvelling at the animals at the Masai Mara game park and walking among thousands of pink flamingos at Lake Nakuru. A short trip to the ancient spice trading route of Zanzibar to scuba dive in the turquoise waters and drink cocktails on the beaches. But it was the trekking with the gorillas at Bwindi Impenetrable Forest that was the 'once in a lifetime' experience that Mum had been dreaming about since she was a little girl.

It was lovely to connect with Mum again. To tell her of my excitement at entering the public health world, and the details of the project I was working on in Kitgum to stop open defecation, as I found it such a fascinating approach. The day after the gorilla trek we decided to explore a nearby village. On our way back, walking along a dirt path, Mum suddenly went into a panic.

'Krissy,' I could tell it was serious by the look on her face, 'I *really* need to go to the toilet!'

'Mum, we're only ten minutes away, just hold on.'

'Oh no, I can't, Krissy. I have to go.' There were no toilets in sight and although there were not many people around, we spotted a few boys walking herds of goats in the distance.

'Ones or twos, Mum?'

'Twos!'

'MOTHER! You are *not* shitting in the bush. Please, just wait ten minutes. Come on, let's just walk faster.' My voice was stern and I grabbed her hand to walk faster along the track.

'Krissy, I can't . . .' She tore her hand away and wandered off.

'MUM. DON'T YOU DARE!!! We are so close!!!' I walked faster ahead and was embarrassed to look back as she ducked into some bushes on the side.

Momentarily, I disowned her as my mother. It reminded me of the time when I was a teenager walking my dog, and seeing it stop to cock its leg on the flowers outside the florist. What dog? I don't have a dog? I never thought I would feel this way about my mother!!

There I was in Uganda teaching people to build toilets and to stop open defecation, when my own mother was shitting in the bush. Granted, there were no toilets around but how embarrassing! The poor boy who went to check on the white woman who had wandered off the path must have got the shock of his life.

With the gorilla trek and the poo incident behind us, we continued our adventure in Uganda—visiting my cousin, Kev, who happened to be working in a chimpanzee forest, and stopping at the highest waterfalls on the Nile, as the boat we were travelling in floated past the ominous eyes of hundreds of crocodiles and hippos. We were heading north to my temporary home of Kitgum. I wanted to show Mum where I worked and the reason why she 'shouldn't be shitting in the bush'—something she would never live down!

I was proud to take Mum to Lumkwa village, which is one of the villages where the Community Led Total Sanitation (CLTS) program was being piloted. As we entered, we passed the newly dug grave of a child of one of the village leaders, and most of the community were absent due to another funeral taking place of a little boy who had died of malaria—the biggest cause of sickness and deaths here. The 30 women and men present for our meeting felt sorry that there was not a more grand meeting for my mother and I, who were honoured guests. We felt bad even being there considering they were probably in mourning, yet they still made us welcome—and I was surprised when they carried out a whole couch for us to sit on under a large tree. I had never even seen a couch in one of these villages before. Most *tukals* are barely big enough to lay down mats to sleep on, let alone house a couch. Such hospitality and humble kindness. Mum got up to join the women as they performed the local dance and song to welcome us.

The progress the village had made in the six weeks since my last visit was encouraging. They had truly taken power into their own hands and built several latrines, which were drop toilets with newly woven shelters for privacy. Some even had hand washing facilities, usually in the form of a 'tippy tap' (easily made jerry cans with a string to tip the water up). Their plan was to build a latrine for every household. They wanted to be the first village in the area to stop open defecation and to achieve this with their own materials and labour. Many households were proud to go beyond just latrines, building wash rooms with soak pits, drying racks made out of bamboo for pots and pans, and separate shelter for their chickens and goats. They were proud to be a model village and also that the first Muzungu to visit, now brought her mother! At least now there were toilets if Mum needed one!

We took photos to put in the local paper with a story about their success and, in turn, this influenced other communities to come on board. A little healthy competition to motivate change.

Although it was difficult for Mum to understand why we couldn't transport the whole community back into town in the Oxfam vehicle, I think she really enjoyed the visit and could now visualise where her daughter was when I wrote my emails home.

Gin and tonics in hand, Mum and I sat together quietly on the last night before her departure. Seemingly miles away, she looked at me seriously.

'Krissy, you know that if you don't end up married with children that it's ok. I won't be disappointed.'

'Mum, no, don't say that. I *will* find Mr Right. He has to be out there somewhere. You know I am dying to have children and I don't know what I'll do if I can't.'

Mum hugged me. 'Of course you will, darling, of course you will . . .'

Mum and I have one of those unusual relationships where we actually get along and can be really honest with each other. Besides the odd fight along the way, we were like best friends travelling together for a whole month. I was in floods of tears when her car pulled away the next day.

As the car disappeared into the distance I looked around the compound, feeling lonely. I lay in my small, lumpy bed covered in the blue mosquito net, stared at the concrete floor and cried myself to sleep. But I woke during the night to a vibrant full moon and felt better. The moon always reflected Mum's love for me.

I'm not sure if it was missing Mum, or Dad's increased calls asking me to come home. Or getting photos of Steph's new little one growing up so quickly. Or missing engagements and other friends having babies. But my yearning to return home continued to grow. It was a strange feeling being homesick. Despite the several years I have spent away from home, I have never really wanted to be anywhere else other than the country I was in. I planned to travel for a few months around West Africa after my contract finished but I began to have second thoughts. Maybe I would surprise everyone and come home early for Christmas. But it was only September and I was excited to get back into the public health work.

CHAPTER 24

THE CHICKEN RUN

UGANDA 2009

After several gin and tonics and a couple of shots, I sang, ok, well, slightly slurred, my favourite, and rather sexy, Tori Amos song 'Leather' at Fuglys in Kitgum. I'd never seen the bar on fire like it was that night. There were a few Navy boys in town to scope out a military exercise planned for a few months time. Although the monotonous short back and sides hair styles and loudness were slightly scary and quite out of place, it was nice to have some new people to play with.

After a frustrating day in the office, I had come to Fuglys with a mission to let loose and drink! It seemed that everyone had the same agenda, as the alcohol flowed, guitars came out, the singing started and soon, it didn't matter what brought you to Kitgum—God, humanitarian or military motives—in the end, Fuglys gave us a chance to just be a group of people in a remote location letting go of their stressful work and having fun.

'So I noticed that you were looking at me when you were singing that amazing song . . .'

Mmm . . . cute smile, but that crew cut . . . I don't know! The Navy boy drew closer, after buying me a shot of something strong for 'the entertainment'.

'Really?' I flicked my hair, amused. 'No, I don't think so.'

I laughed and sipped my drink.

'Ouch, that hurt,' he said at the first hint of my upfront honesty and bluntness. As if I was going to pretend. I actually hadn't noticed him until then. They all pretty much looked the same from where I was standing. Same type of clothes, similar muscular body type, same haircuts.

'I'm Dan. And you are?'

This one was a cutie. A little short for my liking, but a sparkle in his eye and a quick wit.

'Krissy.' I offered my hand. His hand felt strong and coarse.

After talking and flirting for a couple of hours, I discovered Dan was a pretty cool guy. He was not what I imagined US military to be. He was intelligent, articulate, funny and open-minded, and calm and considered in his response, as I ridiculed the whole reason that he was there.

'Haven't these people been through enough without having to house 5000 men coming from all over East Africa for a military drill?' He just smiled as I continued. 'How can you justify the costs involved in this operation? Kicking people off their own land so you can use the space and taking massive amounts of water from the local lakes to purify and use for washing!!! WASHING—do you not realise that most people here have to walk for hours just to get drinking water—and you are purifying what little water there is to wash your arses!!!!!'

Dan was clearly amused by me, as he couldn't get that cute smile off his face.

'Yeah, I know, it's ridiculous, isn't it? It's such a waste, but unfortunately it's the way the military work.'

. . . hold on a minute . . . if you agree, what are you doing here?

'And, yes, I agree that the "humanitarian" work we are doing is a bit of show. We hope it does some good, but we know that it's not sustainable for the long term . . .'

This guy was quickly winning me over. Yes, he was in the US military, but he seemed to have a good understanding of the local culture and the potential bad effects of their presence, and after further interrogation (from my side) I found out that he was actually here for civil military liaison, so it was his job to understand these things.

After a few hours of interrogation and banter, he interrupted me mid-sentence. 'I really feel like kissing you . . .' he said, with that cheeky smile. And then that was it.

He was a really good kisser.

Somehow I made it to work the next morning, feeling worse for wear and trying to fill in the blanks from my memory of the night. Luckily, Ramona had been with me most of the night so we suffered in silence together, careful not to tarnish our 'responsible' reputation to the national staff. A few hours later the first text message came.

'Great to get to know you last night, I'd love to see you again.'

Er . . . I think I remember him being nice, but what if it was me just being drunk, what if I don't even find him attractive, what if I made a mistake . . .

'Sure, but no expectations, ok?' I replied, giving myself an out.

'Tonight. 8 p.m.?'

'Make it tomorrow night. See you then. ;-)' I had a big day training community health workers the next day and I didn't want to be hung over. Plus, I could hardly keep my eyes open and needed a good sleep. Dan would have to wait.

⌒

The heat seeped through the open *tukul*, bouncing off the concrete floor. Plastic chairs were arranged in a circle. The fringe of the grass roof protruded just over the top of the rectangular room overlooking the courtyard. I longed for a slight breeze to soften the searing heat, but it didn't come.

There were nineteen people attending the training session. Women in their traditional colourful dresses, puffed at the sleeves, a couple of little ones tied to their mothers' backs. Men in dark pants and shirts, looking professional for the training. We were conducting a Knowledge, Attitudes and Practice (KAP) survey that would give us an idea of the health status and needs of the 70,000 population of the area. For such a large survey, we were training our health workers on information gathering. Everything from random sampling, to interview techniques. A few hours into the training, I watched my colleague explain.

'Each survey question is outlined clearly on the . . .' *SKWAARK* . . .

A chicken bobbed around the courtyard outside.

'Make sure you tick the right box according to . . .' *SKWAARK* . . .

It was so loud, but no one seemed to notice. A man in rubber shoes and a dirty shirt ran across the courtyard, wielding a knife high in the air. *SWAAARK . . . What the . . . ?!*

'How many people in your household? And make sure you mark down male, fem . . .' . . . *SWAARK* . . .

I couldn't concentrate. All I could hear was the ruffling of feathers and the pitter patter of chickens' feet, until I saw the grubby legs of the man with the knife.

'Question 9: Is anyone in your family sick? If so, what ...' ... *Oh my God, is he going to kill it right here ... oh no ... concentrate, Krissy, act professional ...*

I looked intently at the survey, reading along. *SWAAAAAARK!!!!!*

'Why is hand washing important? Is it ...' ... *Stomp, stomp, stomp* of the man's feet ... *pitter patter pitter patter* of the chicken across the yard.

'Be friendly, approachable. If they are unsure then ...' ... *Pitter patter, stomp, stomp* ... and back they came the other way. I felt like I was in the middle of a bizarre cartoon.

'Now it's your turn to practise. Turn to the person next to you and ...'

SWAWK SWARK CHOP SWAAAAARK ... CHOP CHOP ...

... silence ...

'Great, now, once you have run through the survey, swap partners so you can all ...' The training continued without interruption.

Look normal, Krissy, look normal.

I looked up to see one of my colleagues laughing at me. He could see me wince as I heard the chicken come to its loud, screechy death. Luckily, no one else seemed to notice.

As everyone munched on their freshly cooked chicken stew that lunch time, I stuck to the stale bread and overripe banana. A forced smile stuck to my face.

⤳

Standing at Fuglys' gate with Ramona, I swallowed hard. I knew where he would be sitting, and I knew he would have a full view of anyone entering. *Breathe, Krissy, breathe . . . if you don't like him, you don't have to speak to him.*

I cringed as the iron gate clanged when I closed it behind us. The 50 metres distance leading to the bar where I knew Dan would be sitting felt like the length of the Sahara.

And there he was. Staring straight at me, red wine in hand and that cute smile. I greeted his two mates at the table, gave him a kiss on the cheek and sat down. *Well done, you've come this far. Keep up the good work.*

Besides getting up to fill our glasses, Dan and I barely left each other's side. The glow of the flames highlighted Dan's dark features. He had gentle eyes and a round face with a dimple in his chin that really showed when he smiled. He leant forward as he spoke. His voice was deep and sexy and I loved his American accent. Occasionally, he placed a hand on my arm or leg as he emphasised a point in our discussion. Soon enough, no emphasis was required. Our conversation flowed as smoothly as the imported merlot that filled our glasses.

He told me about the time he was shot at when taking photos from a rooftop in Iraq. I told him how I walked down the streets with placards protesting that very same 'illegal' war. He told me how strict the Navy was with their protocols and about its conservative views, but that he didn't fit the mould. I told him that when I was five I was kicked out of the Brownies because I didn't want to wear shoes. That I have always been adverse to authority and discipline.

He loved books and writing, and had secret dreams of being the next Hemingway. He was currently reading Tolstoy's *War and Peace* . . . (tick)

His dad was also a military man but they were not close. He hardly saw his parents. (cross)

He didn't seem to have close friends either. A bit of a loner. (cross)

Too much bullshit to sift through, he said. Except for his kids. Yep, he had two young kids under the age of ten. They were the light of his life and he spoke passionately about them. (tick . . . I think)

He had been separated for a year now and, in the midst of getting a divorce. (tick . . . at least he was single . . .).

He wasn't religious but had strong values of social justice. (tick)

He loved travelling and discovering new cultures. (tick)

He was in the Navy to make a difference to the world but was starting to question the way this was done. (tick)

I didn't quite get him; yet he intrigued me. We continued to unpack each other's lives. Like opening a pass the parcel at an eight-year-old's birthday . . . unwrapping each layer carefully, wondering what you will get. Excited, yet apprehensive in case you didn't win the prize. I pressed him more on Iraq as it was a sore point for me. He actually didn't agree with the war either (tick), but he had enjoyed the experience and what he had learnt there. It's being a part of history, right? You see, for me, it's simple—if I am ethically against something, I won't support it and certainly would never work for an organisation that I was fundamentally against. But he voted for Obama and hated Bush. (tick)

'Have you ever shot anyone?' *Please say no, please say no, please say no.*

'Only with my camera,' he smiled. *Thank God!*

Dan's role wasn't on the front line. And no, he wasn't a doctor. He was a communications specialist who had spent the last twenty years moving up the ranks in the Navy. Although he was modest about it, it sounded like he was quite high ranking—not that I understood the difference between a 'lieutenant commander' and a 'petty officer'.

213

The Navy was all he knew. It was in his blood. I guess how I felt Oxfam was in mine—except he had known no other job.

'So why do you do what you do?' I asked him.

'I want peace and justice in the world and think the military have a role to play in this . . . oh, and it's great to travel, see the world and have adventures in places people have never dreamed of,' he replied.

'And you, Krissy, why do you do what you do?'

'The same reasons, really . . .' We stared at the fire in silence for a while. The shadow and light of the flames danced between us.

I respected the reasons he was there: the travel opportunities, the diverse situations he had been able to work in. But I couldn't really understand how someone who was 'left wing, open-minded and creative' could work in an institution with such a disciplined, conservative agenda. Actually, despite my lack of understanding, it is one thing that I admired most about him. That he did have a different life and political view than the majority of his colleagues and the institution. He went against the grain and hoped to bring about change from the inside. Although not quite convinced, I appreciated his ability to be critical, to analyse and question the environment in which he worked. I thought that took strength and independent thought, and I really liked that about him.

'What have you done to me? I am mesmerised by you.' I hoped the glow of the fire would mask my embarrassment. 'I just want to know everything about you. I could talk to you forever.'

He continued, 'I don't usually like socialising or meeting new people. Most people bore me, but you . . . I feel like you have put a spell on me.'

Um . . . I was not really sure what to say, so I just laughed it off. While I liked Dan, I was still figuring out if I 'like, liked' him. For one thing, I could not believe he was another man in uniform. Rob

214

in the Army, SS in the police force and now the Navy! What was it with me and men in uniform? Uniforms to me just represent discipline, authority, conservatism. I was never one of those women who get turned on by the whole uniform thing . . . except, possibly, a fireman! Regardless, I thought I was over that stage!

The night was getting quieter and people started to leave. There was no way to get home after about midnight as the few motorbike guys who worked in town would be asleep. I wouldn't feel safe walking alone . . . no street lights, no electricity in town except for those lucky few to have a generator. I didn't know whether I wanted to go home anyway. I knew that uncomfortable stage would soon be here, when I would have to decide whether to stay or go. To be safe, I checked in with Ramona.

'Hey, Mona, let me know when you're leaving, I'll get a lift with . . .'

'No way, girlfriend, you're staying.' She nodded towards Dan. 'He's gorgeous . . . and anyway, my car's full.'

Ramona drove a big Land Cruiser that seated ten. She had one other person to drop off that night.

CHAPTER 25

VILLAGE BY DAY, LOVE DEN BY NIGHT

UGANDA 2009

'So, um . . . I've decided to stay with you if that's ok?' I whispered shyly to Dan.

The red wine was obviously not enough to throw away my inhibitions like on the previous night. He pulled me close and kissed me for the first time that evening.

'I'd love that.'

With whispers and muffled giggles, I snuck into his room like a guilty teenager. It was like a university dorm, only just separated from the rest of his 'boys' by paper thin walls. When the flimsy single bed broke as we gave it a good work out, there was no more keeping our secret. We laughed uncontrollably, kissing and huddling close. It was quite a feat on a single broken bed, tucking the mosquito net around us without much success. A persistent mozzie relentlessly buzzed around my ear all night. After what could only have been a couple of hours sleep, my eyes snapped open. It was 6 a.m. Already awake, Dan smiled at me. His face uncomfortably close without the cloak of red wine to protect me. *God, I need to brush my teeth!* I tried to breathe through my nose.

'I've got to get up . . .' His one day growth tickled my face as he kissed me gently.

'No, let's just say in bed all day,' I moaned and rolled over. I nestled my back against his chest, feeling his arms around me. *What do I say now . . . God, I hate the morning after . . . hope my breath doesn't smell . . . um . . .*

I pretended to be falling in and out of sleep as he got up and dressed. Busy days for both of us lay ahead. He was to visit some villages to suss out a location for their massive military operation and I was dreading going to the office for some serious partner meetings. I could hear his crew getting ready beyond the thin walls. The sound of someone brushing their teeth. The toilet flushing. A loud belch. I shrunk smaller in the bed. *Oh no, they must have heard everything.*

'I'll call you later, ok?' Dan gazed at me gently as he sat on the edge of the small broken bed, tying the laces of his metal-capped boots.

I nodded lazily, still naked under the white sheets. 'Ok.'

'I can't get this stupid grin off my face.' He leaned over and kissed me again.

The door closed behind him and I was left in the box room planning my escape. I peered out the curtains of the small window, straining my eyes across the courtyard behind the bar. There were a couple of jeeps with uniform clad men lumbering in. It took me a few self-conscious minutes to find all my clothing strewn across the room. I dressed quickly and listened intently at the door before I dared to run across the hall to use the shared toilet.

I heard one of the guys walk past and held my breath and my bladder mid stream as I put my pelvic floor muscles into use. *Oh no . . . shhhh!*

'Yeah, I'm comin', I'm comin . . .' he yelled.

As soon as the coast was clear, I ran back to the little room. The walls looked even more bland in the light of day. Not that I was concerned with the colour of the walls the night before.

I peered through the curtain again. I couldn't see anyone. The jeeps had gone and there was silence. I guessed it was safe. That damn mozzie buzzed around my head. *SMACK* . . . I slapped it against the wall as my (or Dan's) blood splattered against the peeling paint work. *Little bastard—better not be malarial!*

Taking the walk of shame home, I arrived to find my housemates making coffee and getting ready for work. I managed to slip through to have a shower without being noticed. I wondered if they noticed I didn't come home last night. I was now the only girl in the house as Selma's contract had just finished and she was on her way back to Somalia. I wished she was there to tell. She loved these stories. A single girl herself, she was also on the look out for Mr Right. Although in her case, it was likely she would have an arranged marriage.

'What's it like?' she asked me one night as we talked about the eternal search for Mr Right.

'What's what like?'

Selma was inquisitive and open-minded. It was the first time she had worked, let alone travelled, outside Somalia. I even suspected having friendships with western women who were more liberal about sex and relationships was also relatively new. She was curious and asked lots of questions.

'Well, the first time can hurt a bit . . . but then it can be fantastic. It depends on the man, really . . . the connection you have, the mood you're in . . . it's hard to describe.'

Although I wondered what Selma would feel at all—without a clitoris and much of the other sensitive areas around the vagina.

'I'm so terrified of my first time. I don't know what I'm going to do.'

'Oh, Selma . . . I can't imagine . . .' We both squirmed.

'I have heard stories of my friends, of their husbands just ramming into them until they rip open. They say it's so, so painful.'

'Can't you do something?'

'Some people have operations, to make things a bit more normal down there.' She looked at her hands. 'But Somali men don't like that, Krissy, they wouldn't want to marry you.'

'No, Selma, you are a strong, educated woman. I'm sure if you find an educated, liberal man . . . surely he'd understand?'

'You don't know how it is, Krissy. My culture is so traditional.'

No, I didn't know how it was. I can't even imagine being in that situation. Poor Selma was terrified at the thought of sex. It was no wonder. I'd be terrified too if I was her. There was so much that I took for granted as a western woman from Australia. It was conversations like these that taught me more about gender issues than any academic journal I would ever read. I missed Selma in the house, and who knows whether I would ever see her again. The nature of emergency work meant that you often made incredibly close friends in a short space of time who you may never see again.

Back at work, I stared at the computer hungover and sleep deprived—but this time with a big smile on my face. This time, knowing that it was not a drunken mistake.

'I can't stop thinking about you . . .' came the first of many texts that morning.

Beep. 'I'm dreaming about kissing you.'

Beep. 'Can't wait to see you again.'

Beep. 'What have you done to me?'

I put my phone on silent but kept it in sight and skipped a breath each time it lit up.

It was so nice to feel wanted. I caught my reflection in the window, my smile a permanent fixture. I glowed from the inside.

The next three days and nights were spent in much the same way, but each night had a different flavour—a new feeling—and was a unique adventure. By night, there was growing passion. Hours spent making love, talking, laughing. We explored the depths of each other's minds, each other's bodies. By day, lacking sleep, trying to concentrate on work yet both with minds wandering to the growing romance. Exchanging romantic text messages that would warm our hearts and excite us for the night ahead.

We continued to sneak around like teenagers, not wanting the word to get out. The military operations were already controversial among the aid agencies. It was a bit like I was sleeping with the enemy. I felt like we were the leads in a romantic movie. Australian aid worker meets US Navy man in the remote plains of post-conflict northern Uganda. It was the most unlikely match in an unlikely situation.

Thank goodness for Ramona letting us stay at her house. There is no way I could have him in my female dominated compound, where we all shared a bathroom and living space. Ramona also got lucky with one of the other Navy crew so we nicknamed her house the 'Kitgum Love Den' for a while. It was all a bit of fun, although the connection between Dan and me seemed to grow beyond a frivolous fling.

'Girlfriend, you are definitely not wearing your Emergency Goggles this time. He's great!' Ramona teased.

'Ha ha . . . what about you, then? I'm just glad your house is big and has thick walls!' We both laughed.

During the days that Dan and I spent apart, I longed to look into his gentle eyes. To admire the weathered smile lines that crinkled up every time he laughed. To lie my head on his chest, his hairs tickling my cheek. The more time I spent with Dan, the more ruggedly handsome he became. He had a strong physique and I felt safe and protected when he put his muscular arms around me

Dan was kind, intelligent, liberal minded and creative. He was considerate, sweet and a good listener. The ticks started to outweigh the crosses—even if 'military status' was worth a fair few crosses! The more I discovered about Dan, the more I wanted him. He told me more about his two young children, who he missed desperately. He said the only thing he really didn't like about his work was being away from them. That he looked forward to the time when he would be based at home and have more time with them. I wondered if he wanted more children but I wasn't going to ask.

By day, I'd be out in communities talking to people about rebuilding their lives, latrine building projects and working with our engineers to talk about safe water collection and disease prevention. Dan continued to visit communities to prepare them for the military exercise, as well as planning for short-term medical clinics to be opened while they were there.

By night, we would share stories of each other's days. Successes, frustrations, interactions and hopes. And then we would melt into each other once again.

The night before Dan's departure, we lay in bed talking. Lightning flashed across the sky and fierce winds rattled the shutters. The might of the thunder reflected the strength of the growing passion within me. Our tea light candle flickered as we brewed our own storm. It was three in the morning and we had to be up at six. We were both still wide awake.

'Once upon a time, there was a little girl with curly blonde hair . . .' *Oh my God, he is going to tell me a story.*

'She was skipping up a mountain singing with the sweetest voice anyone had ever heard.' He stroked my hair. 'The little girl's voice was so beautiful, that the angels of the mountain were captivated. "The magic of her voice", they cried. "This is what we have been waiting for".'

I felt like I had gone to heaven. I lay in the arms of this man I had known for only four days, as he dreamt up a fairytale about me. I wondered if he could feel my chest expand as my heart opened wider.

'The angels took the little girl under their wings and bottled up the magic of her voice. She would sing and sing and sing and those magic bottles were brimming with healing powers.'

'And what were they used for?' I asked, trying to quell my excitement.

To be honest, it didn't matter. This man was telling me a fairytale. A fairytale!!!

'Um . . .' His lips pressed gently against mine. 'Well . . . the angels then delivered the magic bottles to cure all the sick little boys and girls of the world.'

I giggled as if I was five again. Was this man for real? Would this fairytale have a happy ending? I wished he didn't have to leave and wondered if I'd ever see him again. Or was I just another girl in another port?

'Goodnight, angel.' Dan's breathing got heavier and he began to snore. But I couldn't sleep anyway.

Dan told me he was returning in a month. Perfect timing to celebrate my birthday. I promised I'd keep the night free for him and him only. What a wonderful present. Next time he would be back with 5000 other military types from all over East Africa and North America, but I didn't care—there was only one that I was interested in.

CHAPTER 26

SITTING BY A MUD HUT

UGANDA 2009

'Steph. Help. I'm completely freaking out . . .' I wrote in a desperate email. I'd been sending daily reports to Steph after every night with Dan. When he left Kitgum I felt content and philosophical, but as the intensity of his contact grew—so did my feelings. And I was terrified.

'Steph . . . *OH MY GOD, I CAN'T BREATHE RIGHT NOW! It's all moving too fast. What should I do? Am I falling in love? I think he is. He told me he is having visions of moving to Australia and meeting my friends. He just texted me for the fifth time today: "I see your face everywhere . . . I adore you" . . . ARGH, WHAT AM I DOING! I CAN'T FALL FOR A MILITARY MAN . . .'*

Yes, I really liked Dan, but his feelings seemed to have transcended into more depth than mine. As the weeks went by and we were in daily contact, usually via text messages, I felt like I had started falling for him too. I dreamt of being in his arms again, imagining our reunion out here in the middle of nowhere—running into his arms just like they do in the movies.

I forwarded copies of emails he sent and quoted text messages to Steph for dissection.

'When he writes "loving you" here, does this mean he is saying "I love you"?? There is a big difference, you know!' If men only knew how much we shared with our best friends!

Stephanie was my saviour as usual. 'Just breathe, Krissy. And enjoy! Finally a man is seeing you for the wonderful woman that you are. It's fantastic he can be so open about his emotions. Relax, enjoy and take it day by day.'

I tried, I really did try. I buried myself in my work. Our team continued the massive study that would tell us the health, water and sanitation needs of 70,000 people. *I wonder what he is doing now.* Biostatistics haunted me in full swing as I struggled to work out 'confidence intervals', 'chi-square tests' and X x Y / AB = God knows what . . . !! *Can't wait to kiss him again.* We mobilised the community health volunteers we had trained earlier to interview a random sample of a ridiculous amount of people on their knowledge and behaviours. *Mmm . . . I wonder if he would get along with my friends.* It was an intensive process that saw us walking for hours between villages, through brush, in rain, under the hot sun. *I want a garden wedding. Yes, a garden. Under a beautiful . . . STOP IT. STOP IT. STOP IT.*

On our first day out to test the survey, the first person we interviewed was a woman in her late twenties named Ayaa. Her long floral skirt brushed the black dirt ground and she wore a red scarf wrapped around her head. A few teeth missing, Ayaa smiled shyly and generously agreed to be interviewed, baby suckling on her breast as she continued to sort through greens in the cane basket next to her.

My colleague and I sat on two unsteady wooden stools that she provided for us, while she sat in the doorway of her round mud house with overhanging straw roof. I observed as my colleague asked the set of questions we had meticulously designed to gain information on general demographics, health status, access and usage of water and hygiene practices.

Dusty, half naked children giggled as they popped their heads around trees, taking a look at the strange white woman in their village. A few chickens walked around the compound and a grotty pig snorted by. As we spoke, I saw women cleaning around the village, and tirelessly grinding sorghum that would be used to cook the staple starchy brick that would fill their families' stomachs. Where possible this would be complemented by some green leafy vegetables mixed with ground nut. But there was an ongoing drought and the annual rains were well overdue. Many crops were set to fail and food was scarce. Most families had only one meal a day and meat was a luxury and only for special occasions.

As I had witnessed across Ethiopia and other parts of Uganda, young children and women tirelessly sowed the land, with a large possibility that their efforts would be fruitless. Mothers knew that if rain didn't come, in a month's time there would be no food to feed their children.

At least now Ayaa and her community could live in freedom, after living in fear of Kony's Lord's Resistance Army for so long. Her children were no longer at risk of being stolen in the middle of the night. The women could collect wood for a fire without the fear of being attacked or raped. She was helping to rebuild her village away from the overcrowded, disease-filled camps. I wondered what consolation this was when the chance of malnutrition and early death increased with every week that went by without rain.

Ayaa sat patiently with us, despite being taken away from her daily chores. She had already been working the fields for the last few hours, and collected water in the bright 20 kilo yellow containers that she carried on her head, baby wrapped tightly on to her back.

How much water do you use per day?

Who collects it?

Where from and how long does it take?

Do you own a latrine?

Where do you defecate?

Do your family wash their hands? When?

Why is it important?

Has any member of your family been sick in the past week?

Simple, almost irrelevant questions in the West are those that help to save lives here. Around the world over two billion people live without toilet facilities and hundreds of millions live without clean water. We were working to change that.

If Ayaa and her family build and use a toilet, wash their hands with soap and drink clean water, they will have a greater chance of living a healthy life. The child suckling on her breast will be more likely to live past his fifth birthday, unlike the 1.5 million children who die before their fifth birthday from diarrhoeal related diseases each year. 1.5 MILLION children!!! I am not into numbers, but it's these types of statistics that hit hard and give some sort of under-standing of the severity of the situation. Deaths that are completely preventable.

As Ayaa patiently answered the questions, I became hyper aware of my surroundings. Sound became muffled and diminished—I was floating out of my body. Looking down at myself like a spectator on my own life, I watched myself sitting on a tiny stool, by a hut in a village in northern Uganda, Africa—working in public health. It was surreal. Finally, I was doing it. I had been visiting villages such as this for almost a month, but it was only at that moment, interviewing Ayaa, that it dawned on me. I was actually living my dream. A light breeze brought me back. Colours were more vibrant, voices were clear and strong. The rustling of the wind in the trees was comforting.

I had got through my Master's degree, worked in other emergencies, survived my back operation, and given up on my dream of Africa just to renew it again. I took risks by quitting secure jobs, I left relationships . . . and now . . . as I sat there . . . I felt porous to all the breathings of the world. I was a sponge, soaking up the moment. And it all seemed worth it.

This had been my dream for so many years. And here I was actually living it. I was really living it. Focusing back on the interview taking place, I swallowed back tears and smiled.

Driving down the uneven dirt road out of the village, hiding my tears behind dark glasses, I was lost in thought. Was this it? Had I achieved my dreams? I finally felt like a fully fledged aid worker— and what of Mr Right? Could Dan be the one? The Mr Right I was looking for? Is it possible that both my dreams were being fulfilled at once? I looked into the beautiful but harsh land, passing by the old camps that people were slowly moving out of. And my tears of happiness all of a sudden did a back flip and turned into tears of sadness.

Was I really that blind and selfish that I failed to see? Was I still that naïve girl who hobbled into Oxfam's office on crutches all those years ago? Yes, I was now an aid worker, but I couldn't even pretend to understand what these people had been through and the challenges they still faced just to survive.

For twenty years they lived in fear. Fear for their lives, fear for the lives of their children, fear that at any time their boys and girls would be stolen by the LRA and in some cases forced to come back and kill their own families. Fear that in simply going to collect wood to make a fire in which to cook the small amount of food they had, they could be killed, or raped, or taken.

The people had so much hope and resilience, and incredible skill and willingness to work. But is that enough? Hope that I was afraid would be dashed by inaction by their own government and the international community. I had faith that this study we were conducting could help to make a difference, that we could improve the lives of the poorest of the poor. But I was also scared because the program funding was drying up and the donors might not extend it. This meant we would lose our staff and not be able to deliver the new well, or the health education, or latrines that we had spent so much time planning for. I had seen all of our staff work with commitment and courage, but at the whim of funding bodies this could be taken away, a whole program closing down.

These people were not asking for new cars, the latest laptop or toys. They were asking for clean water, health clinics they could access, schools for their kids, the ability to work and make a living to bring up their families and to feel safe.

Yes, I had become an aid worker . . . and with it, developed a healthy dose of cynicism. I had learnt to question, to analyse, to know that everything is not roses. To know that sometimes, despite how hard we work, we work in a global system that isn't fair.

I imagined what it would be like if more people became aware of these issues and took action. If more people cared what was happening over the other side of the world. Gave more to charities. Made better choices in the products they bought, or the political parties they voted for. If we all changed our lives a little for the good of others the world would have to change, but it would take more than the handful of people who currently care enough.

And, more importantly, if our governments would dedicate more resources and take preventative action to help people out of poverty. I believed it was possible, but a lot would need to change on so many levels. I still believed but I was no longer naïve to the politics involved, the layers of bureaucracy, corruption and greedy alliances that would need reform.

I was happy to have met my personal goals, but as a result I was even more aware of global goals that needed to be met to make a big enough impact for sustainable change.

～

Heading back to Kampala a week later, I was preparing to run a team development day. I was looking forward to a bit of city life and luxuries. Maybe a movie, drinks and a dance. Big supermarkets, fresh fruit, vegetables and other goodies. On approaching Kampala, there was tension on the streets. And with each detour and emergency call over the radio, my cravings slowly crumbled away. Political rivalries and tensions meant Kampala city and outskirts were full of riots, tear gas, violent police and army. People burnt tyres and fourteen people were shot dead by the military. Oxfam staff were under lockdown for three days. Everything calmed down pretty quickly and I was able to run my workshop, but it was a reminder of the volatile nature of Uganda.

After the workshop (and a good helping of broccoli), I was keen to return to Kitgum. With only a month left on my contract, I had major deadlines and was starting to stress that I wouldn't be able to complete my projects. That night was filled with dreams that felt like a bad acid trip and I woke up feeling like I'd been hit by a bus. Fever. Explaining to a colleague that I would be ok, I collapsed midsentence and was rushed to the hospital.

CHAPTER 27

FEVER

UGANDA 2009

Lying in the waiting room, with its white walls and babies screaming, waves of severe jaw-clenching shivers took hold of my body. Malaria. My reward for not taking antimalarial tablets. *Damn it, I can't be sick. Shit.*

It seemed that people in the Kitgum office were sick with malaria almost weekly, but as adults their symptoms were light due to developed immunity. A mild fever and headache that passed quickly with medicines prescribed over the counter. A headache: 'it must be malaria'. A fever: 'it must be malaria'. Often I felt it was misdiagnosed, but who am I to say. If you live through childhood in a malaria zone, most adults are immune—or at least they get sick but don't die from it as often. But young, malnourished children under five years old are still especially at risk. Like the young child who was buried recently when I took Mum to Lumkwa village. He was one of the children who die every minute from malaria in Africa. Every minute!

230

Talking to children from the surrounding villages of Kitgum, Uganda, 2009.

Beautiful Karamoja women, facial scarring symbolising beauty, northern Uganda, 2009.

I came across this dancing/singing ceremony on the way back from a field trip in Karamoja, Uganda, 2009.

The men chanted in a deep baritone to compliment the women's dancing. The energy was vibrant. Karamoja, Uganda, 2009.

Woman collecting water from the nearly dry river bed in a major drought-affected area of Northern Uganda, 2009.

Ugandan women carrying 20 litre jerry cans filled with water, often walking for hours from the nearest water point. I could hardly lift one of them, let alone carry it on my head. Uganda, 2009.

Jerry cans cued up at a water pump as women and children take turns to collect water. Uganda, 2009.

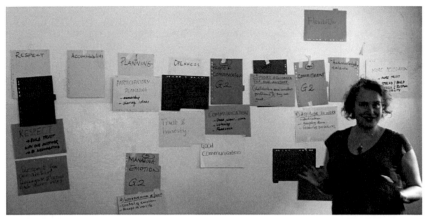

Facilitating a team development workshop as part of the change management process for Oxfam staff in Kitgum, Northern Uganda, 2009.

Community mapping as part of the community led total sanitation program in Lamkwa village, near Kitgum, Uganda, 2009.

Proud owners of the new latrine this couple built as part of the community led total sanitation program in northern Uganda, 2009.

With mum at the start of our Gorilla trek in Bwindi Impenetrable Forest, Uganda, 2009.

Girl in traditional canoe in cholera affected waters—in which children play, bathe, go to the toilet and drink from—before the hygiene promotion program began. Sepik River village, PNG, 2010.

Toilet over the water, just metres from stilted houses built on the same river, PNG, 2010.

Loading hygiene kits onto boats for distribution to cholera affected islands on the Sepik River, PNG, 2010.

Setting up a distribution point for community collection of hygiene kits, PNG, 2010.

Illiterate community members had to 'sign' using their thumb print if they were not able to write their name when collecting hygiene kits, PNG, 2010.

A child looks out through a window, observing one of our monitoring visits, Sepik River, PNG, 2010.

Monitoring visit with village health workers to find out progress of hygiene promotion program. Sepik river village, PNG, 2010.

I thought back to the villages in Kitgum where I worked, and how on many occasions there would be a fresh little grave for the children who had died from malaria. A disease that is often preventable and easily treatable.

For non-immune adults like me it was dangerous, and I was lucky I was in a well-resourced hospital with the right medication.

'Hi, Anne, you were right, it's malaria.' I was starting to feel a little better after the fainting spell.

'They say I'll be out this afternoon, so can you organise a car back to Kitgum tomorrow, please?'

'Ah, Krissy, I don't think you'll be going anywhere.'

'Look, it will be fine, I don't feel too bad now.'

'Have you had malaria before, Krissy? It's different for you Muzungus.'

'Please, Anne, I can't afford any time off work. Please send a car in a few hours.'

Lying there on the stretcher in the hallway of the hospital, I willed myself better. I only had four more weeks before the end of my contract and I had every day planned out down to the hour to meet my deadlines. I couldn't believe after a whole year in Africa, that one bloody little mosquito could knock me down. I wondered if it was the little bastard I had squashed in Dan's room back in Kitgum all those weeks ago.

'Take these and we'll keep you for observation for four hours. Then you should be able to go.' I sat up to swallow the tablets.

'You may get worse before you get better, depending on how you react to the drug. That's why we observe for a while.'

I lay back and thought about the million and one things I had to do to finish off my final project. I hated the thought of leaving the country with unfinished business.

Within the space of four hours, my busy brain full of reports and deadlines had been replaced by fear.

'What's wrong with me?' I held back tears as I asked the nurse.

'It's the drugs. They work to kill the malaria parasites in your blood stream. Often the symptoms can be mild, but your tests show a severe case, which means the dying parasites will be a little bit like poison in your blood stream. You are likely to get more sick before you get better.'

OH GREAT!

'So, you really need to drink lots of water to flush it out of your system.'

A few hours later the driver came to pick me up as instructed, but I could hardly focus on him. The look of shock and concern on his face would usually have worried me more, but I was delirious with fever. The waves of shivers continued shaking my bones and my teeth were clenched tight. *I want my mum.*

One night in hospital turned into two, turned into three. In a windowless room there was no natural light, and I wasn't able to see the moon that always comforted me that Mum was with me, even if on the other side of the world. Every night, I would toss and turn. The purple and orange striped singlet I had worn in was drenched with sweat. I couldn't hold down any food and was so weak I needed a nurse's aid to walk me to the bathroom.

'Please, you need to drink more water.' The nurses softly yet sternly encouraged me to drink as much water as possible. But my stomach became bloated from trying to force down so much water and eventually they put me on a drip. As much as I hated needles, I was not in a state to care.

Mum and Dad called daily. It was comforting, even though I could hardly muster the energy to talk. I had other visitors, which was lovely, but it's not the same without family and close friends.

What did pull me through were beautiful text messages from Dan.

'I feel so helpless being so far away. I wish I was there to look after you and hold your hand.'

'I miss you, beautiful, how are you today.'

'Can't wait to be there with you.'

My sheets and clothing were drenched as I shivered with cold sweats. I felt barely conscious, yet these simple messages from Dan made me smile on the inside and warmed my heart. I didn't get it. How could this man who I had only spent five nights with care so much, want to be here with me while I was sick? I knew it was genuine, that it was real and it made me fall for him a little bit more.

Four days later and feeling like a new person, the senior doctor told me off for not taking antimalarial tablets.

'You people come in thinking you are invincible. Do you know I sent a girl about your age to Kenya in an emergency helicopter with cerebral malaria last week?'

Fair enough. It was stupid of me. I just figured I would be in Africa for a whole year and I did not like taking drugs every day for so long. A mistake I vowed never to make again.

And then the doctor released me with a week's medication and a few more months of antimalarial tablets, which I promised to take religiously. Malaria knocks it out of you. All I can say is thank God I was in Kampala and near good private hospitals. If I had been in Kitgum, who knows where I would have ended up and on what medication.

Back in a room at the humanitarian coordinator's house in Kampala, the contact with Dan intensified. We texted at least five times a day.

233

All hopelessly romantic and each tugging at my heart strings even further. He would surprise me with a phone call every now and then and we would talk for hours. Must have cost him a fortune. It was so beautiful and I loved hearing his voice . . . Could it be that I was falling in love? No, surely not, I thought, love doesn't happen so quickly, does it? All I knew was that despite being in recovery from malaria, and the growing frustration at being stuck out of action, it felt great to have Dan in my life—even if he was living on the other side of Africa.

~

'So, have you found Mr Right yet, then?'

'Well, actually . . . maybe . . .'

'Hubba hubba . . . Krissy . . . who is it?'

'DAD . . .' I was embarrassed. 'It's probably nothing . . . his name's Dan.'

'Is he a doctor?'

'Ha-ha . . . no, Dad . . . he's in the Navy.'

'Navy!?'

'I know . . . I know . . . and American too!'

'What . . . another man in uniform!' Dad was such a dad, with dad jokes and all. 'So, are you coming home for Christmas?'

'No, Dad, I already told you. I'm going travelling and . . .'

'Krissy, come home, we miss you . . .'

Despite my travel plans, and if I was honest with myself, although I had recovered from malaria I was suffering from something else. I was homesick for the first time. I had planned on spending New Year's Eve in Timbuktu and travelling in West Africa before going home. But with each day that went by, and hearing

234

Dad's sadness at me missing another Christmas, I started to doubt my decision.

I missed going out to my favourite café and having my favourite 'summer breakfast' in East Brunswick. I missed going out for champagne with my girlfriends, seeing a local band at the pub with my mates. I missed being able to go into a supermarket and buy fresh vegetables or to go out to one of the diverse cosy restaurants that Melbourne has to offer. I missed ordering my favourite green chicken curry and stuffed tofu with peanut sauce from the Thai restaurant down the road. Picnics with friends, dinner parties and barbecues. And I missed my family.

I was sick of cold showers, of sharing a house with six other people who changed constantly, intermittent electricity and goat curry. I was sick of sleeping on a bad mattress with a lumpy pillow and of having to always tuck the sides of the mosquito net in before I went to sleep. But it would only be a few more months on the road and Australia is so far away from Africa. When would I have the chance again to travel in West Africa?

My 34th birthday was fast approaching, which meant a countdown to seeing Dan.

'Come to Kidepo Game Reserve. We'll spend the weekend, celebrate your birthday in style,' some of the Fuglys crew offered. Ramona and most of my good friends had already finished up their contracts and the social crew of Kitgum was quickly dwindling.

'Thanks, guys, but I'm waiting for a "friend" to arrive to celebrate.'

I had it all planned. I'd already requested permission for a guest to stay in the compound. I'd chosen my outfit from my limited clothing options. I knew the meal I wanted to cook. And I'd played in my head the first words I would say, how I would embrace him,

235

when we would first kiss—a million times in my head. It was going to be the most romantic birthday I had ever had with a man who could potentially be Mr Right.

The day of my birthday, I heard military helicopters landing in nearby fields. Dan would be on one of them.

Champagne I had brought all the way from Kampala for this very day was chilling in the fridge. I adjusted and readjusted the freshly picked flowers on my desk. The mirror got sick of my reflection as I checked my hair.

The phone rang.

'Hello!' My voice had risen three octaves with expectation.

'Happy birthday, Krissy!'

'Thanks.' I could hardly breathe. 'Where are you?'

'Bad news, I'm afraid.'

I couldn't respond. What was he going to say?

'I'm in Uganda but my chopper's been delayed. I won't make it for your birthday.'

Oh no! Oh no! . . . be calm, Krissy . . .

'That's ok.' I forced a smile even though he couldn't see it. Maybe it would take the disappointment out of my voice.

'But I'll be there tomorrow and we can celebrate, ok? I really wanted to be with you for your birthday. I'm sorry.'

'It's ok. It's not your fault, I know you want to be here.'

'I'll see you tomorrow, ok, beautiful? I'll make it up to you.'

So for the very first time in all of my 34 years, I spent my birthday alone.

Tomorrow came, again, with a 'sorry I have been delayed, but I'll be there tomorrow' phone call. I took off the pretty dress I had been saving yet again, so I could wear it when he finally did arrive.

Three days later and finally when I was about to give up hope, Dan arrived in Kitgum. We planned to meet in the evening, but he called from his truck full of twelve of his Navy team, lost and needing directions to the UN office. It happened to be around the block from Oxfam.

'Just come to my office, I'll show you.'

And then there he was, standing in front of me. Thank God he wasn't in uniform, as a military person visiting the Oxfam compound would not have looked good. There is always an uncomfortable divide between the military and non-government organisations because NGOs are neutral and have a mandate to protect all, whereas military are usually fighting for one side or another. NGOs have to be careful with the way they interact with the military so that they don't compromise their neutrality and can serve all. As it was not a conflict situation this was not as pertinent, however, I was still slightly nervous as to how my 'interactions' would come across. I could see my colleagues pretend to work as they watched me greet Dan formally and take him to the upstairs room, pretending he was here for a meeting.

The door closed behind us. An uncomfortable silence. We stood a few centimetres apart. I could feel his heat. What to do. What to say. I had played this scene in my head a million times but I didn't imagine it like this.

HOOONNNKKK!

His truck's horn blared aggressively. I couldn't believe his colleagues were hurrying him. Didn't they understand the importance of this moment?

We hugged. Finally—touch. Searching each other's eyes for a sign. A sign that this was real. We hadn't made this up. The month of growing tension was not just a fantasy. He was standing next to the filing cabinet in the empty office. Our kiss was brief but intense. It was real after all.

HOOONNNKKK!

His truck beeped the horn again. It had only been five minutes, if that. *GO AWAY!!!!!* I wished they'd leave me to get lost in his eyes, his lips, his embrace for just a bit longer . . . but as soon as he had arrived, he had left . . . left me addicted and wanting more.

Five minutes was all it took, for me to know that he was a drug I wanted more of. I looked forward to that evening, with the promise of another hit. Five hours is all I had to wait. Wait for the call telling me to come and meet him on the corner . . . to take him back to my den, where we didn't have to hide. Where we were free to explore each other.

The phone call came half an hour late but I didn't care. 'Be there in three minutes,' I said, my bag already over my shoulder as I prepared to run down to our meeting spot.

'Krissy, wait . . . I can't come . . .'

'What!' *Please say you're joking!* 'Are you serious?'

'I'm sorry, it's harder to leave than I thought. They are literally checking everyone in and out here, and I have hours more work to do.'

'But . . . I . . . I . . . please, Dan . . .'

'I wish I could. It's killing me. God, you looked good today . . .'

I knew he was really disappointed too and couldn't blame him. He was working from 5 a.m. to midnight every day, he had not predicted the workload or the difficulty in security for him to leave his barracks. There was always tomorrow.

Every day I was waiting, expecting him to arrive any minute and every day I would get that phone call. Three more days came and went with 'I'm sorry, sweetheart, I just can't get away, tomorrow it will be better.' It was torture. We spoke every night for an hour before I went to bed, but it wasn't enough.

How could he be in the same small space as me, working on the hospital down the road, but I could not even see him? I toyed with the idea of going to him, but it would not have been feasible with all his troops around and the last thing I wanted was an audience for our reunion. I was nervous enough as it was. They were all staying half an hour's drive away, in a compound that sounded as tough as Alcatraz to get in and out of. I tried to be patient, but remained hopeful. It had been four days since he had arrived and it was nearly a week after my birthday. And my contract was ending in five days' time. So not only was I fretting over him coming, but I was finishing up the work of my whole deployment.

I knew we had planned a romantic getaway for after our contracts ended in a few weeks time, but I wanted to see him a week ago as planned.

'Please tell me you're coming tonight . . .' I was reduced to begging now.

'I wish I could say so, Krissy. I really do.'

Silence.

He continued, 'It was such a hard day, the communities were fully rioting to try to get to the medical clinic we set up. We had to get security to push them back. They all wanted the medicine we were handing out and . . .'

Keep it together. Don't cry. Don't cry. Be strong.

I pulled myself together to speak: 'Look, I can't talk now. I have to go.' I hung up the phone without waiting for a response. I hoped he couldn't hear my voice crack.

It wasn't fair of me. I knew it wasn't his fault. But I didn't care any more. I didn't give a shit about the stupid riots, I didn't care about his ridiculous team and all I could see was the fucking bottle of champagne sitting on my bench, willing me to give up and drink it alone.

Crying like a baby, I started to talk myself out of Dan and headed on a downhill spiral that saw me struggling for breath.

Five minutes after I sent a 'He's not coming. Call me' text message to Steph, she was on the phone.

'Krissy, what is it?' God bless her heart.

I balled down the line. Cried and cried and cried. I couldn't speak.

'Krissy, stop crying, I can't hear you.'

'Stepphhhh . . . I give up . . . What's the point of meeting with him at the end of my trip, it's never going to work anyway. We come from different worlds. There is no point. He lives on the other side of the planet . . .'

'Krissy!'

'. . . already has children and life with him would be full of disappointments. That's it, I'm going to call it off. What's the . . .'

'Krissy!'

'. . . point of putting myself through pain. It's only going to get worse. It's not fair. Why does this have to happen to . . .'

'KRISSY . . . STOP IT!'

'But Steph . . . I . . .' I sobbed uncontrollably.

'NO, STOP IT. Take some deep breaths. Listen to yourself!'

I could always trust her to be straight with me. Get me out of whatever hole I was in. Sometimes it took tough love and it startled me out of my tears.

'What are you afraid of, Krissy. Falling in love?' I didn't respond. 'Are you going to stop all of this in case you fall in love?' More silence. 'Are you going to do this with every man that you . . .'

'Well . . . I just don't see the . . .'

'Think about it. You are going to stop this just in case it doesn't work out. That's ridiculous. Life is full of uncertainty. That's what adds the richness. You know he wants to be with you, don't you?'

'Yes.'

'And you know he is not doing it deliberately.'

'Yes . . . but . . .'

'Well, this is life. Don't run away from love, Krissy. Otherwise you'll always be left wondering . . .'

Later that night, Dan called me for the third time that evening. Each time we spoke for at least half an hour. I lay in bed, alone, phone tucked to my ear, imagining that he was beside me. I became at peace with the fact that we wouldn't see each other in Kitgum and dreamt instead of our romantic getaway that we had started to plan. The distance only strengthened our desire to see each other, and with every word, every breath I heard over the phone, I knew I didn't want to be left wondering.

〜

It was my farewell and the Kitgum staff gathered under the Oxfam *tukal*. It was lovely to hear their speeches, to receive their thank yous and the recognition of me fitting in, trying to speak the language, always with a smile and contributing to the Ugandan people. 'You fit in here like you have always lived here,' praised one of my colleagues. 'You tried to speak our language and you became our friend and we want to thank you for coming from your country to help our people.'

In my time in Uganda, I had trained all 150 staff on performance and change management, worked with teams to ensure they understood each other and developed better ways of working, ran leadership training courses which meant staff were more confident managers, and advised on how to ensure a smooth restructure.

In a couple of months volunteering with the public health team, I had worked with a team to conduct a large knowledge, attitudes and practices study that would inform the future planning of the program, and the newly developed Water User Committee training manual suitable for illiterate communities to ensure sustainable water systems was looking to be taken on by the whole district. I had worked with a department of health consultants to develop and implement the Community Led Total Sanitation (CLTS) pilot program—the first ever to be run in this district—and while not all villages caught on, we saw some great results from villages such as Lumkwa, which Mum and I had visited most recently. I was proud of my achievements, but knew the program was slowing down and could lose funding altogether. And while we can help with improved water systems, the effects of climate change were apparent and the worsening drought meant that the seeds and hoes distributed as a part of our agricultural program may come to nothing without the rain. I was sad but ready to go.

Taking the eight-hour journey south from Kitgum back to Kampala, I focused on my growing excitement and nerves at seeing Dan again. A romantic trip in a luxury tent at the source of the Nile in Jinja was awaiting. Despite the disappointment in Kitgum with his no shows, at least we had that. Well, I hoped we had that. By that stage I wasn't sure I could rely on anything and I prayed that he wouldn't cancel again.

Back in Kampala, that phone call I was waiting for arrived. I held my breath as I answered it.

'Hello?'

'Hi, it's Dan . . .'

CHAPTER 28

ROMANCE ON THE NILE

UGANDA 2009

Walking down the hallway to Dan's five-star room in Kampala felt like it took an eternity. Dressed in a little red dress I had picked up from the second-hand market in town, champagne in hand, I could hardly contain myself. My heart was racing and the walls of the corridor seemed to get narrower with each step I took towards room 326. I doubted I could maintain any type of composure.

Breathe, Krissy . . . just breathe . . .

I knocked tentatively at the door, smoothed over my dress for the umpteenth time, and fixed a smile on my face that I hoped would hide my nerves.

Dan opened the door wearing a crumpled white t-shirt that had lost its white, and a cheeky grin.

'Anyone for champagne?' I exclaimed, my voice unnaturally high.

'Look at you . . .' He took me in his arms and kissed me passionately. 'Look at you!'

Gotta love second-hand clothes!

I couldn't believe that Dan was actually in front of me. If he was nervous he didn't show it, but I was struggling to breathe.

Unsure of what to say, I opened the champagne . . . *POP!*

'Woo hoo . . . the best sound in the world!'

Dan smiled and stared at me incredulously as I poured us each a glass. It was as if I was the first woman he'd ever seen. The bubbles quickly settled into my blood stream and I started to relax. But not for long, as clothes began flying in all directions. Months of wanting was unleashed in raw passion. We melted into each other's bodies. Desperately making up for lost time, but with all the time in the world.

It felt so good. It felt so right.

It scared me.

Finishing the champagne, Dan brought out a bag of birthday gifts.

'I had these ready for you in Kitgum. I'm sorry it's taken so long to get them to you.'

'Ohhh, thank you, Dan. You didn't have to . . .' I was embarrassed. Seeing him was gift enough.

I opened the bag, pulling out each item one by one. A nineteenth century book by an adventurer in Uganda. I didn't have to read beyond the first page to know that I already loved it. He wrote on the first page about our meeting in Kitgum. How the meeting had been enchanted by the Acholi spirits of the region and how lucky he felt to have met me. A little rhino teddy, which I immediately fell completely in love with. And for me the most touching gift was his Navy pin. I had only seen these gestures in Hollywood movies. Guys in Australia never gave things like 'pins'. It was a gold pin of an anchor with three stars on top, indicating his rank. I was speechless, but we didn't need speech.

Wearing matching 'his and her' crisp, white hotel gowns, I lay on the bed watching him. We had just finished our room service dinner and Dan was up pouring what was left of our second bottle of wine.

'Are you scared of falling in love?' he asked out of nowhere. *Oh my God. Is this man reading my mind? Why is he asking me that? What do I say to that . . .*

Silence.

Silence.

Silence.

'Terrified.' I replied.

Silence.

Silence.

Silence.

'So am I,' he said, as he looked at me across the room.

And that was it. We didn't talk about it any further but it was pretty clear what we were both thinking. We only had five more days together. Soon we would go our separate ways, Dan back to the States before his next deployment with the Navy, wherever that might be. And I was returning to Australia, and then . . . Who knew what I would do? It was unspoken, but we both knew the turmoil that would follow our time together if we did fall in love.

I decided then and there at the start of our brief holiday together that I couldn't afford to fall in love with him. So I committed myself to just take things day by day and not to fall in love. I told myself that we would just have fun and then we would return to our lives. I ignored the fact that I was probably already halfway there. That night we fell asleep in each other's arms. We were in a luxurious king size bed, but we could have been back in the half broken single bed in Kitgum, and we still would have fallen asleep with smiles on our faces.

I wanted to stay in bed forever but we had to meet Battle Buddy and be on our way to our luxury tent in Jinja. Yes, Battle Buddy. Dan had warned me of this but I kind of hoped it was a practical joke. Although on holiday he was still formally under Navy custody while in Uganda, which meant he was unable to go anywhere without another team member. That team member they called Battle Buddy. Traditionally, it was a mate who would watch your back during battle.

So our romantic week away would be us plus one. And, no, I am not joking!

Luckily, Battle Buddy turned out to be Ramona's fling from Kitgum so I had met him a few times before (and shared a Kitgum love den). Regardless, I still felt like I was entering into some bad porn movie and made jokes with them that if Dan got tired, he would be called in to take over . . . Da de daaaa . . . (insert superhero music) BATTLE BUDDY to the rescue. What other role would a Battle Buddy fulfil outside the battle field?

All I could do was laugh about it and berate myself for once again getting involved with a man in uniform. What else could I expect? Of course there would be a Battle Buddy accompanying us on our romantic week away. How silly of me to presume we were two free adults.

Battle Buddy turned out to provide hours of entertainment. He had me in stitches doing comedy skits and impersonations as we downed our sunset beers overlooking the Nile on our tent patio. He even instigated a midnight skinny dip in the hotel pool. Naked in the moonlight, with two military men. This seemed a bit much for Dan as he told me that Battle Buddy was trying to take over his turf. Jealousy already. I teased him but I was not at all interested in the younger man, despite his bigger muscles. All I wanted was Dan.

The next few days were filled with sex, long walks down to the

246

source of the Nile, sex, cocktails watching the most magnificent sunsets over the water, sex, reading in the hammock, sex, long sleep-ins and lazy breakfasts, sex, white-water rafting, sex, and oh yes, in case I failed to mention it, sex. We explored each other's bodies, but we also explored each other's minds.

I told Dan about my temination in Sri Lanka; he told me about the difficulties of his divorce. I told him about my close connection to my family; he told me why he hardly spoke to his. We discussed the importance of honesty and openness in a relationship; he told me that he tends to compartmentalise things that get too hard, and to push them to the back of his mind.

'I think you call it repression,' I teased.

'It's the way I cope with being away from my children for so long.'

'But that issue is still going to be there, it ain't going away.'

'Yeah, but at least I don't have to think about it . . . it's too painful if I think of how far apart we are.'

'Do you do that with everything you don't want to think about? Just pop it away in a little cupboard in your brain?'

'I even tried to compartmentalise you when we were apart, to focus on other things . . .'

'Gee, thanks!'

'You were way too distracting . . . I couldn't focus on anything with you on my mind . . . But you seeped into every damn compartment in my head!'

'There is no escaping me!' I laughed, as I straddled him on the bed and held down his arms above his head.

'I don't want to escape from you, Krissy. I could live very happily as your captive.'

'Mmmm . . . Now, where are those whips and chains then?' I teased.

The next morning I enveloped myself in the hammock, reading. Dan ventured into the Nile for a white-water rafting adventure with Battle Buddy. He returned in the afternoon to find me still in the hammock. The way he looked at me filled my heart with so much joy that the hammock could have been a cloud.

'Do you like me coming home to you?' he asked.

The answer was in my gentle kiss and the lingering look into his eyes.

Over the next couple of days we'd lie together talking for hours on end.

'You are so amazing, Krissy.'

He didn't say it, but I knew he was in love with me, I could feel it. And I was falling so fast and hard myself that it was making me dizzy. Sometimes I would catch myself. *Stop it, Krissy. You CAN'T fall in love with this man. It's not realistic. There are too many things against it. Just stop it.* But it was like stopping a Karamoja warrior's spear flying at full speed in the air, heading straight for my heart.

One evening, we were talking about love and marriage and he told me that he didn't want to get married again. He had been there, done that and the piece of paper meant nothing to him. After he went to sleep, I lay awake thinking about what he said. Tears came to my eyes as the realisation hit me. I knew I must be in love, because of the feeling of sadness that consumed me, when I realised we wanted different things in life. The feeling crept up on me like a slowly brewing storm and it was too late to back pedal. I was in—mind, body, heart and soul. Silent tears escaped into the pillow as I lay next to him, watching the rise and fall of his chest as he slept. He was at a different stage of life. He already had children and he didn't want another marriage. All I wanted was marriage and children.

The next day as we lay in bed watching the Nile flow by, I opened up to him.

'Dan, last night, when you told me that you didn't want to get married, I realised that we must be on really different paths. And that's totally fine but I have a problem.'

'What is it, sweetheart?'

'Well . . . I'm in . . . I mean . . . I think I. No, actually, I know . . .' *Say it. Just say it.* 'Dan, I love you . . . and I'm scared. I'm terrified. I know we are going our separate ways, and I haven't been in love for so long, and it feels so unreal.'

'You are pure magic, there is no other way to describe it,' he said, as he kissed me and stroked my hair.

I should have been feeling over the moon. I was finally in love. Wasn't this what I had always wanted? I felt a desperate mix of emotions. On top of the world that I was in love, but already starting to bring myself down to earth with the reality that we would be leaving this love haven in a couple of days. I felt like I was in a delicate bubble that could burst at any second.

Later that night over a few drinks, Dan let his emotions spill.

'Krissy, I love you so much. I knew since the moment we met that there was something special between us. When you told me today that you loved me, I was in shock.' Dan spoke faster and with more excitement as he continued. 'I was so happy. I couldn't believe what I was hearing. How can you love me? I just thought that you were coming for a fun week away. I had no idea that you felt like this. Our story really is like a movie. It's too good to be true. Yet here we are . . . it's incredible . . .'

'Dan, I . . .'

'Let me finish, I'm on a roll . . . I have never felt like this with anyone before . . . no one.' He took a swig from his drink and continued. 'I know we don't know each other well but you are everything that I want in a partner. I can imagine you meeting my kids and trusting you with them. I don't trust anyone with them. Let's make this work, Krissy.'

'But how? We live on opposite sides of the world. You want to stay in the Navy for a few more years and I'm not the type to be a Navy wife, waiting on the shores for my love to return.'

'Well, what if I left the Navy? I was planning on leaving in a few years anyway. What if I left in a year? I could come to Australia and be with you there.'

'Oh Dan, I would love that, but what about your kids?'

'They can come and live with us when they're a bit older. They're with their mother now, but in a couple of years time they will be old enough to come and live with me. This was already my plan. What's the difference between living in America or in Australia? They would love it. Krissy, let's do this, I love you so much . . .'

'But I want babies, marriage . . . I don't think you . . .'

'I'd marry you, Krissy . . . I'd marry you. And I'd have more kids with you. Anything to be with you, Krissy. You make me so happy.'

Dan and I beamed at each other. I felt like one of the Karamojong tribe, jumping high into the sky, my feet suspended for an eternity in the air. Is Dan the one? Is this my Mr Right who I have been searching for all my life? Right now I felt cautious but hopeful. We discussed the realities of our situation. That, yes, it was like a movie. We were in an 'unreal' situation. We could feel differently when we were living normal lives, and not in a remote area of the world where any encounter would be romantic. We knew that things could change quickly, but we also knew how wonderful we felt together and how much we wanted it to work, so we committed to keep in touch and see where things went. No promises. Let's just see.

That night, our final night, we cuddled up with the moonlight shimmering on the Nile, casting shadows inside our luxury tent.

'If you're still thinking of me in three months time,' I whispered, curling up next to him, 'come and get me.'

'I will,' he held me closer. 'I will.'

CHAPTER 29

SURPRISE! I'M HOME!

MELBOURNE 2009

'Surprise! I'm home!'

I rushed into Dad's arms and caught sight of a tear on his cheek. It was such fun turning up unexpectedly. I had organised for Mum and my brothers Cam and Paul to pick me up from the airport. No one else knew. I turned up to girlfriends' engagement parties and weddings to surprise them. Lots of screaming, hugs and tears. 'But you're not home until January!!' they would scream. Stephanie nearly had a heart attack when I stood at her front door. We both fell into a bush, as she bowled me over with a leaping hug.

It took everything I had to keep the secret for months but it was well worth it seeing everyone's expressions. I could go to West Africa another time. A time when I wasn't craving the creature comforts of home.

I was so happy to be back in Melbourne. I was glad to be in the best city in the world with the best friends and family that anyone could ever ask for. I still had moments of sadness, of disconnection and reverse culture shock. After living in such remote places, seeing so much poverty and working with it every day, coming back was always confronting. I knew the feeling well and I knew it would disappear, that I would regain my normal self. Luckily, it was summer in Melbourne, so several picnics and parties, as well as the odd peaceful weekend away with friends, helped to ease the transition. Plus, all my friends and family had helped me through this transition before. They knew to take it easy with me and understood if I suddenly burst into tears, or had to leave a function uncharacteristically early.

My friends understood, but when people I didn't know would ask 'How was Africa?', they were quite taken aback when I'd just burst into tears.

'How was Africa? How was Africa?' How to answer that question? Firstly, that Africa was a continent of many diverse countries, and then . . . 'Great, incredible, amazing, difficult, hard, challenging, complex, sad, happy.' My responses were filled with contradictions and opposing emotions. But I guess so were my experiences. How much do people really want to know anyway? I always felt I would bore people if I talked too much about my experiences, so in general I didn't talk much about them.

And, actually, the main point of conversation with most of my friends was not the Lord's Resistance Army and child soldiers, or the looming food crisis that would affect millions across the region. It was focused on the little gold Navy pin that I wore on my lapel.

The questions came quicker than I could respond to them.

'So is it love?'

'What is it with you and men in uniform?'

'What about the children?'

'What are you going to do?'

'Would you move to the States?'

'Would he really give up the Navy for you?'

'Do you think he's the one?'

I couldn't answer most of their questions. But I did know that I was still in love. It had been six weeks since I'd seen Dan, and while I was a romantic and wanted to give it a go, I was also a pragmatist and knew that our fantastical romance had the odds against it.

But I wasn't worried. I was in love, happy to be home and on the look out for the perfect job. I wasn't sure what I wanted, but I did know I wanted a break from aid work for a while. I wanted stability.

In the meantime, I enjoyed an Australian summer. Picnics at Edinburgh Gardens, day trips to St Andrews market, barbecues with eskys in back yards. And, of course, the ever increasing numbers of weddings and engagements. I was the only single one at our table for my girlfriend's wedding soon after my arrival. But it was ok, because I had Dan. Didn't I? I tried not to feel like the odd one out and was just happy there weren't any slow songs played, where I would be left to dance with the bride's grandfather. Many of my friends were either married, engaged or in long-term relationships by now. While I had travelled the world and worked in remote places, they had been shacking up, buying houses, starting to have kids. I was 34. Luckily, I had enough single friends left so I didn't feel like a complete leper. But I felt time was running out. That blasted clock started ticking a lot louder in my head.

I allowed myself to imagine my turn. I wondered if Dan would like a garden wedding. What dress would I wear? I imagined Dad and me both in tears as he walked me down the aisle. Lots of champagne, strawberries and chocolate cake.

But the more distance that Dan and I had between us geographically, the more distance I felt emotionally. Dan was a shocking communicator and sometimes took a week to get back to even a text message. I don't know what changed, as he was so attentive even when we were living in separate countries in Africa. He was often out at sea, somewhere remote where phones were limited and he was hopeless on email. I started getting upset and he explained that to him, one week was like a day. He had trained himself in the twenty years of being in the Navy, away from his children and loved ones, to be able to live with distance and to make the most out of infrequent contact. Otherwise, he said, it would be too hard. I realised he was successfully locking me away in one of those compartments in his mind. And judging by his dwindling communication, I was no longer 'seeping into every compartment'.

Although I rationalised that this was the way he operated, the way he had trained himself—it wasn't good enough for me. We were newly in love, and although we hadn't made any real commitment we both wanted to make a go of this. Well, so I thought.

The look of happiness on Dad's face at Christmas was worth coming home for. Our usual loud festivities began with 26 of our clan around an elaborately decorated table. Uncles, aunties, cousins, other family, friends. Copious food, wine, sweets followed by the famous Nicholson sing-alongs that would continue long into the evening. Dad's toast included a thought for those less fortunate, and particularly the people who I had worked with in Uganda and Ethiopia. A tear escaped onto my roast turkey.

I was hoping for a phone call from Dan that Christmas Day. I sent him a series of cute photos of me sending him kisses in a Santa hat. He didn't even say thank you or acknowledge them. He did send me a text message saying 'Merry Christmas, am thinking of you'. But thinking wasn't enough for me. I needed action.

'If I was him,' Dad declared, 'I would be ringing every day and sending flowers.'

'Dad, it's not the same, he's in . . .'

'It's all I'm saying. If he was for real he'd . . .'

'Dad!' My eyes clouded over.

'It's just that you deserve the best, my darling.'

Maybe Dad was right. After a few more weeks of lagging communication, I decided that it was too hard. If we were going to have a long distance relationship it would need hard work and commitment, and I was not feeling it from his side. I was sick of waiting for calls that never came. Dan was sailing away. With each nautical mile, I could feel him disengaging.

After yet another promised phone call that never came, I started sending emails to start the painful goodbye process. I packed away the little rhino that I had slept with every night. The Navy pin left a small hole in my cardigan and I convinced myself that it wouldn't have worked anyway. It was a Hollywood love story, but my life was not set in Universal Studios with a guaranteed happy ending. It was time to let go and get on with my life.

I started flirting with other men although, when it came to the crunch, I was still in love with Dan and couldn't let go.

'Sorry, I just can't do it,' I said to a lovely tradie who tried to kiss me at the end of a date. Any other time it would have been a perfect end to a great date. 'I'm still in love with another man.'

My friend Dave joked with me over a beer the following day.

'It's ok, you still have the last member to go . . . Mr Right's still out there.'

'What are you talking about?'

'Well, you've had the policeman, Navy guy and now a workman . . . all you need now is the American Indian—maybe he's the one.'

I burst out laughing.

'YMCA,' he sang with all the arm actions to go along with the Village People's classic. Thank God for friends to make light of the situation.

I had a few interviews lined up with local organisations, when I got a call from Oxfam.

'Krissy, there's a cholera outbreak in Papua New Guinea. Are you interested in going as the public health coordinator?'

'When?'

'Within the week.'

'Can I think about it?'

'You have until 5 p.m. today.'

I wanted to be home. The thought of getting on another plane was nauseating. But it was only for a few months and the opportunity was too good to pass. What did it matter that I knew nothing about cholera. I'd learn. This is why I did my Master's degree. It's what I volunteered in Uganda for. My first public health role where I would actually be managing the program. A week later, I was packed and on another plane.

CHAPTER 30

LOVE IN A TIME OF CHOLERA

PAPUA NEW GUINEA 2010

'Good luck in this godforsaken place.'

A medical non-government organisation had been working alongside Oxfam in the first phase of the response in PNG and it was withdrawing to another remote area as I arrived for the second phase of the response. This was the phrase uttered as the NGO staffer handed over the latest report. Frustrated with the bureaucracy, the inefficient government health systems, the broken promises by authorities, they had built cholera treatment units, trained up local health workers and were moving to another destination.

Oxfam was to be the only NGO operating in the Sepik River area, and basically the team consisted of me, three staff members and two government health workers who had been assigned to work with us.

Apprehensive, yet excited to start my first day, I sat in the Wewak office, awaiting my new team. Wewak was a small coastal city that housed one of the Oxfam offices. It was three hours travel inland to Angoram on the Sepik River, where we would need to set up a temporary office for the cholera response. Armed with 500 documents from my briefing in Melbourne, and all the information I could find out about cholera, I hoped I had made the right decision to take this on. I had never worked on, let alone managed, a cholera program before. I took a deep breath and trusted my experience with other water, sanitation and hygiene related programs would suffice.

Jack, my trusty logistician, was there on time. Coming just up to my shoulder, Jack had deep-set eyes and brown, stained and crooked teeth, his gums red from chewing *bui*. *Bui* was beatlenut, and it was chewed constantly, as a smoker would smoke cigarettes, and unhygienically spat in a red juicy mess onto the ground. On first sight I thought everyone had a bloody gum disease, but chewing *bui* was common among men, women and even children alike. An appetite suppressant and mild stimulant, many were addicted to this teeth-rotting substance, which can cause mouth cancer. Jack was quietly spoken, kind-hearted and highly efficient. He became my right-hand man during the response. He had worked in the first phase of the emergency late last year with the initial outbreak, and was familiar with Oxfam's programming.

We sat under the fluorescent lights and fans of the small office, sifting through the latest situation reports. Although over twenty years old, the 1985 census was the closest official information we had to get an idea of the population we would be working with. Keen to get started, we awaited the newly recruited public health assistant who would be a crucial team member to ensure the success of the program.

A few hours later, we sent someone to her house as she didn't have a phone. It turned out she was participating in a sports event and had decided that she was not ready to take a job based so remotely after all. *Thanks for letting me know now!* Douglas, the government health worker, turned up three hours late with news that the other government worker I was relying on had to visit his uncle in another state and would not be here until next week. In actual fact, he never showed up at all.

I sat there with Jack and Douglas looking to me for direction, not sure whether to laugh or cry. I was responsible for managing a cholera response in nine remote locations, reaching 10,000 people, and half of my already small team were a no show. Welcome to PNG. I was to learn quickly that this was a common scenario.

With the jeep packed to the rafters with barrels of fuel, food for the next few weeks, printouts of emergency needs assessments, stationery, first aid equipment and everything else we would need to set up a small office, we bumped our way through lush forest on our journey towards Angoram. It would be our home for the next ten weeks. Jack joked that the bumpy journey was called the 'PNG massage special', as we were thrown from side to side on the unpaved, potholed road. I wished I had packed my sports bra for the ride!

Angoram is a small, sleepy town cradled by the Sepik River, with no more than a couple of thousand residents. Lush, green and surrounded by palm trees, the *Lonely Planet* description of 'a once bustling town, but it's hard to imagine now' is a serious understatement. The only hotel in town had been closed down for ten years, but had opened again to become the Oxfam office. While our accommodation was basic and clean, there was no electricity or functioning running water system. There was no power in the whole town, no functioning communications, a decrepit half-opened hospital that had been transformed into a cholera unit, one small shop and not a lot else. I couldn't believe the place used to be alive with banks, post office, fancy social balls, water, power and even an airport and golf course! But that was in the colonial days.

We found Helen sitting at the side of the road in the shade, selling knick-knacks and snacks from a plank of wood. Helen was an active member of a local women's group and had been the interpreter for the previous response. She was a solid woman with short dark hair, slightly bloodshot eyes and a broad but cheeky grin. Confident, loud and with a quick wit, I promoted her to be my public health assistant. We now had a small, and I hoped effective, team and got to work straight away.

The program manager in Wewak had briefed me on the situation before we left. Oxfam's first phase of the response started in November last year after PNG was plagued by a cholera outbreak. It had spread rapidly and had now affected over 2000 people. Oxfam had worked to control it in areas of the East Sepik region at the time, but it had continued to spread down the river through infected water, trade routes and markets.

My briefing said that the aim of the program I was managing was: 'to ensure the risk of cholera and further loss of life and suffering in targeted communities in East Sepik Province is significantly reduced. That communities have access to safe water and understand and practice safe hygiene behaviours to prevent transmission of cholera.'

Mmmmmm . . . I studied my notes on cholera. A diarrhoeal disease caused by ingesting contaminated food or water, and through poor hygiene. It is transmitted by a faecal to oral route, which is basically germs from your poo (or *pek pek* as they call it here) getting into your mouth.

Cholera is similar in transmission and prevention to most diarrhoeal diseases so I felt confident. My experience in Uganda, and involvement in most Oxfam programs over the years, had concerned contaminated water and hygiene practices, and this was going to be similar. The big difference between cholera and other diarrhoeal diseases, however, is that cholera can be fatal within 24 hours if not treated. A part of our education campaign also concerned early treatment. There was a lot more time pressure than in other normal hygiene and water programs.

With no time to waste, we were cruising along in a little 7-metre tinny down the Septic, I mean Sepik, River. Calm waters, a perfect blue sky and gorgeous greenery all around, we passed quaint riverside villages, the wind blowing in my hair. The small outboard motor that would not go past 40 km/h just added to the adventure. Tourists would pay thousands for this experience. Well, take away the cholera epidemic and they would! The pleasant three-hour journey gave me a chance to think about Dan and what I should do.

A few weeks before I had been ready to give up on him, but as soon as I started alluding to this fact in my emails he started picking up his game. More frequent emails, texts and phone calls. Promises that he'd try harder. He knew he was being crap, and said that he loved me and wanted to make it work. My heart felt elated once more. With no email or telephone contact out here, I would have to wait until I was back in Wewak before I heard from him. A family in a wooden dugout canoe paddled by, and I smiled confidently at them. Dan and I were back on track. Considering I needed to focus on the cholera program at hand, it was probably best that I didn't have access to romantic emails that would only distract me.

We pulled the boat up through thick mangroves that snaked up to the small strip of land of our first village. Taken aback by the rudimentary wood and bamboo shacks standing on stilts, I jumped onto land, splashing the black, putrid water up my legs. The slither of an island faced on to the ocean and backed on to the lake.

A pig wandered by and a toddler stopped to poo in the shallow water under one of the stilted houses. Nearby, other children played in that same water. After gaining permission from the village chief, we started our assessment.

Having taught my team the good old 'throw the pen in the air' trick to set the direction of our random sampling of household surveys, we split up to cover more ground. Taking off my shoes to climb into the houses, I watched my step so as not to fall through the rotting wooden floors into the faeces ridden water. I wondered how the small children didn't fall straight through the gaps.

Each shack was a large room that slept up to four families. Blackened old pots and pans, dirty buckets for water collection and a small fire for cooking in the corner of the room. Some had old, dirty mosquito nets but no beds—just a hard wooden floor to sleep on. I saw the occasional pack of cards or ancient teddy bear, but this was rare. Children amused themselves with dried seeds for marbles and played in the contaminated water. There was a school but it was run down, full of junk and barely used. The difficulties of attracting teachers to live in such remote areas meant that most children were left uneducated and grew up to be illiterate.

Our emergency needs assessment consisted of the usual questions about demographics, number of illnesses, hygiene practices, where people went to the toilet, where did they wash their hands, did they use/have soap, how and where did they collect their water from and what did they know about cholera and how to prevent it. The people were friendly and willing to speak to us. They had been living in fear, having seen a growing number of their village get sick and die, and were thirsty for knowledge about how to stop it.

Surveying one woman, it was hard to focus on the interview as her toddler—no older than eighteen months—played with a machete twice the size of its head. It wasn't my role to take the knife away from the baby and it seemed perfectly 'normal', so I held myself back.

Everyone here went to the toilet in the mangroves, in which their houses on stilts had been built. Rarely did they wash their hands. Soap was too expensive to buy, and the water-collecting containers that most households used were dirty and without lids, and therefore exposed to contamination. To collect water, the people of this village rowed into the lake for a couple of hours to reach anything drinkable, filled up their dirty containers, and then rowed all the way back again. One meal a day was the norm, consisting of the local starchy sago and fresh fish. Occasionally, they would barter for greens from nearby villages, but since the cholera outbreak the health department had advised against trade as it was a major route of transmission.

Cholera cases were already on the decrease, which from a public health perspective meant the worst was over. However, it was clear that the community still didn't understand cholera, and were scared and didn't know how to stop it or other diarrhoeal diseases that were prevalent.

I met Charlotte on our first visit, when I asked if there were any people living with disabilities or other vulnerable groups such as widows or female-headed households. In an emergency it is often the most vulnerable that get missed. Charlotte was an eight-year-old disabled girl. She couldn't walk by herself, had little control over her bodily movements and limited speech, although she could communicate well with her family, who had learnt to understand her.

'Hallo, Charlotte, you right?' I asked in my slowly improving Pidgin.

'Ahhhh . . .' Her head rolled involuntarily as she tried to retreat.

264

Charlotte seemed scared of me and shouted and cried. Her father looked at me apologetically as I talked to him about Charlotte's needs and told him we would be providing him with extra water containers and hygiene kits to make it easier for his family's special requirements. I didn't want to scare Charlotte any more than I had so I smiled and said goodbye, moving on the next household.

After collecting all the information we needed, we spoke to the village chief to ask for nominations of three women in the village who could be trained as village health volunteers and set up their training for the following week.

The most brilliant sunset of pinks and oranges streaked across the sky and the water rippled like silk around us. Due to the travel time and distance, despite a fourteen-hour day, we had only visited one village. There were eight to go. We needed a new strategy, as I couldn't afford another week just in needs assessments. Despite not really knowing the skills of the team well enough I had to risk it, so the next few days we split up, visiting separate villages. Other villages were only an hour or so away by boat, and within a couple more days we had all the information we needed to plan and start the program.

~

Before that, however, we headed back to Wewak for meetings with the Department of Health cholera team, to use the internet to send situation reports and program plans back to Melbourne for approval and to restock our supplies. Relieved to be back in Wewak in a comfortable hotel room with hot running water, the days were shorter and the gin and tonic at the hotel offered reprieve. The team were busy picking up shipments of buckets, soap and oral rehydration salts, fuel and more supplies. I was putting together the cholera training for the twenty health volunteers we had recruited across the villages to help with education and the distribution of hygiene kits. I also finally had internet and phone access and was over the moon to talk to my darling Dan.

'I miss you so much, Krissy, we have to see each other.'

'I know, it's getting ridiculous. Maybe I can come and visit after my contract? I don't have a job to go back to.'

'Start packing, honey, I can't wait.'

Oh my God. It's really going to happen. I started looking up airfares and let my imagination run wild. I pictured us getting married, I thought about the kind of consultancy work I could get in the US while he finished his year in the Navy. And then we would move happily to Australia and start having children of our own. I also knew the reality of the situation. We could see each other outside the romantic confines of our luxury holiday tent in Uganda, and maybe it wouldn't be the same. But if I didn't go to find out, I might regret it forever.

CHAPTER 31

AN EMERGENCY ROLLERCOASTER

PAPUA NEW GUINEA 2010

Back at the Sepik, I felt like I was on a rollercoaster. Some days went smoothly, like in my first week out here. But other days everything seemed slow, nothing worked and I wondered how the hell I was going to manage. The same boat ride that shimmered with the sunset one day became a nightmare the next, depending on what the gods had in mind. One day the weather turned overcast and the water was rougher than usual. When the Sepik River met the Murik Lakes that day I was tossed up and down, feeling the hard plywood that we lay on in the boat to be more 'comfortable' smash up my spine. Memories of the year I had spent on my back forced me to rest the following day, as I could hardly walk. I needed to rest it, even for one day. Feeling embarrassed, I conducted meetings from my bedside and resorted to paperwork, completed while lying on my back.

Luckily my back came good and it was all systems go again. But there were other frustrations to deal with—late shipments containing our hygiene kits, inefficient government health structures with weak surveillance systems unable to tell us the rate of cholera cases in the area, and a dying generator that forced us to work some evenings by torch light.

The same stale dry biscuits with peanut butter or spam that seemed to be part of an adventure last week now seemed revolting. And the memory of that beautiful sunset seemed distant as we covered ourselves with a tarp to protect ourselves from the wind and the rain on long journeys back to base.

There were some days I felt organised and on top of things, such as just after I spent a day with my team going through our program plan, team roles and expectations, security and logistics. I felt on top of it all, had a good rapport with my team and felt everything was achievable. We were on schedule to reach the villages most in need. We had trained village health volunteers and organised transport. The shipment of hygiene kits suddenly arrived and the communities were starting to take action to prevent cholera. All was planned out nicely for a successful program. The team were motivated. We had some wonderful interactions and were building relationships with people in the communities and were set to go.

And then the very next week, I found myself hitting my head against a wall once again. I began to understand that there was no such thing as planning in PNG, as something always happened to change that plan. I felt frustrated and that we were not moving fast enough—and then the situation would change again. A new outbreak of cholera in a completely different area in urgent need of assistance came to our attention. As there was no one else working in the region it was up to my small team.

The organised plan went out the window. A new plan was devised, and despite it being a logistical nightmare to reach this new village we were good to go. We just needed to figure out contingencies for the bad road that we nearly got bogged in five times when we had last used it. As to how we were going to truck in containers of hygiene kits, I didn't know! I did know that one of the last big trucks that took that road fell off the top of a ravine, killing the driver and passengers.

On cue, the charger to my satellite phone—my ONLY means of communication—blew up, and to top it all off I got my period, and my back was in need of a good physiotherapist . . . *BREATHE* . . . *BREATHE* . . . *BREATHE* . . .

~

By some sort of miracle and despite all the challenges, things came together. And this was partly due to Larisa. Yes, Larisa. I knew head office were looking to send an international logistician to assist me, but it was a shock when I read Larisa's name in the email. I was excited but also a bit nervous.

I met up with her in the Wewak guesthouse. 'You silly bitch!' she teased, as we embraced on her arrival.

I screamed in delight. It was so good to see her again. She pulled out a bottle of duty free booze to catch up on old times. It had been five years since our tearful farewell at Colombo Airport. No time wasted, we relived our time all those years ago. We gossiped about news on our 'Sri Lankan boys'. Laughed about those tuk tuk rides with hangovers, stopping for fresh coconuts on the way to work. And we remembered fondly our status as the 'Queens of Colombo'.

'Ah, those were the days, hey?' she smiled at me. It was great to see her. She looked the same but with a slightly shorter hair cut. 'So what happened to you then, hey? You dropped off the face of the world.'

'Oh, Larisa, I'm so sorry.' I stared into my drink before looking up to continue. 'It's hard to explain . . . I just . . .'

'Don't worry about it, girl, what's past is past, we all went on with our busy lives . . .'

'No . . . I really want to explain.' She paused and looked at me. 'I know you must have felt me distance myself after Sri Lanka and it's true . . .'

Larisa shifted uncomfortably. We couldn't always hide behind frivolity and alcohol.

'Yes, well, actually, I did feel a little hurt. I thought we were good friends.'

'I know, we were. We were inseparable. I couldn't have lived without you in Sri Lanka.' I watched the waves crashing against the rocks from our guesthouse patio. 'I guess I felt like I lost myself . . . spiritually, I mean.'

I didn't think Larisa would understand as she was not spiritually inclined, but I wanted to explain.

'You see, while I had a fantastic time in Sri Lanka, I really felt ashamed about some of my actions.'

'Ashamed!?'

'Yes, I felt like we reverted to teenagers.'

'And . . . what's the big deal with . . .'

'No, there isn't anything wrong with that . . . It's just that so many of our friends at the time were so full of lies. Their whole lives were a lie. They lied to their families, they lied to us . . .'

'Yeah, but we knew that at the time . . .'

'And at the time I just let it slide. I was having such a fun time, but I felt that in the middle of that I let my values slip. I don't know . . . it's hard to explain.' I breathed heavily. 'I don't even know that I understand it myself, but I do know that I became hard and that

I knew I didn't want friendships that were not based on trust and honesty.'

'I never lied to you.' Larisa looked hurt.

'I know you didn't. I know you didn't and that's why I feel bad. I clumped you into the same category as the boys. And you were such a good friend to me, Larisa. I think I just look back at that time and don't like myself like that . . . so I have pushed away anything to do with that time . . . which included you.'

Silence.

'I'm sorry, Larisa.'

'Forget it, Krissy. Leave it in the past. We had fun. We move on.'

'So you're not angry?'

'No, you stupid bitch. Just don't do it again.' Larisa always had such a way with words.

'You know I had the time of my life, though. In Sri Lanka, I mean.'

'I know . . . we were the Queens of Colombo after all, now get these spirits into ya,' she said as she filled my glass. We burst into laughter and that was that.

We didn't mention cholera once that evening, but the next morning I gave her a full briefing and we got into action. Thank God she was there. Having someone who has managed several large-scale distributions before, this was a piece of cake for Larisa. In a few days we managed to get twelve boats and two truck loads of hygiene kits from the port in Wewak onto little boats to nine villages. I hired several more casual staff to load and unload, and despite a boat that broke down due to a submerged log and one truck that didn't arrive due to the driver being arrested for drunk and disorderly the night before, everything actually went to plan.

With the help of our newly trained health volunteers and the enthusiasm and new knowledge and practices of much of the community to whom they had passed on their knowledge, we read out names and handed over brand new, bright green buckets full of soap, jerry cans, oral rehydration salts and educational materials to proud owners. Such simple products, but with the ability to prevent illness and save lives.

Some villages greeted us with traditional song and dance, while others were completely unprepared and unmotivated—each experience was different.

Larisa left the week after; it was only a short deployment that not only made sure the cholera program was a success but gave me a chance to release guilt I had held on to for years.

~

On my final evaluation visit to the first island we had visited, I stopped to say goodbye to the little disabled girl, Charlotte. Charlotte had warmed to me after several other meetings over the ten weeks we were there. And now, instead of being scared, I was greeted with laughing and cuddles.

'Likem you, Charlotte,' I said, cuddling her, surrounded by other children.

'Yah . . . likem you . . . hehehe.' She hugged me closer, as her family gave me a traditional, woven, homemade *bilim* bag in gratitude.

Her father told me that Charlotte had been telling her mother about a new friend she had made. They wanted my address to send me a bigger gift for recognising the extra needs of their daughter. Of course I declined, saying the bag was enough and a beautiful reminder of Charlotte for me.

It was great to see there hadn't been any more cholera cases in Charlotte's village for a while now, and we could see the Oxfam hygiene kits being used and people's knowledge increasing. But the situation was challenging in all the villages in East Sepik and there needed to be a longer-term water and sanitation program, improved health and education systems, and income generation activities to reduce the risk of outbreaks like cholera. I left as an Oxfam engineer was assessing the situation to look at how we could help further, so that families such as Charlotte's could have hope for a healthy future.

As the boat pulled away from the shore on my last day on the river, Charlotte and her community waved.

'Goodbye, Krissy, thank you.'

Winding back through the mangroves, kids waved from the water.

'Likem you, Krissy. Bye bye . . .'

I was touched. I didn't realise that so many people here knew my name. I looked at my team with pride as we began our final three-hour journey back to base.

Considering most of the program was run by only the core team of four, with some amazing helpers along the way, it was incredible how much we actually achieved. How many people benefited from our hard work. I'd miss them. And I'd miss the beautiful communities we worked with; the boat rides up the Sepik and all the adventure that entailed. But I was looking forward to getting back to some creature comforts, hot water and, most importantly, my emails from Dan.

After reflecting on our program as we cruised along the river, waving to villagers as we went by, my mind switched to Dan. The pragmatist in me took over from my hopeless romantic heart. If I was honest with myself, it had been a rollercoaster ride with Dan, too. Sometimes I felt I was rushing so fast, full speed ahead with hands up in the air shouting for joy. Other times I'd be left confused, not hearing from him for weeks on end and with the broken promises of phone calls. I started to consider how realistic this relationship really was. And was it really what I wanted?

How prepared was I to leave Australia again after being homesick for so long? How would it work with his children? Surely their mother wouldn't want them leaving for the other side of the world? Despite the calmness of the river that evening and the crimson sunset reflected off the water, one question led to another and sent my mind spinning out of control. Maybe Dan wasn't right for me after all?

There were two things I was sure of. One, I wanted to have my own children. Two, I was happy to live overseas for a year or two, but I definitely wanted to settle in Australia. I loved Dan, but realistically we had only just met. I needed to know before exploring our relationship further, before I booked those flights, whether we wanted the same things or not.

There was no point going over to the other side of the world if we didn't ultimately want the same thing. So when I was back in Wewak, I sent him a long email explaining my feelings. I told him that I'd understand whatever his response. I knew it would be difficult for him as he had his own children, but I also knew what I wanted. I cursed myself for being so analytical. Why couldn't I just throw caution to the wind and follow the romance? But, ultimately, I knew that it would protect my heart in the long run. If I went to America and it worked between Dan and me, would he be willing to eventually settle in Australia and have more children?

After a LONG week of finalising program issues, writing reports and WAITING—the email finally came. I couldn't face reading it in the office so I printed it to read in the guesthouse, where I'd have time to myself.

Walking on the beach that evening as I came back from the office, the ocean was calm. The waves came in ebbs and flows as if they were the breath of the earth. Inhaling, exhaling, inhaling, exhaling. 'Why are you so calm?' I screamed silently at the ocean.

I sat on a rock, the water just touching my toes as it approached in an exhale. And I read the letter.

He said no.

CHAPTER 32

EMERGENCY JUNKIES

MELBOURNE 2010

Emergency junkies. That's what they call those hard-core aid workers who jump from crisis to crisis. Earthquakes to war zones. Tsunamis to droughts. Feeding off the adrenalin of fast paced, high stress, dangerous environments. You can pick them a mile away. They've been at it for years. Highly skilled but often burnt out and cynical. The deep lines in their faces reflecting the myriad stories they could tell. Usually alcoholic smokers with a series of broken relationships behind them.

They wear a standard uniform of cargo pants with worn out t-shirts (with or without an organisation's logo), sporting a pair of Teva shoes or closed toe, hard-core boots. If you're lucky, their multipocketed vest will hold the essentials: flashlight, pens, pocket knife. They have no place they can really call home, they lost that connection years ago. Returning to the place they grew up in they feel alone, left behind. No one understands them. They get frustrated at the complacency. The waste.

Emergency junkies rock up to their old mate's place. A white picket fence and 2.3 children. A mortgage. A news flash of the latest earthquake in some unknown place. 50,000 people dead and 1 million displaced. 'Oh, how terrible, you've been to places like that, haven't you? It must have been awful,' their friends mutter, as they switch the channel to *The Simpsons* and continue eating a three-course meal, not thinking twice about the luxury of turning on the tap to get a glass of water.

This time, they say, this time I am going to try to settle down. Yet after three months of feeling disconnected, having little in common with their friends and getting bored in their newfound 9 to 5 jobs, they start to fidget. The next emergency strikes and they are off again. Like a vampire to their next victim. Comfort in crisis. It's what they know, live and breathe.

There is a certain breed of aid worker and the hard-core variety can be slightly strange. Certain stereotypes may fit—socially awkward, cynical, a naive do-gooder or just lost (fit everywhere but nowhere), an emergency cowboy. Of course they are generalisations, but often true.

I don't think I'm an emergency junkie but I get it. Aid work is pretty addictive. It's also a hell of a lot of hard work. It's an existence of extremes. Extreme conditions, extreme suffering, extreme stress, extreme resilience, extreme parties, extreme love affairs, extreme insecurity.

I know the feeling all too well of itching to get back to the field. When I see a new emergency strike in a faraway land, I have to hold myself down. I feel helpless staying in the comforts of my own home, guilty for not taking action. But it's something I have to get used to if I am ever going to have a chance at a normal life, to find and maintain a stable relationship in my own country.

And that's what I wanted. I had to give up the adrenalin rush. I didn't want to risk falling in love again with someone who lived on the other side of the world. I didn't want to risk leaving again, to lose the opportunity of meeting Mr Right in my own backyard.

I had had my 'rushes' over the years. Now it was time for that white picket fence, 2.3 children and a golden retriever. And it obviously wasn't going to be with Dan.

⤳

Back in Melbourne, I re-read Dan's letter. He didn't just say 'no'. The rejection was cushioned in a bed of love and roses and petals and memories and adoration. But it was a rejection all the same. Why didn't I just go to the States as we planned? Why had the pragmatist in me overridden the romantic? Why did I question him on the long term when I could have just lived in the extremely romantic now?

In his email, he said the reasons were that he was not ready to leave the Navy yet, and he wanted to be near his kids. Fair enough. The type of man I want will want to stay in close proximity to their children. Of course I was sad, but I understood. Maybe I was being inflexible, not willing to give up my life and move to the other side of the world forever. But I knew that I couldn't have children without my family around me, and after being away for so long I just wanted to be at home. I could sacrifice a few more years away to be with him, but not forever.

So I packed up my fantasies of marriage, folded the beautiful wedding dress into the recess of my mind and convinced myself that Dan wasn't really Mr Right. I wrote an emotional goodbye letter, promising he would always have a piece of my heart and that I would remember our time in Uganda with love. It was time to move on, but despite his decision he wouldn't let go. The emails and text messages continued.

'Why can't we be friends?' he asked in a text message.

'Because we are still in love—how are we going to let go and move on if we are still in contact?'

'But surely we'd get past that, it's too hard, maybe I've made the wrong decision. I love you.'

'Love is not enough, Dan, please, let's just say goodbye, it's too painful . . .'

'I want to speak to you, darling, can I call you?'

'Sure, is it going to be a goodbye call?'

'No, definitely not. I can't say goodbye now. I just want to talk to you. Hear your voice. I'll call tomorrow. I love you.'

And with that our texts ended and I went to sleep, expecting an emotional phone call the following day.

'Love is not enough.' Did I really write that? I can't believe I came to that conclusion. I've always thought that love could conquer all. But in my relationship with Dan, I realised it couldn't. The time has to be right. The place. Circumstances beyond us. Was I sabotaging myself? Maybe these are all excuses and I should just get on that bloody plane! But there was no point now.

Tomorrow came and went and there was no phone call. And the next day and the next. I texted. Emailed. Started to worry that he'd been in an accident. Weeks went by with nothing. And I realised this was his way.

Dan couldn't say goodbye. So he didn't.

I never heard from him again.

CHAPTER 33

POWER OF THE HUMAN SPIRIT

MELBOURNE 2010

Starting with a blank canvas, I felt like an artist. I stood at the easel and started drawing my life again. My future. I had the opportunity to apply for the emergency public health adviser position at Oxfam but I declined. It had been my dream job for years, but if I had to get on a plane to face another emergency I'd burst into tears. For the first time in my life I was following a strong desire to set up roots and stay in one place. Being on the move for so long had taken its toll and it was definitely time.

After eight rewarding years with Oxfam I was in search of a new job, a new man and a new home. A new life. Closer to depression than I'd ever been, I was teary with feelings of hopelessness reverberating through my body.

What was I going to do? Who was I without Oxfam?

Oxfam was my blood, my life, my identity for so long. It cradled me through thick and thin. It challenged my sense of self, the world, what is right and wrong. I grew up with Oxfam and made lifelong friends. I had developed as a person and a professional. The opportunities thrown my way saw me realise my dream of becoming an aid worker and working with some of the most disadvantaged people in the world.

Although I felt lost and a lack of belonging without Oxfam, I knew I had to move on.

I lay down alone on my queen size bed and wondered what my life would have been if I hadn't become an aid worker. Maybe I could have achieved that other dream of mine. Maybe I would have been married with two children.

Would I swap it? I thought. Is that the life I would have preferred? The answer was clear—no way in the world.

Was I resigned to a life of singleness? Have I given up on my search for Mr Right? Not a chance.

Oxfam would always be a part of me and I knew I could return at any time, but I needed a new focus.

A couple of months on, life started to get on track again. I embarked on a group facilitation course, landed a fantastic job based in Melbourne working with young refugees, and I was even consulting as Humanitarian Trainer for RedR Australia. I moved into an awesome home above a shop in Brunswick, was back sipping cappuccinos in my favourite cafés, drinking sav blanc in my local bars and juicing life for all it's worth. My eyes wide open to how lucky I was.

When I heard of bombings in Kampala that killed 74 people I felt sad and reflective. One of the bombs went off in the Ethiopian café that I used to frequent. A year earlier I could have easily been a casualty of that blast. Another number in the death toll. But instead I was safely at home and was thankful that none of my Ugandan friends were injured.

And when floods ravaged Pakistan that year, affecting more people than half the population of Australia, I nearly scratched my eyeballs out with helplessness. It took all of my might to stay put in my new job, when all my cells were screaming at me to drop everything and get on the next plane.

I thought of Dan often. But time, and a few flirtations, heal all wounds and I forced myself to gain my own closure. And after a while I felt completely happy as a single woman. It felt liberating. I figured that when it was right, it would happen and I was just going to go with the flow. I had a blank page and I was going to fill it with the most vibrant of colours. Create new dreams. I was busy living life and my calendar filled up with the usual dinners, parties and picnics. I was a strong, independent woman and Mr Right would arrive in my life when he was meant to.

I needed to reinvent myself. Not to start from scratch. Oh no. But to move on to the next chapter of my life, armed with a wealth of knowledge and experiences to help me on the next part of the journey. I felt like the luckiest woman on earth.

I looked back at all that I had seen and done with my work around the world. I thought about the potential Mr Rights, the flirtations, the fun, the love. I had learnt so much from each man. I had learnt more about myself and more about what I did and didn't want in a relationship.

I had achieved my dream to become an aid worker; it was time to open myself up to achieving my other dream. To find Mr Right. But with no pressure. No expectations. I sat down with pen in hand to right out another list.

'Mr Right will be . . .'

I stared at the blank sheet for an eternity and slowly put my pen down as a smile spread across my face. I don't want a man who fits into a neat little box. I want complexity . . . difference . . . spontaneity. I can't describe that in a list. If I have learnt anything from the men who I've dated and fallen for over the years, it's that some of the most beautiful treasures can be found in the most unlikely of places. I wanted to be open to those treasures. I needed to let go of expectations and just be open to possibilities.

When I found Mr Right . . . I would know. I'd just know.

~

Out with the old and in with the new. I set up my new house perfectly, placing relics collected from my travels around the house, giving it warmth and character. The old wooden carving of a crouching man from PNG sat on the bench; an elaborate silver necklace from Pakistan was displayed in my bookshelf; framed photos of the Karamojong people from Uganda livened up my walls.

Sitting in my room on my deep red Afghan rug, I was in the process of culling clothing, a cleansing yet gruelling process for any woman. I pulled clothes out from the mountain on the floor and developed three piles: 'Keep', 'Throw' and 'Maybe'. The 'Maybe' pile would be revisited for further scrutiny and the 'Throw' pile wasn't nearly as big as it should be.

The little second-hand red dress I wore with Dan in Kampala—Throw; a tattered but favourite black t-shirt—Maybe; a bright yellow *shalwar kameez* I wore to the field in Pakistan—Throw; the grey corporate suit that I wore to my first Oxfam interview—Throw.

I pulled out a green Oxfam t-shirt from the pile. It was oversized and ugly and I never liked wearing it, but it travelled with me through many a field trip. I hugged it close to my chest in silence. And then I felt a deep rumbling volcano erupt inside me and began to cry.

Images and feelings that had been buried deep in the recess of my mind rushed through my body. My tears were uncontrollable. I cried for the deformed beggars with arms outstretched in Bangladesh. The woman who let go of a child to save her others in the tsunami in Sri Lanka. The bodies hidden beneath piles of rubble after the earthquake in Pakistan.

I cried for the mothers and babies who died during labour in Ethiopia. The women scraping the bottom of the dried up lake in Uganda. And those poor children who were forced to be soldiers and kill their own families.

I looked at myself in the mirror—red, tear-streaked face and puffy eyes. I hugged the green t-shirt closer. And kept crying. For the thousands who had died, for the millions who had suffered . . . that still suffer, all around the world. My tears could have filled an empty well.

As I looked back at all I had seen and all I had experienced, I realised that it wasn't until that second that I was able to let myself grieve. My feelings had been buried for too long. So deep. To enable me to keep on going. To keep working in disasters and difficult situations.

And then I stopped and looked at myself in the mirror again. What right do I have to cry? Sitting here in my comfortable room, throwing away hundreds of dollars worth of unnecessary clothing. The spoilt little white girl who has seen too much. Who was I to be sad?

It's ok, Krissy. You're allowed to cry. Let yourself cry about this. You don't have to feel guilty.

So I kept crying. And after feeling deep sadness, I took some deep breaths and my mind shifted. I started to think about the strength and resilience of all the people in all the places I have worked.

How in the face of absolute poverty and destruction people go on. They have hope. They have faith. They are passionate about rebuilding their lives. They work hard. They learn. They are resourceful. They sing. They dance. Their cultures are rich. Their faith in God is strong. Their sense of family and community is tight. And their skills are many.

I dried my tears and reached for my photo albums on the bookshelf. I flicked through the visual history of all the programs I had worked on. I thought of the hundreds of thousands of people whose lives were improved, even if only a little, because of these programs. The countless new wells and water storage systems, the new tools, and seeds, and boats that would help families be more self-sufficient and earn a living. The women who have been trained and empowered to demand their rights. The communities that are now open defecation free and suffering less illness as a result. The knowledge that whole communities are able to live longer, healthier lives. I felt so blessed to have been a part of that.

The fulfilment I found through my work, from following what was true to my values, was something I could not have achieved if I had stayed at home, even with marriage and a family. It would not have been the same. Despite not finding Mr Right, there is nothing I would have done differently. The choices I have made, the people I have met, the places I have travelled, have shaped the person I am today. And I still believe that focusing on what I love and what I am passionate about will attract that other type of love and passion that I now feel ready for.

My life had been an amazing journey up to that point, and I knew there was so much more to come. Sitting on my bedroom floor, reflecting on my time working with disasters, it was the strength and resilience of the people I would hold on to forever. And if I was to learn anything on my journey, it was to have faith in the absolute power of the human spirit. And it's that spirit I was determined to carry with me. Whether it be with the choices I made in daily life, the way I dealt with problems that came my way, the work that I choose—and even my attitude to finding Mr Right.

I took a few deep breaths, folded the green t-shirt, and placed it on the 'Keep' pile.

EPILOGUE

'You can't end it like that! Readers will be disappointed. You lead them on throughout the book and achieve your dream of becoming an aid worker, but you don't find Mr Right. You need a stronger ending, Krissy.' Jess took another sip of her Corona. Her comment threw me into confusion.

'But I don't want to make something up, do I? I don't want to lie.'

'All I'm saying is that readers won't be happy with the ending.'

'Great, what am I meant to do, then? Maybe I could end with a dream or something, and leave it ambiguous . . . like it could be a dream but it could be reality . . . then I wouldn't be lying.'

'I reckon you could just make something up. It is "creative" non-fiction—and it will make for a better story.'

'No way, just tell the truth. Readers know life isn't a fairytale! Just be your beautiful powerful self,' said Stephanie, as she blew me a kiss. There were four of us old school friends enjoying a cheese platter and drinks around the table at my house.

'Shit, I don't know what to do!!'

'Don't worry—just write and it will come to you,' Stephanie reassured me.

'I bet you'll find him when you're writing the book! How awesome would that be! It's sooooo gonna happen,' squealed Gini, as everyone laughed with excitement.

'Imagine that . . .' I looked off into the distance smiling. 'Imagine that!'

╰╮

In the process of writing my story, I had several conversations like this with my girlfriends, however, I decided to stick with the truth. I was scared that my ending wouldn't be satisfying for readers, and I toyed with making up a Mr Right . . . or at least the prospect of one to satisfy all those romantics out there. But I had told stories of some of my most incredible adventures and romances along the way. And I had achieved a major dream of becoming an aid worker. I was happy. I was content as a single, independent woman. I didn't give up on my dream of finding Mr Right, and I actually thought my ending was quite liberating and hopeful. I thought it might appeal to some of the single women out there who, like me, were still looking. I wanted it to be inspiring. Plus, after being so honest about my whole journey, I didn't want to fabricate the ending.

But guess what . . . Gini was right . . .

╰╮

'I hope you know that I am completely, madly and utterly in love with you.'

Oh my God, what do I say . . . If I say I love you back does that mean I am committed for life? Does that mean he will move over here? I need more time. KRISSY . . . SAY SOMETHING. The poor guy has just told you he loves you . . . SAY SOMETHING . . .

But I couldn't say a thing. I was speechless like I've never been speechless before. Overwhelmed by emotion. So I just kissed him.

The fire blazed and the crowd around us danced to the tribal beat of the twenty African djembe drums. We were at ConFest, my annual hippie festival in the bush, and all my dreams were suddenly coming true.

'Krissy, I love you so much. All I want is your happiness. If I can play a part in that, it would make me the happiest man in the world.'

GULP!!! Oh my God, it's happening, it's really happening . . . just say it, Krissy, say it . . .

'That's so lovely, thank you.' I kissed him again. *SAY IT. SAY IT. SAY IT!!!!!!!*

I hugged him, feeling his warm arms embrace me tightly. I looked up at the moon as I struggled to find words. It was full. The moon was willing me to say it. I didn't know why it was so hard—it felt great, I couldn't get the smile off my face—but my head was spinning with 'what ifs'. The truth of the matter was that I had to stop myself several times that week from telling Scotty I loved him, as I woke in his arms in our tent.

'I'm scared,' I admitted. 'I love hearing you say it, but I'm so scared.'

'So am I, Krissy, but all I know is that you are the most amazing woman that I have ever known, and I want to be with you.'

My whole being was alight. My heart beat faster than the drums and my head spun like the fire twirler spinning around and around us. The moon above shone brightly, beckoning me to open up, to let go of fear, to release to what I already knew.

'I love you too,' I whispered. His face lit up and he let out a sigh of relief. The poor guy must have been holding his breath.

'I feel like I've won the lottery,' he exclaimed, as he hugged me tightly.

'Honey, this is way better than the lottery,' I replied. We laughed and moved together to dance as one.

'My cheeks are sore from smiling.'

'It's my life's work to keep that smile on your face every single day.'

～

Now I know you must be thinking 'Heard it before' as you have just read several accounts of my journey to find Mr Right with different men. But this was different. And while I was terrified, it was so normal, so natural, and it just felt right.

Where did he come from, you ask? Well, he has been in front of me all along. Can you believe it—while I have been searching in the wilds of East Africa, the waters of the Pacific and the depths of South Asia—he was always there. Following my journeys.

Scotty has been my dear friend, occasional 'friend with benefits', my 'back-up plan' over the last thirteen years. He is the one I mentioned earlier in the book who reneged on the whole back-up plan thing. I never took it seriously, and despite falling for him on and off over the years I never imagined it would be him. But as predicted by my girlfriends, when I took a year off work to finish my book in Europe, I met up with my Scotty for a week in Cornwell, in southern England.

The week was relaxed, fun and intimate. We fell comfortably into each other's arms and as with our friendship (and beyond) over the years, were completely at home with one another. I left the week feeling a bit loved up but also marvelling at the fact that we could have such a strong friendship and that such intimacy didn't actually get in the way. I also knew that if we spent more time together, the friendship dynamic would have certainly changed to romance. I didn't really entertain the thought of more as I knew Scotty didn't want more, children or marriage, and I was on my way home to settle down and find just that.

Little did I know that in our time together, Scotty had fallen in love and started the journey of a major paradigm shift in his thinking, leading him to me. He went from not wanting more kids or marriage to flying over the other side of the world, declaring his love (under the moon at ConFest), and committing to my happiness and all that entailed—and yes, that meant kids and marriage, which he cannot stop talking about.

No, he isn't a doctor, but he is so much of what I want in a man. And even though I threw that list away, I can't help but chuckle that he meets nearly all of my old criteria (except for his table manners—but I'm working on that!!). He even serenades me with the guitar . . . (melt . . .). And I am so in love and so sure that Scotty is the man I want to spend the rest of my life with. Even writing this now, I still can't really believe it. I can't believe he was my 'back-up plan'. Scotty would never be a 'back up'. He is the number one, forefront, best man I could ever imagine. And he is mine.

I was reticent to include my happy ending here. I thought it would be unfaithful to those single women out there who, like me, had dreamt of finding Mr Right for so long and were still searching. I liked that my book was strong and hopeful without the predictability of a Hollywood movie ending.

But at the same time, I just want to stand on the edge of a mountain and scream to the world: Yippppppppppppppeeeeeeeeeeeee eeeeeeeeeeeeeeeeeeeeeeeeeeeeee!!!!!!!!!!!

I truly am one lucky woman, who really is going to get my 'happily ever after'.

Scotty is moving to the other side of the world to be with me—the most romantic gesture that anyone has ever made for me—and I am already starting to look at wedding dresses and venues! I have landed a new job as Water, Sanitation and Hygiene Manager for Plan International Australia, a child rights organisation. After a year in the Australian community sector, I realised my passion really was in international aid. My job gives me the best of both worlds. I am based in Melbourne with regular travel to Africa. And my focus is water, sanitation and hygiene, which keeps me in the public health field.

So for all the romantics among you, I have my happy ending in every possible way. I achieved and continue to live my dream of being an aid worker, and I found my Mr Right. I can't wait for the next chapter of my life to begin . . .

HOW TO BECOME AN AID WORKER

Lots of people have asked me over the years how to become an aid worker. Unfortunately, it is not as easy as showing up and saying you want to help, as the industry is extremely competitive and professional. The advice I give is to think about the following areas.

Motivation: Why do you want to become an aid worker? Is it something you want to experience as a 'one off', on a voluntary basis, or would you like to make it your career? In what ways do you feel you can contribute in an emergency response? Or would you be more suited to longer term development work? Do you want to volunteer or be paid and make a career out of it?

Organisation type: There are several types of aid and development agencies. Research what would suit you. It could be not-for-profit, the United Nations or Government agencies and partners. Check whether it is secular or religious, child focused or community focused, specialist in a certain area or a cross section of areas. Have a look at the vision and mission statements of agencies that interest you and find one that matches your values.

Specialisation: What type of role do you want? Aid workers are many and varied with different skills. There are front line roles such as doctors, nurses, nutritionists and engineers, or generalist options in program management, monitoring and evaluation, and gender advisors. Business/support roles in human resources, finance, logistics, administration, communications, advocacy and information technology are also available. There are a myriad of opportunities, so think about what your skills, experience and interests are and focus on that area.

Learning needs analysis: Once you know what area you want to work in, have a look online at some job descriptions. Think about your own skills and experience at the moment. What are the gaps you need to fill in order to meet the selection criteria? Make a plan for how you can do this. Competencies required for all aid workers include: flexibility and adaptability; cross cultural communication skills; team work; ability to live away from home, often in basic conditions; multi-tasking and working under pressure; human resource management; problem solving and analytical skills; and stress management.

Education and Training: In many cases aid workers are required to have higher education, whether it be a specialised degree such as an engineering or nursing degree, or a more generalist degree such as a Masters of International Development or Public Policy. There are also several short training courses available, such as those run by RedR (which I highly recommend) and Red Cross humanitarian training.

Informal learning, by reading relevant books and journals, and visiting websites that cover humanitarian topics (such as those listed in the references section at the end of this book) are great ways to build your knowledge. Attending conferences and talking to professionals in the field will also help.

The best resource I can recommend is *The Australian Aid Resource and Training Guide* (AARTG). It provides an extensive list of relevant organisations, education and training suitable for everyone, from practitioners to students, wanting to connect to the humanitarian/development world.

How do I get the experience?

Study is important, but it is field experience that is valued the most. Even if you have a doctorate in international development you will still need experience to back it up. And this is the difficult and most competitive part to achieve, even for a volunteer role. Some ways to gain experience include:

- Volunteering overseas – reputable volunteer agencies include Australian Volunteers International or UN Volunteers.
- Volunteering in a head office in your own city (most states have volunteering websites that list opportunities).
- Applying for an internship with an aid organisation.
- Checking out government initiatives. For example, in Australia there is the Australian Youth Ambassador in Development (AYAD) Program for those under 30, and for those older (or younger), you can try Australian Volunteers for International Development.
- Applying for jobs and asking for feedback if you are not called for interview. You can only learn from these and find out what skills you need to build upon.

If you are from the corporate sector looking for a role in the business/ support side, you will need to take a drop in salary but you can make the swap into the NGO sector a lot more easily than for program/ front line jobs that usually require field experience.

Network: Speak to people in the industry, go to information sessions, use your networks to meet others who may have experience, and generally put yourself out there.

Don't give up: It can be a long and frustrating road. But be persistent, committed and passionate and if you are in the position to volunteer, study, and persevere, you will eventually succeed.

Some people suggest just going to a disaster zone and chipping in. I don't advocate this. Usually for bigger disasters it can cause more coordination and logistical issues than actually helping the people in need. It is best to go with a professional organisation that has the skills and experience to assist with your deployment.

Don't want to become an Aid Worker but want to help?

If you don't have the skills, time or inclination to work in emergencies but want to help, there are so many ways you can do this. Here is a list of a few that come to mind:

- Educate yourself and others—read, research, discuss.
- Donate money to your favourite aid agency—either as an individual or by participating in fund raising events and have fun too!
- Volunteer your time in Australia—it could be anything from general administration to volunteering at an event

such as Oxfam's *Trail Walker*, or Plan's *Because I am a Girl* campaign. Nothing is too small and all helps the cause of ending poverty!

- Talk with peers about key issues— raise awareness and take action where you can.
- Write letters to your local and national leaders on injustices occurring in the world that are important to you.
- Vote for political parties that have the best humanitarian policies.
- Buy fair trade products.
- Be environmentally conscious—use resources carefully, such as energy and water, and recycle.
- What other ideas do you have?

Write a list of three things you can do NOW!

_____

_____

_____

AND FOR THOSE LOOKING FOR LOVE . . .

As well as learning more about emergency work, it is also my hope that you have had some fun along the way with my romantic (and not so romantic) interludes. If you have found the love of your life, treasure every moment and never take him/her for granted. If you are single and looking, I wish there was substantiated research and websites that could outline the laws of attraction for 'how to find and keep Mr/Mrs Right'.

We know how to prevent major diseases around the world— it will take international pressure, political will and good practice to make it happen. Unfortunately, all the political will in the world won't be able to prevent heartbreak, or lead us to the person of our dreams. Yes, there are many websites that can give you tips, and I think internet dating and social forums are a great avenue to meet people. But I think what it comes down to is to know who you are and be the best person that you can be. Live your dreams. Be happy. Believe in yourself. Throw away your lists . . . don't give up.

The right person is out there somewhere. You just have to be open to the possibilities and actively put yourself out there. Well, who knows—as you have read, I am obviously not an expert in this area.

Good luck xx

REFERENCES AND HELPFUL INFORMATION

It is my hope that after reading this book, you will be more aware of some of the issues facing people surviving disasters and living in poverty. In particular, gender issues that cross over all spheres of life. References for facts I have included in this book are freely available through the internet. I have listed some of these sources, as well as other sites of interest below. Where possible I have chosen easily accessible, simplified web pages that highlight key information on relevant topics. I encourage you to do your own research for more complex analysis and up to date information of these topics.

* All web pages were accessed in April 2013. Due to the nature of the internet, the sites may be updated or changed.

Chapter 3
RedR relieves suffering in disasters by selecting, training and providing competent and committed personnel to humanitarian relief agencies worldwide. The RedR Humanitarian Training is referred to

throughout my book, and I am now employed by the organisation as an Associate Trainer. RedR Australia: http://Redr.org.au

Chapter 4

Bangladesh life expectancy
World Health Organization (WHO) Country Cooperation Strategy At a Glance 2008 – 2013, Bangladesh: http://www.who.int/country-focus/cooperation_strategy/ccsbrief_bgd_en.pdf

Child marriage
United Nations Population Fund (UNFPA) – Child Marriage Fact-sheet: State of World Population 2005: http://www.unfpa.org/swp/2005/presskit/factsheets/facts_child_marriage.htm

Facts and figures on violence against women including dowry violence: http://www.unifem.org/gender_issues/violence_against_women/facts_figures.php?page=3

Chapter 5

Honour Killing
Human Rights Commission of Pakistan: State of Human Rights in 2011: http://www.hrcp-web.org

Unite to End Violence Against Women
Launched in 2008, the United Nations Secretary-General's Unite to End Violence Against Women campaign aims to raise public awareness and increase political will and resources for preventing and ending all forms of violence against women and girls in all parts of the world.

It offers information, resources and fact sheets that cover most gender issues raised in my book: http://endviolence.un.org

Chapter 7

Qawwali Music Translation from song by the great Nusrat Fateh Ali. Song: Ye Jo Halka Halka Suroor: http://nusrat.info/

Pakistan: Country Cooperation Strategy at a Glance, World Health Organisation, 2006: http://www.who.int/countryfocus/resources/ ccsbrief_pakistan_pak_06_en.pdf

Chapter 8

The Sphere Handbook: Humanitarian Charter and Minimum Standards in Humanitarian Response: http://www.sphereproject.org/handbook/

Chapter 12 and Chapter 19

Maternal mortality
World Health Organization: WHO Maternal Mortality Fact Sheet: http://www.who.int/mediacentre/factsheets/fs348/en/

Safe termination
Marie Stopes International offers quality reproductive and sexual health care to women all around the world: http://www.mariestopes. org.au/how-we-help/safe-abortion

Chapter 15

Amnesty International article about seventeen aid workers murdered in 2006 'No Justice for Humanitarian Workers Murdered in Sri Lanka': http://www.amnesty.org.au/news/comments/23553

2004 Indian Ocean Tsunami: five years on

Oxfam End Of Program Report 2008: http://www.oxfam.org/en/emergencies/tsunami

Chapter 21

Northern Uganda Conflict
Civil Society Organisations for Peace in Northern Uganda (CSOPNU), March 2006. 'Counting the Cost: 20 years of War in Northern Uganda' Oxfam Great Britain website: http://www.oxfam.org/en/policy/report-CSOPNU-nuganda-060330

Report on Northern Uganda conflict with a focus on the Child 'Night Commuters'. 'When the Sun Sets We Start to Worry'. An Account of Northern Uganda, United Nations OCHA IRIN Publication November 2004: http://www.irinnews.org/pdf/in-depth/When-the-sun-sets-Revised-Edition.pdf

Chapter 22 and Chapter 26

Water, Sanitation and Hygiene (WASH)
'Safe Water Means Better Health' Oxfam Water Campaign: http://www.oxfam.org.au/explore/water-sanitation-and-hygiene/safe-water-means-better-health/

Diarrhoeal diseases fact sheet
World Health Organization: http://www.who.int/mediacentre/factsheets/fs330/en/index.html

WaterAid Australia provides some great development information sheets on key issues around Water, Sanitation and Hygiene: http://www.wateraid.org/australia/learn_zone/1612.asp

Female Genital Mutilation Fact sheet
World Health Organization: http://www.who.int/mediacentre/fact sheets/fs241/en/index.html

Chapter 27

Malaria fact sheet
World Health Organization: http://www.who.int/features/factfiles/malaria/en/index.html

Malaria Consortium
International not for profit organisation aiming to control malaria: http://www.malariaconsortium.org/

Chapter 31

My three minutes of fame video clip in PNG
Oxfam Australia Cholera response to Cholera outbreak in East Sepik area of PNG: A great YouTube clip on the program that I managed: http://www.youtube.com/watch?v=PiyefHGKScE

Chapter 33

Kampala bombings July 2010
BBC News article: http://www.bbc.co.uk/news/10593771

Pakistan Floods Progress Report July 2010 – 2011, Oxfam International: http://www.oxfam.org/sites/www.oxfam.org/files/pakistan-progress-report-floods-jh-en.pdf

East African Food Crisis 2011-2012, Oxfam Australia: http://www.oxfam.org.au/explore/conflict-and-natural-disasters/current-emergencies/east-africa-food-crisis/

GENERAL

Oxfam Reports

Throughout the book I refer to Oxfam's aid and development work. Oxfam produces countless documents, reports and resources on the impact and effectiveness of their work. As the website links change and are updated frequently, it is best to refer to Oxfam's main search engine to access information on the specific contexts in which I have worked, or any other aspect of the organisation's programs globally:

www.oxfam.org.au.

Jobs, information and training

There are numerous websites that provide reliable and relevant humanitarian information, news and analysis including jobs, training and development. I have named a few that I like.

The Australian Aid Resource and Training Guide (AARTG) has been around since I first started at Oxfam. It is designed to provide useful, practical material for development practitioners, students, and other interested people. http://www.torqaid.com/

The Australian Council for International Development (ACFID)
ACFID unites Australia's non-government aid and international development organisations to strengthen their collective impact against poverty. It lists jobs and volunteering opportunities with many of the big Australian Agencies. http://www.acfid.asn.au/

Oxfam Relief Register
This is the register that I started on at my career with Oxfam. However you need to be an experienced aid worker to get onto this register: https://www.oxfam.org.au/about-us/working-at-oxfam/humanitarian-relief-register/

UN Volunteers: http://onlinevolunteering.org/en/index.html

Australian Volunteers for International Development Program: http://www.volunteering.austraining.com.au/

Australian Youth Ambassadors for Development (AYAD) Program (18 – 30 year olds): www.ayad.com.au

Red Cross oversees volunteering program: http://www.NATCD Volunteering@redcross.org.au/volunteer-overseas.aspx

Relief Web: http://reliefweb.int/

Alert Net: http://www.trust.org/alertnet/

Make Poverty History
A coalition of more than 70 aid and development organisations, community and faith-based groups working to achieve the United

Nations Millennium Development Goals and halve global poverty by 2015 and beyond: http://www.makepovertyhistory.com.au

Dealing with Stress and Psychological Support
Mandala Foundation promotes the prevention, mitigation and treatment of stress in humanitarian aid and development staff: http://www.mandalafoundation.org.au/

Organisational Development and Human Resource Practice in Emergencies
People in Aid: http://www.peopleinaid.org/

Child Rights

Plan International Australia: http://www.plan.org.au/

Gender

Association for Women's rights in development: http://www.awid.org/

BRIDGE supports gender advocacy and mainstreaming efforts by bridging the gaps between theory, policy and practice: http://www.bridge.ids.ac.uk/

Because I am a Girl
Based on a nine-part series of reports titled, 'Because I am a Girl: The State of the World's Girls'. Published annually since 2007, the reports examine the rights and needs of girls and young women in developing countries and explore how they are uniquely placed to break the cycle of poverty. http://www.becauseiamagirl.com.au/2011/

ACKNOWLEDGEMENTS

A heartfelt thank you to Mum, Dad, my family and friends who have supported me to believe in myself and to follow my dreams. Your encouragement helped me to write this book. To my best friend 'Stephanie'—a combination of Mara, Fleur and Rachael, who are always there for me.

To those who proof read, advised, or listened to me reading chapter after chapter including Mel, Mum, Anne Maria and Rochelle. Special thanks to Holly Stanton who put so much work into my initial edit. I don't know where I would have been without you.

Thank you to the team at Allen & Unwin, including Julia Cain for copy-editing and Christa Moffitt who designed my beautiful cover. Particular thanks to Tracy O'Shaughnessy, Laura Mitchell and my agent Jacinta Di Mase, for your feedback and advice on how to negotiate this new and strange world of books and publishing. It feels like years ago that I began writing this book and I can't actually believe I am here now!

To the courage of all the aid workers and communities I have worked with, and to those who continue to live in poverty and disaster—your strength is humbling. To my Oxfam colleagues, friends and the Mr Wrongs I have met on my travels: thanks for providing me with lively stories to tell. To Oxfam as a whole, not only for supporting my career, but for the incredible emergency and development programs that contribute to the alleviation of poverty globally.

And finally to my husband Scotty. Who knew at the beginning of my writing this book about my search for Mr Right, that I would actually find you! Thank you for your love and support—and of course for enabling me to end it with 'and then she lived happily ever after'.